TO JEFFNIFER

JOHN 8:32

FREE at LAST

FREE *at* LAST

LARRY HUCH

WHITAKER
HOUSE

FREE AT LAST: Removing the Past from Your Future
expanded edition

You may contact Pastor Larry and Tiz at:
Larry Huch Ministries
P.O. Box 610890
Dallas, TX 75261
phone: 972.313.7133
www.LarryHuchMinistries.com / www.newbeginnings.org

ISBN-13: 978-0-88368-428-3 • ISBN-10: 0-88368-428-4
Printed in the United States of America
© 2000, 2003, 2004, 2010 by Larry Huch

Whitaker House
1030 Hunt Valley Circle
New Kensington, PA 15068
www.whitakerhouse.com

Library of Congress Cataloging-in-Publication Data

Huch, Larry.
 Free at last : removing the past from your future / Larry Huch.— Rev. ed. with study guide.
  p. cm.
 Includes bibliographical references.
 ISBN 0-88368-428-4 (trade pbk. w/ cd insert : alk. paper) 1. Family—Religious life. 2. Blessing and cursing. I. Title.
 BV4526.3.H83 2004
 248.8'6—dc22
                    2004013630

7 8 9 10 11 12 13 14 ய 16 15 14 13 12 11 10

Contents

Dedication

To Tiz,
my wife, my friend, my inspiration,
my dream-come-true,
who knew me before
I knew this.

Foreword

E ven the title of this book has the power to ring the sweet bell of freedom in the mind and spirit of anyone seeking deliverance and renewal from the chains that bind him or her. Pastor Larry Huch is living the life of freedom he proclaims in *Free at Last*. Delivered from anger and issues that plagued his family for years, he speaks with authority as one who, by the power of God, is "free at last."

Pastor Huch's practical and concise teaching shows us that *help is on the way* when we allow the power of God to transform us and break those bondages passed down from one generation to another.

In *Free at Last*, Pastor Huch's personal and biblical examples come alive, not so much to inform us as to transform us. The more of this book you read, the more you will discover about the power and purpose of God to transform us into people of true godly character who are able to live free from the clutches of the enemy.

Within the pages of this book, you will discover that it's not about becoming good but about pursuing the heart of God in order to experience—for you and your family—the power of the cross to deliver all believers from the bondages passed down for generations.

At its core, this is a book about the urgency of the hour. The clock of heaven is winding down and about to chime *liberty* for your life and family. As you read through the pages of this amazing book and as you walk through its corridors of liberty, you will encounter a journey of faith and courage, rekindling and igniting a hope for you and your family as you come to fully realize that you, too, can be *Free at Last*.

—Marcus D. Lamb
President and founder, Daystar Television Network

Introduction

I WAS BORN AND raised in an area of St. Louis called South St. Louis. If you have ever been through St. Louis, you have probably seen the Gateway Arch on the Mississippi River. My old neighborhood is located near the Arch. The main sewage river ran right past us, and not far away was a brewery that gave off the smell of hops. A few blocks away in the other direction was a slaughterhouse. On warm summer evenings, there was always an overpowering stench hanging in the air.

My school was the oldest high school west of the Mississippi River. Because of frequent stabbings and shootings, armed guards stood patrol there. Once, in the middle of the school day and in broad daylight, a rival gang aimed their guns at the school and blasted away. The environment I grew up in was filled with physical violence and the stress and hopelessness of poverty.

Years later, after Jesus had helped me to put my past behind me, I was on a platform in Anaheim, California, with Benny Hinn. As we were singing and worshipping, the anointing of God was so heavy and so powerful that I was literally being swept up in the Spirit of God. All of a sudden the Lord spoke to me and said, "Larry, open your eyes and look at these people." I looked out at the crowd and saw about twelve to fifteen thousand people in that Anaheim stadium.

The Lord spoke to me again, "Do they deserve to be healed?"

I said, "Absolutely, Lord, that's why they're here. That's why You've raised up Pastor Benny."

He said, "Larry, just as much as they deserve to be healed, they deserve to be set free. I want you to go and bring deliverance to My people."

Immediately, I began to argue with the Lord because I thought that deliverance would mean people screaming and demons manifesting all over the place. So I said to the Lord, "Lord, I don't know that I want to do this."

And the Lord said, "They shall know the truth, and the truth they know shall set them free. What I've taught you in My Word you're going to teach them, and the moment they see it, the truth will set them free." (See John 8:32.) In Hosea 4:6 God says, *"My people."* He's not referring to those who are in the world or to those who are not serving Him, but He says, *"My people"* are destroyed because of one thing, a lack of knowledge.

God said, "I'm going to show you how to teach deliverance, so that whoever has ears to hear and eyes to see and receives the teaching, that truth will instantly set them free."

We receive letters from Christians who say, "We're born-again Christians, but we're in bondage." They are in bondage to depression, anger, insecurity, drugs, alcohol, food, and a host of other things. A lot of Christians haven't been willing to confess their faults because they have been saying, "Well, we're Christians, and we are supposed to be free." I carried the same shame these people carry. There was a time when I refused to get help from our pastor because I was too ashamed. *Christians aren't supposed to be this way,* I thought.

I am going to speak very directly and straight to the heart because there is too much at stake to play games. I tell my story of going from cursing to blessing so it can become your story. By the blood of Jesus Christ you too can be set free from your prison—whatever that may be.

For all those who have called or written to us, and for all those who are still waiting for the storm of oppression to end in their lives, my story and your story are intended to end in such a way that our healing and our subsequent lives give glory to God. God is not pointing a condemning finger at you. He's reaching out a healing hand to touch the innermost parts of your life and to make you every bit whole. It is time to stop the storm that rages inside. It is time to get out of the war zone and get into the winning zone!

Introduction

In this book, I'm going to show you the truth. This is not just a book about the curse of anger or drugs; it's about anything in your life that is trying to destroy you or the blessing and future that is already yours in Jesus Christ. I am going to walk you through the steps that have set me free and have kept me and my family free. Acts 10:34 tells us God is not a respecter of persons. What He has done for us, He will do for you, and today is your day to be set free.

> *The word which God sent to the children of Israel, preaching peace through Jesus Christ; He is Lord of all; that word you know, which was proclaimed throughout all Judea, and began from Galilee after the baptism which John preached: how God anointed Jesus of Nazareth with the Holy Spirit and with power, who went about doing good and healing all who were oppressed by the devil, for God was with Him.*
> —Acts 10:36–38

Part One

Identifying and
Understanding
Generational Curses

Chapter One

Getting a New Life

I DON'T KNOW if it was the way the cab driver responded, or didn't respond, or just our imaginations, but all of a sudden, something seemed wrong—real wrong.

Just a couple of minutes after we had gotten in the cab, another car had pulled up next to us as we went down the road. They started yelling at our driver, "Stop that cab! Let those gringos out! We will kill them!" They used a few other descriptive words as well. Then they drove on. I was finally realizing what a bad idea this outing had been. We needed to get back up the mountain to my ranch as quickly as possible. We would be safe there.

I was sitting in the backseat of the cab, right behind the driver. Jim was next to me, and Laura was in the front because her Spanish was better than ours. We were somewhere outside the city of Medellín, Colombia. It was almost dark, and those roads grew even more dangerous at night. Still, we thought we would be all right as long as we kept to the main roads where there were more people. But the driver made a turn instead of staying on the main route like we had told him, and he suddenly pulled onto a side road leading back up into the hills. We got very nervous and started to question him, "Why did you turn off? Where are you going?"

"It's okay, it's okay," he kept saying. "This is a shortcut, a quicker way."

I'd been living in Colombia nearly a year, and in all that time, no cab had ever taken us this way. By this time it was pitch black outside, and there were no houses, no lights, and no one else

14

around. Could they be thinking we were drug agents to be gotten rid of, or did they know we had a lot of money to buy cocaine? Maybe they were going to kill us, take the money, and just keep the cocaine. I began to realize that, any way you cut it, they would get what they wanted, and we would be dead.

We kept shouting at the driver, "Turn around! Take us back!"

But he wouldn't do it. "Just up ahead," he kept saying as we drove further and further up into the hills.

Then out of nowhere two cars pulled out, not at the same time, but one in front of us and one behind. I've never been so scared in my life. Everyone was screaming and yelling at the same time, some in English and some in Spanish, which just added to the confusion and the intensity of the fear. Jim and I didn't understand everything being said and the driver didn't speak English. But, while the words may have been lost, the meaning was coming across quite clear. We knew that we were being set up to be killed and robbed and that our driver was in on it. "It's just up ahead," he cried. "It's just up ahead."

In that part of Colombia, people disappeared all the time, never to be found again. Just the week before we'd heard on the radio that two tourists had their hotel room door broken down. The man was robbed and then killed, and the woman was raped. This was a dangerous place.

Panic had hit us all, and I felt we needed to kill the cab driver and take over the cab or we were dead. I took my belt off and screamed, "Tell him if he doesn't pass that car I'm going to kill him!" Laura was yelling at me in English, "Not yet, Larry, don't do it!" and at the driver in Spanish at the same time, "Pass him! Pass him!"

Jim was shouting at both of us, "We've got to do something! We've got to get out of here!"

The two cars were on us bumper-to-bumper. I figured it was now or never. I gripped the belt in my two fists and got ready to put it over the driver's head and around his neck. I yelled at Jim, "I'll pull him to the back, you jump in front and grab the wheel. Don't stop for anything!"

Just at that moment we came over the hill and saw the lights of the village. The other two cars turned quickly off the road and disappeared into the night. The taxi driver had been telling the truth. We had never been in any danger, and I'd been ready to kill him for nothing!

As he let us out at our ranch, I was split between panic, anger, and relief; I hardly knew what to think. When I had awakened that morning, I never thought that by nighttime I would be thinking about killing someone. That was bad enough, but what really upset me was that it didn't really seem to bother me that I had been ready to kill someone so suddenly. I realized then and there that my anger—and my life—were totally out of control.

We meet and hear from people nationwide who are desperate for answers and are about to give up on themselves, their friends, or their family because of some bondage in their lives. Some people get shocked into reality when the hopes and dreams they had for their lives or for their children's lives have been shattered. Others fear they are losing their grip on a lifelong battle against their own private demons of drug dependence, gambling, lying, cheating, anger, violence, sexual abuse, divorce, or sickness.

> Some people get shocked into reality when the hopes and dreams they had for their lives or for their children's lives have been shattered.

I often speak to men and women with great ambitions, talents, and promise for success who just can't seem to get ahead. Their lives consist of repeated failures in business as a result of a spirit of poverty or failure. Depression seems to be at an all-time high in men and women from every walk of life. Many have finally accomplished their life's dreams but are plagued with a shadow of darkness or hollow emptiness. I've ministered to professional entertainers and athletes who have achieved great fame and fortune yet have lost it all.

Situations like these beg an explanation. We yearn to make sense of such destructive events—especially when they are happening to us or to someone we love. There has been a lot of talk in the news about medical researchers trying to determine why certain sinful traits are passed from one generation to the next. Researchers recognize that there is a definite pattern, but they can't pinpoint the reasons. Is it genetic? Is it environmental? These all play a part, no doubt, but I believe there is a spiritual reason that is the main determining factor. Some reports have called it "family baggage." It is a family curse.

To understand the awesome delivering power of God in my life, you must first see what I was delivered from. I was an extremely angry and violent person, but my life has been transformed by the supernatural power of Jesus Christ. And here's good news for you: What He has done for me, He will do for you! *"God is no respecter of persons"* (Acts 10:34 KJV).

I think it's obvious that the violent anger I experienced that day in Colombia didn't just pop into my life overnight. Anger, drugs, divorce—the numerous battles we face are spiritual. These are spiritual strongholds that get into our lives and into our families. Unless we know how to find them and get rid of them, they will stay with us, grow, and be passed to our children and our children's children.

I can remember the very day the spirit of anger began to grab my life. A terrible thing happened to me that left me feeling unwanted and alone. I was very young, and I remember going into my room to cry. Lying there on my bed, I suddenly stopped crying, wiped away my tears, stood up, and with clenched fists and gritted teeth, made a promise to myself. *Nobody will ever make me cry again.* With that declaration, I opened a door to the spirit of anger, rejection, and violence. And from that point on, it seemed like I was always angry and looking to even a score with someone. If anyone looked at me wrong or said something I didn't like, I would take it personally and anything might happen. I would fight at the drop of a hat, with words, fists, bats—or whatever I could find to use as a weapon. Most of my targets were strangers, so it was impersonal and didn't seem to matter, but I didn't care whom I hurt. This behavior released a Bible principle into my life:

> *Do not be deceived, God is not mocked; for whatever a man sows, that he will also reap.*   (Galatians 6:7)

One night I was sitting at a hamburger place in South St. Louis with some of my friends, and some guys came by in a car and began to yell at us. We immediately jumped into our car to chase them. Just another street fight, nothing new. But what I didn't know was that this was a setup.

As we chased these guys down the street, they suddenly pulled into a parking lot and got out, waiting for us. Six of them and four of us. Not bad odds, I thought. This is going to be fun. But all of a sudden the fun turned serious. From behind the wall came a couple dozen other guys who'd been waiting for us. Then I suddenly found out that they weren't actually waiting for us; they were waiting for me. The three guys I was with took off, and none of the others moved to follow them. I was the one they were after.

They beat me with bats, boots, and fists. The next thing I remember is coming back to consciousness in the backseat of a car going down an alley. Without stopping, the car door flung open, and I was tossed out onto the pavement. As I slowly got up, the only thing I could think of was revenge.

You would think I would have begun to seek a change at that point. My life was becoming a continual hell. But I was growing more and more uncontrollable as I progressed through my teenage years and into my early twenties, and many times I scared myself as well as those who were close to me. I was in constant trouble with my school, the law, and anyone else I thought might threaten me. It seemed that I had enemies everywhere, but in truth I had only one: the spirit I was allowing to control my life.

For we do not wrestle against flesh and blood, but against principalities, against powers, against the rulers of the darkness of this age, against spiritual hosts of wickedness in the heavenly places.
(Ephesians 6:12)

I didn't want to be controlled by this spirit of anger and violence, but I didn't know what to do. Truthfully, I didn't even know what was happening to me.

After returning from Colombia, I remember going back to see a girl I had dated in college. We had split up because of my anger and drug abuse. I wanted to see if we could get back together. I assured her that I had changed, turned over a new leaf, and was a different person. "Larry," she said, "I've heard that before. I know you mean it. I know you want to change, but you never will—not until you find Jesus Christ as your Lord and Savior. Anger is in your family and now it's in you. Only Jesus can change you. It will take a miracle."

While I had been in Colombia, my old girlfriend had become born-again. She was the first "Jesus Freak" I'd ever met. Even though I didn't want any of this religious stuff, there were two things I knew she was right about. One was that I couldn't change on my own. I'd tried too many times before and knew it was impossible without help. The second was that I had become everything I had hated all my years growing up. But isn't it that way in all of our lives? We become the things we hated as children, the things that scared us, the things that pushed us away. "Like father, like son; he's just like his dad" or "She's just like her mom." That's what the world says, but the Word of God says that the iniquities of the fathers (parents) are visited *"upon the children and the children's children to the third and the fourth generation"* (Exodus 34:7).

My girlfriend from college was right. No matter how hard I tried to change, that old nature kept rising up and taking over. I was desperate to live differently, but I couldn't do it on my own.

I started using drugs when I was a senior in high school. The Vietnam War was being fought, and the rebellious hippie movement was spreading around the nation. A few of my friends began smoking marijuana. Eventually, I gave it a try.

The following year, I went off to college at Southeast Missouri State on a football scholarship. While I was there, drugs became more and more available. I started doing acid, LSD, psilocybin—whatever came along. Not only did I find drug use enjoyable; I found out there is a lot of money to be made by selling drugs.

Money Must Be the Answer

It seemed lack of money had caused my mom and dad to live under constant stress and hardship. I promised myself that I was not going to live the rest of my life that way, no matter what it took.

My plan had been to go to college and then into sports to make money, but I discovered it was easier to make money selling drugs.

I began selling LSD and marijuana, and a door opened for me to go to Colombia. I lived in Medellín, worked with the drug cartel there, and smuggled dope back into the United States. At that time, I was the only American in the history of that country to live in that area.

> I didn't know who God was, if He cared about me, or if He even existed, but I found myself saying, "God, there must be something else."

I had a ranch high on top of the Andes Mountains. I was surrounded by chauffeurs, bodyguards, and the servants who cooked our meals and manicured the lawn with machetes every day. I walked around with fifty or sixty thousand dollars in my pocket all the time. I had all the good and all the bad that money could buy.

While I was dealing dope, I had kilos of cocaine available to me in my house every single day, and I began using it. I started snorting it, and soon I was mainlining it. I was using eight to ten thousand dollars worth of cocaine a day.

I didn't know who God was, if He existed, or if He even cared about me if He did exist, but I eventually found myself saying, "God, there must be something else." During this time, I was listening to gurus and reading all kinds of bizarre books. As strange as it sounds, I really thought maybe I could get so high that I would find God.

Right before I went to Colombia, I played college football and lifted weights competitively. I weighed about 215 pounds and was bench-pressing close to 500 pounds. I had finished sixth in the nation in a weight-lifting competition. Then I moved to Colombia. In about eight months I went from 215 pounds to 145 pounds because of my drug use.

Having It All and Losing It All

Laura and Jim, the friends in the cab with me the night I almost killed the driver, were living with me in Colombia. We did drugs from early in the morning until we passed out at night. We went for days without eating, just doing drugs. I kept getting weaker and weaker, and I kept doing more and more drugs. Laura started noticing my weight loss and she would fuss about me all the time saying, "Larry, you are going to kill yourself." She would try to make us eat. She brought us food, but we would just nibble on it and then take more drugs.

One time, Jim and Laura were gone for the day. No one else was around. I had been doing dope and drinking all day long and had just finished a deal. I was feeling good. I said, "Man, I'm really going to get high." Not realizing how stoned I already was, I doubled the amount of cocaine I usually used. I put it in the syringe and stuck it in my arm. I didn't realize I had put the needle right through my vein, so I took that amount and doubled it again.

When a person mainlines drugs, the drug is injected into the vein and that vein carries it directly to the heart. I had been hitting up ten to twelve times a day, so all my veins were in bad shape. I tried over and over again to get the drugs into my veins. Finally, on that one last try, after doubling the dose several times, I took the needle, stuck it into my vein, and I hit. I fell to the ground, began to vomit, and my body began to convulse. There was no one there to help me, and no one could hear me. I can't tell you how I knew, but I knew I was dying.

> In every one of us, there is an "emergency button" in our spirits that calls out, "God, help me! You're the only one who can give me the miracle I need."

Have you ever noticed what people do when they get really desperate? You can call yourself an atheist, agnostic, or whatever you want, but the moment you get into trouble and nothing can help you except a miracle, you cry, "God, help me!" In every one of us, there is an "emergency button" in our spirits that calls out, "God, help me! You're the only one who can give me the miracle I need!"

I didn't believe in heaven or in hell, but I cried out, "God, don't let me die." I had made it out of the city, into college, and down to Colombia. I had everything I could want with one exception: I didn't have whatever it was that was going to make me happy. "God," I pleaded, "don't let me die until I find out what happiness is."

By a miracle of God I started coming to. I recovered, and God was put on the back burner again.

Sometime later, I went to Mexico City to meet some "mule" runners carrying a shipment of cocaine from Colombia. While I was out of Colombia, bandits broke into my house in the mountains. Our servants had tipped off the bandits that I was gone and had driven them up the mountain to the house. Armed with guns and machetes, the intruders got into the house and attacked Jim and Laura. The two somehow managed to get out alive, took all the money, and skipped the country.

In just a few months, I went from having everything I could possibly want to having absolutely nothing. While I was sitting in my motel room in Mexico City, I admitted to myself that, despite my denials, I was a drug addict. Laura had told me over and over that I was an addict, but I had denied it and thought I could quit at any time. Now I realized the full truth: I couldn't even get up in the morning without drugs. Drugs were my life.

Changing the Outside
Doesn't Change the Inside

I returned to the States and moved into a farmhouse way out in the woods of Missouri. I began to live like a recluse—life was just me and my dogs. I did everything I could to change. I let my hair grow long, pierced my ear, and even became a vegetarian. I thought I was really changing, that I could live in peace with anyone and everyone. Then something happened that made me realize that even though the outside circumstances had changed, I hadn't changed at all on the inside.

There was a man on the farm next to mine who couldn't tolerate having a hippie living near him. One day as a friend and I were leaving the farm to go into town, I noticed that one of my dogs was missing. He was a Great Dane pup, and he was as big as a house at six months old. It was very unusual for him not to be with the other dogs. My friend and I looked everywhere, but we couldn't find him. We had to go into town, so we quit looking and hoped he would be back by the time we returned home.

As I was driving down the road, I saw my neighbor. I stopped and asked him if he had seen my dog, Eric. I thought it would be just like him to lock up Eric out of plain meanness. When I asked him if he had seen him, he said, "Yes, the dog trespassed on my property, so I shot him." I laughed, thinking he was joking, and said, "Oh, right, so where is his body?"

"Down by the pond," he responded. Just to humor him, I walked the few yards to the pond. There Eric lay—dead, just as the man had said.

I turned around and saw my neighbor eyeing me with a smug look on his face, and I snapped. I knew I was going to kill him—not just hurt him—I was going to kill him! I ran at him and threw him up against the barn. His wife and kids were screaming and crying. He was begging for mercy. My friend pleaded, "Larry, don't!" They all knew I had lost it. At that point, I didn't care what happened to me, even if it meant going to prison for murder. All I wanted was revenge. I couldn't stop myself.

Even then, the God of love and mercy was moving in my life. As I reached up to grab this man by the throat and kill him, my arms literally froze to my sides. I couldn't move them. In a frenzy, straining to lift my hands, I cried out, "God, let me go!" Finally, I gave up the assault and took off. I picked up the bloodied body of my dog and carried him home to bury him.

As I was digging the grave, two highway patrolmen drove up. With my long hair, earrings, and my dog's blood all over me, I must have been a sight. The police officers got out of the car and nervously walked toward me. They told me I had really shaken up my neighbor, who had called them, terrified for his life. "Larry," they said, "we know how you feel...." I cut them off, "You have no idea how I feel. You tell him I'm coming back and I'm going to kill everything he has." Though I meant every word of it, I never did. I was still selling drugs at the time, and I soon found out the guy I had been selling to was a narcotics agent. I knew it was time to get out of town, so I packed up and moved to Flagstaff, Arizona.

When Everything Changed

Many people have to hit bottom before they can find their way to the top. It was that incident that showed me that, in spite of any external changes I had made, I was still the same out-of-control Larry I always had been. After struggling to make my life different, I was no closer to becoming the person I really wanted to be.

Right after the incident with my neighbor and before I moved, I met up with a friend who had just returned to the States from the Middle East. Knowing I needed to leave, we chose to move to Arizona because I had been reading some books on the Indian religions and thought maybe I could find the peace I was looking for out in the desert. It sounds crazy now, but I was desperately looking for God—whoever and wherever He was.

We moved to Arizona, and just a few days after settling in, God arranged for me to meet a brand-new, born-again Christian. This young man asked me to go to church with him. I didn't especially like Christians, but for some reason I agreed. I went with him to a little church of about thirty people, where I saw a movie on the life of Jesus.

I walked into that church with long hair, wearing thong sandals, a poncho, and earrings. I was also high. I didn't know how to pray, and I certainly didn't know anything about getting saved and being born again. The movie began, and I saw how Jesus hung on the cross and died. Somehow I knew He died for me. I knew I had found what I was searching for. I ended up kneeling and weeping at the altar in the front of the church, and there I said, "God, if You are real, then be real to me."

There is no way I could ever explain to you what I felt the moment Jesus came into my life. I knew He saw right through all my facades and understood everything about me. He took out all the pain and poured in His unconditional love. The years of sin and guilt lifted immediately. As I saw Jesus give His life for me, I gave my life fully to Him.

Ten days later, I went back to the church and was baptized in the Holy Spirit. The next morning, I was rolling my marijuana to smoke as I walked my dogs. I looked at the joint and said, "I am so 'high' on Jesus, I don't ever want to smoke that stuff again and come down."

Free Indeed

We had a saying where I grew up on the streets of South St. Louis, "Once a junkie, always a junkie." According to that, once you became an addict, you could never change. Thank God there's another saying that not only applies to the people on the streets, but to loved ones in our homes, colleagues in our workplaces, friends and acquaintances in our neighborhoods, classmates in school, and to Christians we worship with—literally to every person in every situation and circumstance, in every place around the world. That message is this:

If the Son makes you free, you shall be free indeed.

(John 8:36)

I was a drug addict, putting needles in my arms sometimes ten to twelve times a day. But twenty-five years ago I was set free by the power of a compassionate, loving God, and for over twenty-three years I have traveled the world sharing my testimony. From prisons to churches and from schools to government meetings, I've told the story of how Jesus miraculously set me free from the stronghold of heroin and cocaine addiction. But I also experienced God's deliverance in another area of my life.

Discussion Questions

1. Do you have something in your life that is trying to destroy the blessing and the future that is already yours in Jesus Christ? If so, what is it?

2. Do people think you have changed on the outside, yet you know on the inside you are still the same?

3. Larry found satisfaction and enjoyment in drugs. What do you feel joy in that you know you should be feeling conviction for instead?

4. Larry thought money must be the answer to the problems in his life. What answers have you found?

5. What are/were the results of those activities?

6. According to John 8:32, what will set you free?

7. Read Hosea 4:6. Why are God's people destroyed?

8. Do you identify in any way with the following excerpt where Larry Huch wrote,

There were two things I knew my friend was right about. One was that I couldn't change on my own. I'd tried too many times before and knew it was impossible without help. The second was that I had become everything I had hated all my years growing up. But isn't it that way in all of our lives? We become the things we hated as children, the things that scared us, the things that pushed us away. "Like father, like son; he's just like his dad" or "She's just like her mom." That's what the world says, but the Word of God says that the iniquities of the fathers (parents) are visited *"upon the children and the children's children to the third and the fourth generation"* (Exodus 34:7).

9. If you are struggling to make your life different but are no closer to becoming the person you want to be, read John 8:36. How do you know you've been set free?

Chapter Two

Generational Curses

As I was getting ready for a TBN *Praise the Lord* interview a few years ago, my good friends Laverne and Edith Tripp came in and asked, "Pastor, what do you want to talk about tonight?"

I said, "Well, you know I've always shared my testimony about how God delivered me from drugs and from a life on the streets, but instead of my testimony, let's just share something about what God has been showing me in His Word."

Laverne graciously agreed, but during our live interview, Laverne said to me, "Larry, I know we're not supposed to talk about your testimony, but I feel with all my heart that God wants you to share something that will set people free tonight."

I had always been willing to share about how I was a dope dealer and a drug user, but I had never shared about one particular part of my testimony for two reasons: one, I was ashamed of it; and two, I battled this problem even after I became a born-again Christian.

Now I began to share it publicly for the first time. When I was born again, God delivered me from drugs immediately, and people prophesied that I would go into the ministry. Everyone said I was going to be a man of God. So I would go to church, lift my hands, and praise the Lord. I ministered on the streets and people got saved. Everything appeared to be okay, but there were internal wounds that hadn't healed.

These wounds festered deep within me, and no one knew it—no one, that is, except my wife, Tiz. At times she would have to use makeup to cover up the occasional black eye or fat lip that resulted when my inner scars erupted in a raging anger toward her. No one else guessed my dark secret, except the occasional stranger who was driving too slow for my liking or the man who cut me off on the highway. Those people were also targets of my erupting rage, the manifestation of generations of anger and violence.

In those days I'm sure our neighbors were totally confused. We witnessed to them about the love of Jesus, they saw us go to church several times a week, and in between they heard me yelling and cussing at a young wife, whom I supposedly loved with all my heart. With little provocation, this anger would explode inside of me, and I am ashamed to admit that I hit my wife several times—even when she was pregnant. Yes, I hit my lovely, pregnant wife hard enough to knock her down.

Everyone has their bad days, but my bad days were full of anger, which sometimes escalated into days of uncontrollable rage. In the early years of our marriage, Tiz tried time and time again to get me to talk to our pastor, but I wouldn't go. I felt embarrassed and ashamed. The thought of having an anger problem was, to me, a humiliating disgrace. I hated this part of myself. I desperately wanted to change, but I couldn't. I wondered if I could ever find freedom from this curse.

When we had been married for about five years, I was pastoring our second church in Australia. One day my son, who was a little bitty guy, did something that angered me and I shoved him up against the wall. Although the drugs were gone and the long hair was cut, I realized that on the inside there were times when I was still out of control. "God," I pleaded, "why am I like this? It's time to quit denying it. I've got a real problem and I need help." That's when I began to study the Scriptures and learn how to break the curse of anger that was in my family and in my life. But, because of my embarrassment and shame, I never taught it or shared it with anyone—until that night on TBN.

After the interview, we were getting ready to leave, but they couldn't find the driver who was to take us back to the hotel. Finally we learned that, along with people from the studio audience, our driver had to be placed on the phones because there were so many phone calls coming in. My story about my problem with anger and how God set me free caused their phones to light up worldwide.

From that one interview, we got thousands of letters and phone calls asking us to pray with people, just in the area of anger! Some people wrote, "I'm a man of God in the pulpit, but I'm Attila the Hun when I get home." Others related to my testimony, saying that my experience was exactly what they were going through.

In Need of Repair

Most of us think that when we receive Jesus as our Savior, we are automatically going to be perfect. Unfortunately, that's not true. I have heard it explained like this: "The church is like a body and fender shop—various wrecks in various stages of repair." We come in with all kinds of problems that have to be sorted through.

I want to make it very clear right now that the Lord never condemns us for our past. It is the devil who accuses us, condemns us, and tries to convince us that God is mad at us and that we are a hopeless, helpless, lost cause. We must always remember that God is not pointing an accusing finger at us; He is reaching out a hand to help us. Jesus never tells us, "Go get cleaned up and then come to Me." He tells us that when we have a burden or problem, we are to come to Him.

> *Jesus never tells us, "Go get cleaned up and then come to Me." He tells us that when we have a burden or problem, we are to come to Him.*

Come to Me, all you who labor and are heavy laden, and I will give you rest. (Matthew 11:28)

Our salvation and ongoing relationship with Jesus is a "come as you are" party.

Being confident of this very thing, that He who has begun a good work in you will complete it until the day of Jesus Christ. (Philippians 1:6)

Generational Curses

Before we go any further, let me briefly explain what a family or generational curse is. The first time the word *iniquity* is used in conjunction with generational curses is in Exodus 20:5. The scene is this: God was giving Moses the Ten Commandments. In verse 3 He commanded us to have no other gods but Him. Then, in verses 4–5, He commanded that we should not make idols or bow down and worship them or else our iniquity will visit our children and grandchildren.

God forbids bowing down and worshipping an idol, which is anything we love and reverence more than Him. What He is saying is that, when we worship an idol, we are allowing something other than Him to rule us, to make us bow down and serve it. When we do that, the spirit that operates through that idol will come into our lives and not only make us bow down to it again and again, but it will pass from us to our children and our children's children, making them bow down to it. So this spirit of iniquity becomes a force on the inside that causes us, and generations after us, to bow or bend to its destructive nature.

A spirit of iniquity could be in your life because of something you did, or it could also be something that has landed on you because of something a member of your family did years before you were born. It could be an iniquity, or family curse, that has passed from one generation to another because of something that has happened *in* your family or something that has happened *to* your family.

Let me give you some examples. If there is an unnatural anger in a family, Dad or Mom may have had it, and now their children have it. If Dad or Mom or even the grandparents had a history of divorce, their children may be facing a divorce. See what I mean? This spirit of iniquity—in this case, divorce—passes on from one generation to another. Iniquity can come in many forms: drug abuse, poverty, eating disorders, suicide, children being born out of wedlock, etc. There is no limit. Every time I think I've heard every family curse there is, I hear something new. But I want to assure you, Jesus always comes and sets free those who are bound!

Destructive personality traits and behavior patterns, addictions, suicidal tendencies, divorce, sickness, depression, anger, and dysfunction can usually be traced back through a person's family history. Statistics have shown, and it is now common knowledge, that a person who was physically or emotionally abused as a child has a strong probability of becoming an abuser as an adult. Children of alcoholics who hated their parents' behavior often become alcoholics themselves, and the list of examples goes on.

A sad example of this is the child who has been physically or sexually abused. This child has gone through the turmoil, heartache, and pain of being abused by a parent or a relative. You would think that a person who has suffered the trauma of such abuse would be the last one to inflict that horror on someone else. However, that individual is very likely to become a child abuser or, if not an abuser, to become angry and self-destructive. Why? The spirit of iniquity—the thing that drives them to do what they know they're not supposed to do—is passed down from generation to generation.

Generational curses—curses that are handed down from family member to family member, generation after generation—have been around since Adam's disobedience. Who was the first sinner? Adam. Who was the first murderer in the Bible? Adam's son, Cain. Who was the second murderer? Cain's descendant, Lamech. Why? Because of the iniquity that passed down through the generations of Adam's offspring. (See Genesis 4:8, 23.)

Sometimes the spirit that is passed from one generation to another is the same one, but the devil tries to disguise it and make it look like something completely different. One time I was praying for a lady who wanted to break a family curse that was holding her and her children. When I asked her what it was, she told me that for several generations various family members had died from obesity, never being able to control their eating. Now people in her family were suffering from anorexia, starving themselves. It was the same spirit that destroyed through eating habits but with a different operation. In this situation, the curse was *in* the family, but there are also curses that come *on* a family.

Let me give you an example that everyone in the world can relate to: the one the press has called "The Kennedy Curse." We first became aware of this with the assassination of President

John F. Kennedy, but it came into the news again with the tragic death of his son, John Jr. The media calls it a family curse, and even if they don't understand it, they're absolutely right. Actually, prior to President Kennedy there were others who died before their time; and there have been other deaths in his family between his death and his son's. They may not know exactly what it is, but it seems obvious that there is a force in their lives that is bringing destruction and is being passed from one generation to the next. Without someone in their family standing up and breaking it in the name of Jesus and through the blood He shed on the cross, it will continue.

In your family there may be sickness or disease, financial disaster, or even an irrational fear that stems from a family curse. Any spirit that tries to bring hurt and pain to you or members of your family could be there because of something in your family's past that you don't even know about. I would love to let the Kennedys and others like them know that God isn't doing this to them. It's the devil who comes to steal, kill, and destroy.

Later in this book I will go into greater detail, explaining the revelation I have seen in the Word of God concerning such matters. Then you will be able to not only recognize the root of the problem but also receive your answer, whether it's a family curse *in* your life or *on* your life. For now, just let me tell you with absolute assurance that when the Son sets you free, you will be free indeed!

It Can Be Ended

Family curses, generational curses, the iniquity of parents passed down to the third and fourth generation....Sound depressing and hopeless? It's not. Every time the devil brings a problem, Jesus has already brought an answer!

We have an example of hope in Rahab the harlot. Rahab was a Canaanite woman whose house was on the wall of Jericho. Many of us have read Joshua 6 and know the wall of Jericho came tumbling down after the children of Israel marched around it seven times as God directed. As a result, the entire city of Jericho was destroyed except Rahab and her family. Because she had hidden the Hebrew men who came to spy out the land of Canaan before they entered the Promised Land, Rahab was spared along with her family and *"all that she had"* (Joshua 6:25). As a Canaanite, Rahab was under the curse of the Canaanites that began generations earlier when Noah got drunk and his son Ham *"saw the nakedness of his father"* (Genesis 9:22). Whatever perverse act occurred while Noah was drunk, in the end Noah declared that Canaan, Ham's son, was cursed. (See Genesis 9:18–25.) Rahab broke the curse that was on her family through their ancestor Canaan by sparing the lives of the men of God. The cord of scarlet Rahab put in her window when Israel attacked was a symbol of the delivering power of the blood of Jesus. (See Joshua 2:14–21.)

Just like Rahab, you can break the curse on your family. You can bless your family. That curse started somewhere and it can end somewhere. This has been true in my own family.

I told you what my childhood was like and how a generational curse tried to repeat itself in my life. When I was delivered, I broke it off my children and my children's children too. My son, Luke, is an example of how God has broken the generational curse on my family. Last year, he went on a mission trip with the youth group from our church. When he got back, he told us that he and a friend were walking down a street in Kingman, Arizona, and the Lord began to deal with them about witnessing to two men. Luke and his friend said to each other, "We're just teenagers. They'll just laugh at us if we start talking to them about the Lord."

> You can bless your family. That curse started somewhere, and it can end somewhere.

The two men looked like they were really hurting. Luke said that the thought came to him that the truth is the truth whether it is from an eighteen-year-old or a sixty-year-old. He said, "Dad, we went up to these two biker-looking guys and they were really going through it. We found out they were brand-new Christians. They had just been saved at a Promise Keepers' meeting. However, one guy's wife had left him and was living with a boyfriend who was beating up on his kids.

"These two guys were sitting there talking about this situation, and one of them said to the other one, 'Sometimes I wonder if God is really there for me.' That is when we walked up to them and started sharing the love of Jesus with them. These guys began weeping, and then they prayed with each other and said, 'You know what? We know Jesus is real. If He will send two young men like you all the way from Portland, Oregon, to Kingman, Arizona, to witness to two guys our age, we know God is going to take care of things.'"

When Luke told me this, he began to weep. He got up, walked over to me, threw his arms around my neck, and said, "Oh, Dad, I've got such a burden for souls." Not only was I overjoyed for my son, but I praised God that the bondage of curses and iniquities that had been in my family were broken. I thank God that my son could hug me and feel safe with me. He doesn't have to go through what I went through because the blood of Jesus has broken the curse that brought such devastation and destruction on my family. My son and my two daughters are leaders in our church and in their schools. They love God with all their hearts, and I am continually amazed at the joy and freedom in God that is so apparent in their lives.

No matter who you are or what you're facing, God wants to not only break the curse but to reverse it as well. My children don't have the curse of anger passed to them, but instead they have a spirit of peace and joy. The curse has been reversed!

There are many who want help and deliverance but don't know where to turn. They have not heard that the blood of Jesus Christ can set them and their families free of generational curses. Some say, "If I could see a miracle, I would believe." Well, I am a miracle of God! No longer is my life filled with the destructive anger and violence that used to control me. I love telling people in churches, prisons, schools—wherever I have an opportunity to speak—that Jesus Christ can set them free from whatever it is that is keeping them imprisoned in the same way He set me free.

Recognizing Curses

My people are destroyed for lack of knowledge. (Hosea 4:6)

Look again at this Scripture. God says, *"My people."* He didn't say the unsaved, the bad guys, or those of false religion, but God's people. They're the ones being destroyed for one reason: lack of knowledge. In other words, we perish because we don't understand what the Word of God actually says. Many times we hear, "Christians can't be cursed! We have Jesus. His name is the name above all names." In one sense, they're absolutely right. Jesus' name is the name above all names. His name is above drugs, anger, sickness and disease, divorce, and suicide. But we need to recognize when and how to use His name and the power of His blood. Ignoring problems doesn't make them go away. It just allows them to grow and eventually spread to others in our family.

The first thing we need to understand is that curses are real. If you talk about curses in Africa, on the Navajo reservation, in Fiji, or in South America, most people will understand what you are talking about. Stories have been told for centuries about witch doctors, black and white magic, voodoo, and the bizarre supernatural happenings that take place in certain parts of the world.

> We perish because we don't understand what the Word of God actually says.

However, in Europe and North America, people are predominantly logical, Western-thinking people. We don't understand spiritual cause and effect.

How does the devil get a door into our lives to begin a family or generational curse? There has to be a gateway through which a curse enters. If we don't understand how we got into these situations, then we won't know how to get out of them. Events in life are not just accidents or random, unfortunate happenstance. There is an unseen spiritual side to everything that happens in the visible physical world. We may not see gravity, but we see its effects. We may not recognize the curses, but we experience the consequences of them.

When you go to the doctor, before they even see you, you have to fill out a form. It asks questions like, "Is there any history of cancer, diabetes, heart conditions, drug addiction, mental illness, etc. in your family?" It asks for your family's entire medical history. Doctors need to know this so they can quickly get to the root of your present problem and help you avoid health problems in the future. They ask so you can get healed and stay healthy, not to scare you or condemn you.

Likewise, the Great Physician, Jesus, wants us healed and healthy. So He asks, "Is there any history in your family of anger, divorce, suicide, poverty, or some other problem you seem plagued with but can't get rid of?" Jesus teaches us in His Word that current problems in our lives could be caused by iniquity in our family's past. He came to make us every bit whole.

It's interesting that, as far as natural, physical ailments go, doctors know that many problems are based in the blood. What you're about to find out is that, in the spiritual, the answer to all problems has already been given to you through the blood of Jesus Christ.

We see God's people being destroyed in all areas of their lives—in their families, their finances, their willpower, their health, and in their relationships with other people—because they do not recognize curses. There are all kinds of things the devil tries to bring upon God's people through curses. The curse may not be drugs or alcohol. The curse may be a disease. Why is it that individuals with a family history of cancer, heart problems, and mental illnesses tend to suffer from the exact same problems?

The curse can be poverty. There are people who give offerings and who also tithe, but every time they start to get ahead, the devil steals whatever God was bringing into their lives. The curse can be divorce. Some people are divorced four, five, or six times. Then their children get divorced, and that cycle of broken marriages and broken families is repeated. It is not because they are bad people but because the iniquity is passed down from generation to generation.

We must recognize the source of evil as well as the provision God made to break the power of the enemy.

The thief [the devil] *does not come except to steal, and to kill, and to destroy.*   (John 10:10)

The purpose of the enemy is clear, but we need to know what God has for us. What does God want to give us?

Beloved, I pray that you may prosper in all things and be in health, just as your soul prospers. (3 John 1:2)

I have come that they may have life, and that they may have it more abundantly. (John 10:10)

God does not come to steal, kill, and destroy your life. He is the giver of life! Through Jesus Christ, we have victory over the destruction the devil has planned for us, and we can come into the complete blessing of God for our lives. We do not need to be afraid of curses, but we need to be able to recognize them and learn how to destroy these works of the devil in our lives.

My people are destroyed for lack of knowledge. (Hosea 4:6)

The first and most important thing we need to know is that God sent His only Son to die for us. (See John 3:16.) God's desire is that every man and woman—young and old, good or bad—repent and walk in His righteousness and blessing. So no matter what your sins of the past or what your circumstances today, God is reaching out to you, willing to accept you just as you are and set you free. He wants to bless you.

> **God's desire is that every man and woman repent and walk in His righteousness and blessing.**

The events and circumstances of your past that are holding you in bondage cannot be changed, but your future can be. You can be changed from the inside out! God wants only good things for you, but most of all, He wants to set you free. Then you'll be able to receive and experience His richest blessings and be a blessing to others. You can't change your past, but you can change your future!

He will give you *"beauty for ashes, the oil of joy for mourning, the garment of praise for the spirit of heaviness"* (Isaiah 61:3). He will turn what once looked like a burned-out forest into a snow-capped mountaintop! God will give you freedom where there was bondage. He will give you blessing where there was a curse. And, through you, a blessing can pass on to your entire family for generations to come. Today, all curses in your life can be broken forever.

Discussion Questions

1. Did you believe that once you accepted Jesus you would automatically be perfect?

2. Jesus never tells us, "Go get cleaned up and then come to Me." What does He tell us in Matthew 11:28?

3. What reassurance do we have that our salvation and relationship with Jesus is a "come as you are" party? Read Philippians 1:6.

4. Who was the first sinner? Read Genesis 3:6.

   Who was the first murderer in the Bible and what relationship did he have to Adam? Read Genesis 4:1–8.

   The curses continued in Adam's family. What crime did Cain's descendant Lamech commit that demonstrates this is true? Read Genesis 4:23.

5. Read John 10:10. What is the devil called in this verse?

   What does he come to do?

   In the last part of the verse, what does Jesus say He came to do?

6. As a Canaanite, Rahab was under a family curse that came through Noah's grandson, Canaan. How did the curse come on her family? Read Genesis 9:24.

7. Many years after this incident, the walls of Jericho came tumbling down. When the entire city of Jericho was destroyed, who were the lone survivors? Read Joshua 6:21–25.

8. In Joshua 2:15–18, what did Rahab put in her window when Israel attacked that was a symbol of the delivering blood of the power of Jesus?

9. Write down any history of health problems in your family.

10. Do you currently suffer from any of these ailments? If so, which ones?

11. Is there any history in your family of anger, divorce, suicide, poverty, mental illness, depression, anxiety, fear, divorce, illegitimacy, etc., or some other problem you seem plagued with but can't get rid of? List them below.

12. What do 3 John 1:2 and John 10:10 say that God wants to give you?

13. In John 3:16, what is the first and most important thing we need to know that God did for us?

14. What did God say He would give us in Isaiah 61:3?

Chapter Three

Where Did That Come From?

Have you ever asked yourself, "Where did that come from?" Or maybe, "Why am I like this?" Maybe the question is not about you, but about your husband or wife. Or maybe it's about your children or grandchildren. If you're a pastor or a psychiatrist, maybe it's "How do I get to the root of this person's problem so they can live a happy, fulfilling life?" It starts with being bold enough to open up in prayer and be honest about it. When you do, I promise you the Son, S-O-N, will shine through and give you the answer.

I got a phone call a couple of years ago from a minister friend of mine whom I've known for years. He was pastoring at a church in the Chicago area when he called and said, "Listen, brother, I'm not going to be able to make it to the conference this year." When I asked him why, he answered, "I'm leaving the ministry. I'm leaving my church. I'm leaving my wife and children, and I'm moving on."

When I asked him what the problem was, he shared with me that, throughout their marriage, his wife would go into a deep depression every couple of months and at times would not get out of bed, wouldn't take care of the kids, and wouldn't go to church. He said, "It's ruining our marriage, our family, and our ministry. I can't take it any longer."

I said to him, "Brother, before you guys split up, do me a favor and come see me."

When they came and met with us, I asked his wife what the problem was. She began to tell me how depression would sometimes overtake her and totally control her life. I asked her, "When did this begin to happen?"

She said, "Pastor, I don't—"

I repeated my question, "When did this begin to happen?"

She began to tell me the most heartbreaking story. When she was a child, every so often her father would go into a depression. He would sit and braid ropes, make nooses, and threaten to hang himself. Then one day, when she was seven years old, she heard a commotion in the living room. She ran in and found her dad hanging from a rope that had been tied to a beam. She screamed and tried to hold her father up. She yelled for help, and her mother came running in from the kitchen. Thank God they were able to cut the rope, get him down, and save her father's life. However, from that day, the father's depression came on his daughter.

I said to her, "We're going to pray and we're going to break that family curse off you. And when God does this, it'll never come back on you again." We began to plead the blood of Jesus over her life for her deliverance. Later that night her husband called me and said, "My wife is still in the living room. She's lifting her hands, singing, and worshipping God—what do I do?"

I said, "Let her keep worshipping!"

He called me the next day and said, "When I got up to go to work, she was still in the living room worshipping and praising God."

Today, that couple is pastoring a new church, they're having revival, and the church is exploding in growth. Their marriage and their family have never been better. The depression is completely gone and they're finally experiencing all the joy, blessings, and outpouring of God upon their marriage and ministry that had been on hold for so many years. I say it again: *"God is no respecter of persons"* (Acts 10:34 KJV). What God did for these folks in breaking their family curse, He can do for you today.

Cracks beneath the Surface

Some time ago I was in Los Angeles filming our television program. We were staying in a hotel right outside of Universal

Studios. I went into the bathroom to brush my teeth and noticed a piece of paper on the mirror listing the things to do in case of an earthquake. When I looked out the hotel window, I could see many homes, buildings, Universal Studios, downtown Los Angeles, and a highway. On the surface, everything seemed to be fine and perfect. But the reason the hotel posted that list is because they knew that even though everything on the surface looked fine, below the surface there were faults or cracks that ran beneath that city. Although they were dormant for the moment, when the circumstances and pressures were right, these faults could move and cause an earthquake, bringing destruction and devastation to the once-perfect surface. But the word *fault* can also mean a crack or a flaw in your life, in your character, or in your personality that lies beneath the surface.

> *Confess your **faults** one to another, and pray one for another, that ye may be healed.*   (James 5:16 KJV, emphasis added)

Let's take a close look at this verse because it's not the truth that sets us free but the truth *we know*, or the truth *we understand* and act on, that sets us free. Faults may not be the weaknesses that everyone sees from time to time. They can be those hidden, underlying cracks beneath the surface. When the pressure and circumstances are right, those faults can rise up and destroy your future, your marriage, your ministry, and the blessing God has for you.

> It's not the truth that sets us free but the truth we know, or the truth we understand, that sets us free.

Confessing One to Another

When I talk about being set free, I'm not talking about learning how to *control* depression, anger, or whatever the fault may be. I'm talking about being set free and *delivered* from the fault forever! How do we do that? James 5:16 says to *"confess your faults one to another."* We are to confess these faults lying beneath the surface, confess the cracks we are covering with a certain type of personality, and confess the earthquake pressures that could bring destruction at any moment.

The concept of *confession* is very difficult for some Christians to grasp because we have the misconception that we're supposed to be perfect from the moment we get saved. But none of us are perfect. It shouldn't be hard to confess our faults to one another because all of us have things in our lives to which God is trying to bring deliverance and spiritual healing. So when the Bible says to confess these things, we need to do just that. Just because we're Christians doesn't mean we're without fault.

When Tiz and I first got married, every pastor and evangelist who came through would prophesy over me, "You're going to be a great man of God, and God's going to give you a ministry that's going to go around the world." But they didn't realize that I had a very real and very serious anger and violence problem. They didn't know that when I went home, I would hit my wife or that I sometimes would erupt in a raging anger I couldn't control. This anger and violence was destroying my life, and it was destroying my family. It is a miracle that Tiz didn't leave me.

> Just because we're Christians doesn't mean we're without faults.

When I had finally calmed down after a fit of rage, Tiz would say, "We need to get help. We need to talk to someone and get some counseling." But I wouldn't do it because I thought Christians were supposed to be perfect. How could I confess to imperfection and get help? But James told us to confess our faults one to another. He didn't write this to unbelievers; it was written to *believers*. We are to find someone we can confess these things to. Someone to whom we can say, "I've got this problem, and I need help."

One reason I wouldn't confess is because I didn't know why I was so enraged. I would wonder, *Why am I doing this? Why am I like this? Why is this thing still in my life even though I'm a Christian, even though I'm born again, and even though I've been set free from so many horrible things? Why is this thing here?* Again, it's not the truth alone that will set you free, but the *knowledge* of the truth. Remember, God's people are destroyed because of their lack of knowledge.

Where Did That Come From?

You may be suffering from a generational curse, but not because you're a bad person, a bad Christian, or someone who is worse than anyone else. As a matter of fact, it may not even be your fault. We discussed earlier that iniquity can come as a spirit that lands on you or is something you inherit. But however it comes, James said to confess your faults—those things that lie beneath the surface—so that you can be healed. How did those faults get there? The Lord has shown me that faults can land on you or can attach themselves to you from generations past because of the iniquity of the fathers.

No Curse without a Cause

Now as Jesus passed by, He saw a man who was blind from birth. And His disciples asked Him, saying, "Rabbi, who sinned, this man or his parents, that he was born blind?" Jesus answered, "Neither this man nor his parents sinned, but that the works of God should be revealed in him." (John 9:1–3)

Jesus told the disciples that the man's blindness was not because of a generational curse, but what I want you to see is that the disciples thought it was. According to the religious thinking at that time, someone who was born blind must have been cursed by God. Now don't limit this understanding to someone who has a physical ailment or disability. The question is more than, "Why is this man blind?" The question could be, "Why does this person go through so many divorces?" or "Why are they always angry?" or "Why are they so depressed?" or "Why do they have an eating disorder?" or "Why are they suicidal?" or "Why are they always poor?" or "Why is this child always out of control?" or "Why is this curse on this person's life?" or any other number of similar questions.

Jesus didn't say to His disciples, "That's ridiculous! What a stupid question!" because these people understood spiritual transfer, or spiritual cause and effect. They understood that many of life's problems have a spiritual root.

For the mystery of lawlessness is already at work; only He who now restrains will do so until He is taken out of the way. (2 Thessalonians 2:7)

The word *"mystery"* is translated from the Greek word *muste-rion*, whose root word means "to shut the mouth."[1] And the Greek word for *iniquity* is *anomia*, which means "a violation of the law; wickedness, and unrighteousness."[2] So what does that say to us? Someone is keeping their mouth shut about something that's evil!

When we look at the Old Testament meaning of iniquity in its context, we see that iniquity is a spiritual force that pressures us and drives us to bow or bend under its destructive nature. From this New Testament verse, we can see that to be delivered of iniquity, we must speak the truth, name the iniquity for what it is, confess the fault, and declare that the blood of Jesus Christ has set us free.

> *For I, the LORD your God, am a jealous God, visiting the iniquity of the fathers on the children to the third and fourth generations of those who hate Me.* (Exodus 20:5)

The word *iniquity* appears in the Bible over three hundred times. I believe God wants us to know that apart from Jesus and the understanding that His blood has set us free, iniquities are passed down from the fathers and mothers to the children and to the children's children. The iniquity inherited by the children is passed down through a curse that is not the result of something the children did but the result of something that happened in their forefathers' lives and then landed on them. Can it be that something happened in our grandparents' lives, and because of that, a curse landed on us? We then inherited a family curse.

> *Our fathers sinned and are no more* [they died], *but we bear their iniquities.* (Lamentations 5:7)

> *Behold, I was brought forth in iniquity, and in sin my mother conceived me.* (Psalm 51:5)

You and I inherited the iniquity of our forefathers. Through conception, weaknesses were passed down to us, and we inherited an evil spiritual force on the inside of us that caused us to bow under its destructive nature. We inherited the faults of our parents.

Truth and Reason

The question the disciples asked Jesus was something that you and I as Americans, or westernized people, don't understand. They asked, "Why is this man cursed? Was it because of something he did or because of something his parents did?" We're taught in our Western world to think intellectually, not spiritually. We have been taught to think reasonably, logically, and rationally.

I remember hearing about a study the United States government did on many third-world countries after World War II. The U.S. researchers believed that people in third-world countries were not as intelligent as Westernized people, so they asked them this question, "If cotton does not grow in a cold climate and London is a cold climate, does cotton grow in London?" Their answers were, "We don't know. We've never been to London." Immediately the people giving the test said, "These people are unintelligent. They can't even put two plus two together."

If you and I took that test, we would say, "If cotton doesn't grow in a cold climate and London is a cold climate, of course cotton doesn't grow in London." But the third-world people didn't give that answer, so the U.S. government came to the conclusion that these third worlders weren't as intelligent as those in a Western-thinking country.

> There's a dimension that brings water out of a rock, puts gold coins in fishes' mouths, causes blind eyes to see, and causes the dead to rise.

Researchers later found out that these people did understand. They understood that *normally* cotton wouldn't grow in London because it's a cold climate, but they also understood that there is a dimension beyond the natural. There's a dimension that brings water out of a rock. There's a dimension that puts gold coins in fishes' mouths. There's a dimension that causes blind eyes to see. There's a dimension that causes the dead to rise. There's a dimension that turns ex-drug addicts and dope dealers into preachers and men and women of God. So, in the natural, cotton wouldn't grow in London's cold climate, but they knew there is a spiritual dimension beyond the natural that can override the natural.

Free at Last

In our Western-world mind-set, we can accept the fact that someone is paying a price because of something *they* did. We understand that a man reaps what he sows. What we're not taught is that we may reap something sown by our family many generations ago. The disciples knew that curses were passed on to future generations. They understood that the supernatural could transcend all reason and logic. And we must understand this truth to be set free from generational curses.

A Spiritual Force at Work

Like a flitting sparrow, like a flying swallow, so a curse without cause shall not alight. (Proverbs 26:2)

I am amazed when I hear or read about birds migrating to distant continents at various seasons of the year. A bird can fly out of North America, wing its way across the equator into South America, find the exact nest it had before, stay there for the winter season, and then fly home to Alaska and find its way back to the exact nest it left there.

This is a tremendous illustration of the spiritual principle behind curses. Proverbs 26:2 tells us to look at the swallows that fly thousands of miles every year, if not tens of thousands of miles, and return to the same nest. How does that happen? They don't have a map, they don't have a GPS unit, and they're not following road signs. The birds are not guided by radar or air traffic control. They're not just flapping their wings, flying around, and then suddenly, somehow, happen to find their way to the right nests. It is not a coincidence. There is something inside those birds that guides them to return to exactly the same place they were born.

Here in the Northwest, a salmon can be born in one of thousands of streams or rivers and it will go downstream into a bigger river, that will empty into a bigger river, that will empty into a bigger river, and eventually go out into the ocean. It will spend a couple years in the ocean, but when it's time for that salmon to spawn, it will swim back from the ocean to the main river, up another river, up another river, and go to the exact stream where it was born years before. How does that happen? Something on the inside draws the salmon home.

Where Did That Come From?

In a similar way, a curse doesn't just float around in the atmosphere and then, for no apparent reason, land somewhere. Just as there is something that directs the salmon and the swallows, there is something that directs a curse to a person, city, church, or nation. That curse is guided by a spiritual force.

There is a reason why a child grows up to become an alcoholic.

There is a reason why an abused child becomes an abusive parent.

There is a reason why a young man ends up in prison.

There is a reason why a person goes through divorce after divorce.

David repented for committing adultery with Bathsheba and then murdering her husband, but because of David's sin, a curse landed on his family.

> *Wherefore hast thou despised the commandment of the LORD, to do evil in his sight? thou hast killed Uriah the Hittite with the sword, and hast taken his wife to be thy wife, and hast slain him with the sword of the children of Ammon. Now therefore the sword shall never depart from thine house; because thou hast despised me, and hast taken the wife of Uriah the Hittite to be thy wife. Thus saith the LORD, Behold, I will raise up evil against thee out of thine own house, and I will take thy wives before thine eyes, and give them unto thy neighbour, and he shall lie with thy wives in the sight of this sun. For thou didst it secretly: but I will do this thing before all Israel, and before the sun. And David said unto Nathan, I have sinned against the LORD. And Nathan said unto David, The LORD also hath put away thy sin; thou shalt not die.* (2 Samuel 12:9–13 KJV)

The *"sword"* referred to a curse of destruction, desolation, and death on David's family. One son, Ammon, raped his own sister. Another son, Absalom, rose up in rebellion against his own father. (See 2 Samuel 13:14; 15:4–12.) God forgave David's sins when he repented, but the curse of his iniquity was passed on to his family. The wives and the children did nothing to deserve the curse, but they suffered from the curse that landed on them as a result of David's iniquity.

That's why the Bible says to confess, "I have this depression," or, "I have this fault in my life." Having to confess does not mean we're bad people but rather that we have inherited iniquity. This is not to place blame on the parents or the grandparents either but to identify our true enemy. Our battle is not against flesh and blood. Our battle is against principalities, and powers, and rulers of darkness in high places. (See Ephesians 6:12.)

Once when we were praying for a woman, she went down under the power of God. I said to the usher standing next to her, "Brother, pick her up." Then I said to the woman, "Ma'am, I don't know why you came forward to be prayed for, but there's a spirit of suicide on you. Is there a history of suicide in your family?"

The woman broke into tears and said, "Pastor, my family is from England and Ireland, and at different times over the last fifty years, seven of my aunts have set themselves on fire and committed suicide." She continued, "I love God, I love my family, and I love my life, but I'm being pulled toward this depression and suicide." We prayed the prayer of breaking generational curses, and Jesus set that woman free.

Earlier I mentioned a woman whose family suffered from various eating disorders. When I talked to her in a church service, I asked, "Ma'am, what did God set you free from?" She answered, "For generations, my family members have died early from obesity. However, in the last ten years, my family is dying from anorexia." Whether it was obesity or anorexia, each generation was dying from eating disorders. That generational curse stemmed back to someone in the family who was molested. A spirit of eating disorders was birthed into the family from that traumatic event. We began to pray, and this woman's family is now eating right because Jesus set them free.

A successful businesswoman told my wife that at certain times of the year, no matter how well everything in her life was going, a cloud of depression tried to come over her. She couldn't even pinpoint particular reasons, but she had to struggle just to keep her mind together. She would feel like it was dragging her under. Tiz asked her if her mother faced the same thing and she said, "Yes, only much more severely. It would turn into crippling migraine headaches." Tiz told her this was a family curse. They prayed and felt the Spirit of God break it. This woman has been totally free from the oppression for several years, and that freedom has not only blessed her but her husband and family as well.

I was going through an airport on my way to an out-of-town preaching engagement when a man walked up to me and said, "You're Pastor Huch, aren't you?"

I replied, "Yes sir, I am."

Then he said, "We've been watching your program on television. Pastor, can I ask you something?" He didn't wait for me to answer but instead continued. "I've been listening to your teachings on breaking the curse off our lives. I need to ask you, what happened to me? The reason I am at the airport right now is to pick up my children. My wife and I are divorced. We are both saved, and we both love God and each other. But all of a sudden, we were fighting. We didn't know why we were fighting. We didn't really even know what we were fighting about. The next thing I knew—we were divorced!"

He began to weep, and then he said, "I don't know what happened. She doesn't know what happened. But here we are. We're talking to one another now because we have both been watching your program. We are talking about getting back together again, but we need to know what happened. What happened to us?"

I looked at him and said, "Brother, is there any history of divorce in your family?"

He replied, "My mom has been divorced five times and my dad six times."

I told him, "Brother, that's a family curse."

As we talked, a crowd of people gathered around us there in the airport to listen in on our conversation. Perhaps many of them were going through similar experiences and didn't know how they ended up in a place or in circumstances they never intended to be in. Maybe they were also asking the questions, "How did this happen to me?" and "How can I change my life?"

Most likely for the first time in their lives, they heard a confident answer: "That is a generational curse, and the blood of Jesus Christ can set you free right now!"

Discussion Questions

1. Does your life look normal on the surface, yet underneath things are cracking and breaking apart?

2. What does James 5:10 instruct you to do with your faults?

3. What do the following Scriptures say about iniquity?

    Exodus 20:5

    Lamentations 5:7

    Psalm 51:5

4. How does Proverbs 26:2 compare birds to a curse?

5. Read 2 Samuel 12:9–13. Even though King David repented for committing adultery with Bathsheba and then murdering her husband, what happened to his family as a result of his actions?

6. What does Ephesians 6:12 say our battle is NOT against? What is it against?

Chapter Four

Like Father, Like Son—No More!

W HEN WE SEE a young man with an alcohol problem, and we
know his father was an alcoholic, we don't think anything
about saying, "He is just like his dad." Then there is the woman
who is always screaming at her husband and kids, and people who
knew her mother will say, "She is just like her mother." These
statements remind us of another old phrase: *Like father, like son.*
The reason we don't question remarks like these is because iniquity has been passed from generation to generation since the fall
of Adam and Eve in the garden of Eden.

> *Therefore, just as through one man sin entered the world, and
> death through sin, and thus death spread to all men, because all
> sinned.* (Romans 5:12)

When Adam sinned, his iniquity was passed on to all mankind.
That's the bad news. But the good news is that through another
man—Jesus Christ—sin and the curse of sin are defeated.

> *For if by the one man's offense death reigned through the one,
> much more those who receive abundance of grace and of the gift of
> righteousness will reign in life through the One, Jesus Christ.*
> (Romans 5:17)

Some time ago I went to minister at a prison in Beaumont,
Texas, with Mike Barber and Deion Sanders. On our way there,
Mike told me that when he started his prison ministry in Texas
twelve years before, there were ten prisons in the entire state.
Now there are 140 prisons, and all of them are more than filled to
capacity. *Why is this?* I wondered.

As I started to minister that afternoon, I asked the inmates two questions, "How many of you have parents or grandparents in prison?" and "How many of you have children or grandchildren in trouble with the law?" Close to 100 percent of the inmates raised their hands in response to both of the questions.

I taught on family curses and we prayed to break those curses. We had an uplink to four hundred thousand other inmates in prisons around America so they could hear the message. As we were leaving, the warden said, "We have never been able to find the answer. This teaching on family curses is the answer we've been looking for." Overnight we had three hundred other prisons contact us and ask us for the teaching on breaking family curses because they understood that the iniquity of the parents passes from generation to generation.

Why is there a growing need for prisons nationwide? Because an inmate may get out, but he doesn't change. The majority of them will go back to prison. Not only will they return, but the same iniquity that brings them there will also cause their children and grandchildren to end up in prison. This is why the need for prisons keeps growing in the United States. Not only are the inmates not changing, but the iniquity in the inmates passes to their children and their grandchildren. *Like father, like son.*

Defining Family

When talking about family curses, we need to understand what the word *family* means. A family can be as small as a husband, wife, and children, or it can be the church family. It can be as large as your city or state (remember city fathers?), and it can be as large as our nation, including the president and government officials. Certain families have certain characteristics; certain cities have certain characteristics; and certain states, nations, and nationalities have certain characteristics. But we need to understand that we don't have to accept negative characteristics. They don't have to haunt us the rest of our lives. They can be broken.

When John F. Kennedy Jr. was killed in an airplane accident, every magazine and newspaper was talking about the "Kennedy curse." This is something that can be broken with the Word of

God and by the power of the blood of Jesus! These tragedies didn't happen because the Kennedys are bad people but because of something that landed on them. The iniquity, or curse, was transferred from generation to generation. But Jesus wants to set that family free forever.

The man in Atlanta who killed his wife and children, then went into a brokerage firm and killed others before killing himself, was suffering from a generational curse. In a suicide note, he wrote that the spirit of anger that was on his father came on him and then also passed from him on to his own son. This man had a spirit of anger that landed on him. How I wish we could have gotten to him before this happened!

Another horrible incident happened with a man who kidnapped and murdered three women in Yosemite Park. It was later revealed that years before his younger brother had been kidnapped and held captive for seven years by a child molester. The young man finally broke free and was returned to his family, but he brought those spirits of perversion and violence with him, and they jumped on his older brother.

> The reality of spiritual transfer, or of iniquity passing from generation to generation, is not only found in the Bible; it's found all through life itself.

Now these situations are obviously extreme, but it shows us that the reality of spiritual transfer, or the reality of the iniquity passing down from generation to generation, is not only found in the Bible—it's found all through life itself. We need to look at our own lives and ask ourselves, What is causing us to think and behave in an ungodly manner? What is causing us to lash out at our children for no apparent reason? Why can't we seem to hold on to a job for any length of time? It is time to break the curse off our lives once and for all and walk in the freedom Jesus provided for us through the cross.

We recently heard from a young man named Manuel. He was in trouble with the law by age ten and ended up in a juvenile detention facility. We found ourselves asking the same question about him that the disciples had asked about the blind man:

Who sinned—this young man or his parents? The following is his story.

Dear Pastor Huch,

My first childhood memories are of drugs and violence. When I was four years old, my father gave me beer to drink. He thought it was cute. My mother smoked marijuana most of her adult life, and my father smoked it with her.

My mother passed away from a brain tumor when I was nine years old. My dad had been an alcoholic since I can remember, and it got worse after my mom passed away. I wasn't sure how to handle my feelings, and I started causing trouble at school. I began hanging around with some guys who knew what I was going through. I soon realized they were a gang. Since my dad was abusive to me, I thought it would be a good idea to have gang friends to stick up for me. I thought, "This is my chance to show my dad I am a real man." I was only ten at the time, and I began to think of the gang as my family.

After I got into the gang, I started getting into legal trouble from assaults, thefts, and so on. I started smoking marijuana and snorting crank at the age of eleven. Within a year, I was dealing drugs. I was young, and I knew I had to act twice as tough as the older guys. I was a druggie, alcoholic, and a violent person— everything my mom wanted me not to be. Soon, I was stealing from my dad and from old friends to support my habits. I was worse than my dad had ever been.

When I was twelve, I violently raped a teenage girl. I was sent from one detention home to another, and I went from foster home to foster home. Eventually, I was moved to a boys' ranch.

That was the lowest point in my life. I realized I couldn't make a go of my life all alone. With help from a detention home staff member, I gave my life to God. I prayed daily and began to build a personal relationship with Jesus. I started caring about myself and my behavior changed. I was a child of God!

Some youth group members from your church, New Beginnings, came and spent time with us on Christmas Eve. When the Posse, the music and dance group from New Beginnings, came to our detention home, over half of the kids received the Lord.

I have started a Bible study group in my cottage. I am learning how to be a good friend, and I led another resident to the Lord. I am working with him, and I am loving it.

Like Father, Like Son—No More!

I would like to become a youth minister. I wear Christian T-shirts, and when people ask me about them, I tell them about God. I am not ashamed to be a Christian. I try to work with everyone around me, praising God in my daily life. My goal is to get out and move into the New Beginnings men's house, go to college, get a degree, and spread God's Word. I thank God for every challenge I have had and every victory I have had, because it has made me who I am—a Christian who is strong and won't give in!   *Manuel*

This young man's life is a vivid example of generational curses passing from one generation to the next. But through the power of the blood of Jesus, he was able to break the recurring cycle and turn his life around.

Matt Crouch, Paul and Jan Crouch's son, shared this story with me one day. It vividly illustrates how spiritual strongholds can transfer from generation to generation, not because of a sin that was committed, but from an event that occurred. About two months after their oldest son, Calen, started first grade, Matt's wife, Lori, got a phone call from Calen's teacher. She said that Calen was very upset and panicking because he thought that his mom wasn't going to pick him up from school. Lori explained to the teacher that there was no reason for him to be afraid of this. She had never once been late or missed picking him up, neither this year nor in his previous year of kindergarten. But there was no calming him, so Matt and Lori both rushed to the school to talk to Calen. They both assured him, "Calen, we always come back for you. Why are you carrying on this way?" There was no reasoning with him. Seemingly out of nowhere and for no apparent reason, this fear had come upon him.

For the next three months, this fearful behavior gripped Calen's life. In addition to the continued episodes at school, he would not let Lori out of his sight. He clung to her side wherever she went. He followed her from room to room in their house. If she stopped their car and got out to drop mail in their mailbox, he tried to get out with her. He would burst into tears of panic if she tried to leave him even for a short while. Every night would be a traumatic, panic-stricken, emotional scene as they tried to get him to go to bed, even though he shared a room with his brother. All through the night he would try to come and crawl into bed with Matt and Lori, then they would have to go through it all again.

They tried everything to help reassure Calen of their love and commitment to him. They tried discipline as a means of settling his behavior. They prayed over him and with him constantly. They agreed with powerful men and women of God to break the stronghold of fear over him, but nothing was working. It was breaking their hearts. The strangest part of this was that normally Calen was incredibly outgoing, self-confident, and uninhibited in every area of his life. He had no fear of anything else—except being separated from his mom.

One day Matt was talking to his father, Paul Crouch, about the situation. Suddenly, a light came on in Paul's eyes, and he said, "I know exactly what this is. When I was the same age as Calen and starting first grade, my father died. Every day after that, my mother would walk me halfway to the school grounds and try to send me to school, but I would sob so hard that sometimes she would cry too and just take me back home. I was so afraid that I would come home from school one day and my mom, just like my dad, would be gone and I'd be left alone."

Paul and Matt realized that Calen's fear had not originated from something that had happened in his own life, but from something that had happened in his grandfather's life. Once they realized the root of the fear, they were able to break this generational fear of separation over Calen. He was set free because Jesus' blood was placed over the door of his heart. Now the devil can't torment him with that fear anymore!

Power to Break the Curse

The world's solution to temptations and problems is, "Just say no." But believers know that they need to understand spiritual cause and effect. Without understanding the power of Jesus and His blood, we can say "no" until we're blue in the face and still fail every time. We must understand the truth that sets us free.

And you shall know the truth, and the truth shall make you free....If the Son makes you free, you shall be free indeed.
(John 8:32, 36)

In this passage of Scripture, Jesus was speaking to the Jews who believed in Him and already acknowledged Him as Savior. But they couldn't understand why, being the children of Abraham, they needed to be set free. In John 8:33 they said they were not in bondage to anyone. They didn't understand that with every sin committed—whether by themselves, by their great-great-grand-parents, by their city, or by their nation—there was a spiritual curse yoked to that sin. As Christians, we also need to do more than get born again and receive forgiveness; we need to receive our freedom.

Jesus told them in verse 36, "When I set you free, you'll be free *indeed*. I'll not only forgive you, but I'll break the curse on you that's linked to the sin." If the Son has made us free, we shall be free indeed. The word *"indeed"* means Jesus will break the curse and we can actually live free. He'll not only forgive us of our sin, but He will break the iniquity that goes with that sin. It's important to understand that a Jewish person could always have their sins forgiven, but they could never

> As Christians, we need to do more than get born again and receive forgiveness; we need to receive our freedom.

have the *curse* of their sin broken. King David and his family were a prime example. David was forgiven, but the curse of his sin was passed to his family.

Let me explain directly from the Word of God how this works:

> *And he shall take the two goats, and present them before the LORD at the door of the tabernacle of the congregation. And Aaron shall cast lots upon the two goats; one lot for the LORD, and the other lot for the scapegoat....Then shall he kill the goat of the sin offering, that is for the people, and bring his blood within the veil, and do with that blood as he did with the blood of the bullock, and sprinkle it upon the mercy seat, and before the mercy seat....And he shall sprinkle of the blood upon it with his finger seven times, and cleanse it, and hallow it from the uncleanness of the children of Israel. And when he hath made an end of reconciling the holy place, and the tabernacle of the*

congregation, and the altar, he shall bring the live goat: and Aaron shall lay both his hands upon the head of the live goat, and confess over him all the iniquities of the children of Israel, and all their transgressions in all their sins, putting them upon the head of the goat, and shall send him away by the hand of a fit man into the wilderness: and the goat shall bear upon him all their iniquities unto a land not inhabited: and he shall let go the goat in the wilderness.

(Leviticus 16:7–8, 15, 19–22 KJV)

God had them bring two goats to the tabernacle. One goat was left at the door of the tabernacle, and the other goat was brought in, placed upon the altar, and sacrificed. The high priest would then take the blood of the sacrificed goat to the door of the tabernacle, place it on the head of the scapegoat, and confess the iniquities of the people over it. One goat died for the sins or transgressions, the other goat carried away the iniquity—the spiritual force on the inside that caused destruction—to a desert or a dry place. This is how the Jewish people atoned for their sins.

> Through the shed blood of Jesus, not only are we forgiven of our sins, but we can walk in that forgiveness and be set free from the curse of sin.

In our case, Jesus died for our sins on the cross, but He also shed His blood seven times, just as Aaron sprinkled the blood seven times. (See verse 14.) Through the shed blood of Jesus, not only are we forgiven of our sins, but we can walk in that forgiveness and be set free from the curse of sin. Both of the goats represent the redemptive work of Jesus Christ.

There were two goats but only one Jesus. Jesus shed His blood so that we could not only be forgiven of sin but healed of inner iniquities, which are the bruises and wounds of generational sin that drive us to perpetuate the sins of our ancestors. Only the blood of Jesus provides forgiveness and a new way of living. When we are born again, we receive forgiveness for our sins. But then we need to plead the blood of Jesus over our lives to banish the iniquity to the wilderness and walk in freedom.

Shut the Back Door

When the unclean spirit is gone out of a man, he walketh through dry places, seeking rest, and findeth none. Then he saith, I will return into my house from whence I came out; and when he is come, he findeth it empty, swept, and garnished. Then goeth he, and taketh with himself seven other spirits more wicked than himself, and they enter in and dwell there: and the last state of that man is worse than the first. (Matthew 12:43–45 KJV)

The moment we receive Jesus, every force of darkness that's coming against our life flees. It goes to that desert place looking for a place to rest. Our sin is washed away and the cause of the spiritual curse flees to the desert place. But it comes back later, looking for an open door. Even though our lives have been swept and garnished, blood-washed and cleansed, if it finds that we don't understand spiritual curses and we've left a door open, it comes back in and is worse than it was before.

I see this happen in many Christian families. A person comes out of a sinful lifestyle, they get saved, they go into the ministry or they get involved in their church, and they raise their kids in church. Then, when the kids hit the teenage years, they go out and do the same things the parents used to do, only many times worse. We stand in awe and ask, "What happened? What's wrong? Our kids were raised in church, but they're doing exactly what we were doing before we got saved." That's because we swept the house, but we haven't shut the door through the blood of Jesus and realized that we have to break that family curse.

Moses and the children of Israel are an excellent example of turning the forces of darkness away from our homes. When the curse was coming on the people of Egypt, God told Moses to tell the people to take the blood of a lamb and put it on the doorpost of their homes. When the spirit of death came that night, it saw the blood over the doors of their houses and could not enter in. (See Exodus 12:21–29.) Romans 6:23 says that *"the wages of sin is death."* That doesn't just mean death as in dying—heaven or hell. Divorce is part of the death, poverty is part of the death, racism is part of the death, anger that ruins marriages and families is part of the death, and depression and sicknesses are part of the death.

A man in our church told me that all the males in his family died within the year of a certain birthday. After his father passed away, he came to us. We pleaded the blood of Jesus over him and his family and taught him how to break that spirit of death. People get saved but they haven't learned how to put the blood over the door of their tabernacle. When you realize and use the power of the blood of Jesus, those spirits and those curses cannot touch you. Divorce may try to come, but when it sees the blood over the door of your tabernacle, it cannot enter in. Sickness, depression, anger, violence, and every evil thing will try to come against you and your family, but if you have the blood of Jesus Christ on your doorpost, you are living under God's divine protection.

If you are saying, or if you hear someone say, "Like father, like son," apply the blood of Jesus! Nothing can cross the blood. In the old tabernacle made of stone and mortar, the priest used the blood of a lamb to atone for God's people, but it was a temporary answer. Today you are the tabernacle of God, and the blood of the Lamb of God, once and for all, has been shed to forgive the sin and break the curse.

Discussion Questions

1. According to Romans 5:12, how did sin enter the world and how is it passed from one generation to the next?

2. When Adam sinned, his iniquity was passed on to all mankind. That's the bad news, but through another man there is good news. Who is that man and what is the good news? Read Romans 5:17.

3. Read John 8:32, 36. What makes us free? Who makes us free?

4. In John 8:33, what did the Jews say about being in bondage?

5. In Leviticus 16:7–8, how many goats did the high priest present before the Lord?

   In Leviticus 16:15, what did the priest do with the first goat? What was the goat called?

   In Leviticus 16:19–22, what did Aaron the priest do with the live goat?

6. The moment we receive Jesus, every force of darkness that's coming against our life flees. According to Matthew 12:43–45, where does the unclean spirit that comes out of a man/woman go?

7. What happens when it returns?

8. Moses and the children of Israel are an excellent example of turning the forces of darkness away from our homes. When the curse was coming on the people of Egypt, what did God ask Moses to tell the people to do? See Exodus 12:21.

   In Exodus 12:23, how did the Lord prevent the destroyer from entering the homes of His people and harming them?

Chapter Five

Burden Removing *and* Yoke Destroying

WHEN JESUS ASKED His disciples what men were saying about Him, they answered that some thought He might be John the Baptist, Jeremiah, or Elijah. Then Jesus asked, *"But what about you?...Who do you say I am?"* (Matthew 16:15 NIV). Immediately Peter answered, *"You are the Christ, the Son of the living God"* (verse 16 NIV). I can see Peter slapping himself on the forehead as it dawned on him just who Jesus was.

"Christ" is not just a title. It is not Jesus' last name! *"Christ"* defined who Jesus was out of the Old Testament. Notice that Peter didn't say, "You're the Savior" or "You're the King of Kings," although Jesus is all those things. Peter said, *"You are the Christ,"* which literally means, "the Anointed One."

> *It shall come to pass in that day, that his burden shall be taken away from off thy shoulder, and his yoke from off thy neck, and the yoke shall be destroyed because of the anointing.*
> (Isaiah 10:27 KJV)

The burden will be removed and the yoke destroyed because of the anointing. It is absolutely crucial that you understand this part of the teaching. Remember when Jesus said in John 8:32,

"You shall know the truth, and when you know and understand this truth, then this truth will set you free"? The believing Jews thought they had all the truth they needed because they were the children of Abraham, but they were wrong. Their burdens were removed, but they were about to have their yokes, or their family curses, destroyed. Now what is meant by the burden-removing, yoke-destroying power of God?

First of all, Romans 6:23 says, *"The wages of sin is death."* We know that we've all sinned and *"there is none righteous, no, not one"* (Romans 3:10). The wages for the burden, or the payment, of our sin is death. Somebody has to die for our sins. Twenty-five years ago when I received Jesus Christ as my Savior, He removed the burden. I don't have to pay the price for my sin because the price was paid in full once and for all. Jesus is the Christ, which means "the anointed One of God who removed our burden."

Second, His anointing also removes the yoke. That's why Jesus said, "When you understand the truth, you'll not just be free, but you'll be free indeed. I'll not only remove the burden of sin, which is death, but I'll break the yoke of sin, which is the curse." All you have to do is claim this truth through Jesus Christ and His anointing. Every sin will be forgiven, and every curse will be broken off you and your family in Jesus' name.

> Jesus is the Christ, which means "the anointed one of God who removed our burdens."

Let's go one step further. Take a look at Isaiah 53. Although it is a verse that a lot of Christians know by heart, I've found that most don't understand the powerful revelation that God is prophesying to us through Jesus Christ.

> *But He was wounded for our transgressions, He was bruised for our iniquities; the chastisement for our peace was upon Him, and by His stripes we are healed.* (Isaiah 53:5)

If I took some kind of weapon and hit you in the arm hard enough to break the skin, you would bleed. That would be a wound. Jesus was wounded for our transgressions, or our sins. But the verse goes on to say that He was bruised for our iniquities. If

I hit you on the arm without breaking the skin, your arm would bruise, which means it would be bleeding on the inside. And iniquity is a spiritual bruise on the inside that tries to break or destroy our lives.

Isaiah 1:18 says, *"Though your sins are like scarlet, they shall be as white as snow; though they are red like crimson, they shall be as wool."* The word *"scarlet"* implies "twice dipped, or double dyed;...to double, or to do a thing twice."[3]

When God tells us that the blood of Jesus washes us clean, He means we are double dipped! We are forgiven, but we are also freed from iniquity. We are going to heaven, but we are also healed on the inside so that we can live pure, holy, and righteous on this earth. We have the power to resist sin and live godly lives. We have the power to resist anger, violence, drugs, and depression.

No matter what our sins are, no matter how deeply stained our lives are, the blood of Jesus doesn't just cover them, but it washes them away. And Jesus doesn't only wash the sin away, He also washes away the consequence for our sin, which is death. We have eternal life!

Now a wound bleeds on the outside, and a transgression is the act on the outside. So when the Bible says Jesus was wounded for our transgressions, it means that the blood He shed on the outside washes every sin from our lives. He's the burden remover. When He was bruised, He was bruised on the inside to wash away that spirit or curse. He's also the yoke destroyer. He was wounded for our transgressions, and He was also bruised for our iniquities. He's the burden remover and the yoke destroyer. He washes everything away on the outside and He sets us free on the inside.

When Peter proclaimed that Jesus is the Christ, Jesus said, *"Blessed art thou, Simon Barjona"* (Matthew 16:17 KJV). Because of Peter's revelation, Jesus said, "Peter, you are now blessed." We are blessed when we understand Jesus is the burden-removing, yoke-destroying Christ. Look at what happened next. After Jesus blessed Peter with power and authority, He backed it up by giving him the keys to the kingdom of God.

Keys to the Kingdom

And I will give you the keys of the kingdom of heaven, and what-ever you bind on earth will be bound in heaven, and whatever you loose on earth will be loosed in heaven. (Matthew 16:19)

We've all seen people with a big ring full of keys. They may be janitors, maintenance people, or building owners, but they usually have the authority to enter any given room or building. I've even seen people with a bunch of keys who didn't own a car or a house, but boy, they sure had a lot of keys! People like keys because they are a symbol of authority. A key gives someone the power to lock and unlock, to open something up and to close something down, to let someone in or to keep someone out.

How would you like to have the keys? Not the keys to a building or to a car, but the actual keys to the kingdom of God, to God's power and God's revelation. I often tell the people in my church that there is no power in ritual, but there is life-changing power in revelation. Baptism has no power if people are simply going through a religious ritual. But I've seen people who were taught about water baptism through God's Word go down in the water sick and come up totally healed.

> There is no power in ritual, but there is life-changing power in revelation.

The same thing happens with communion. It's not just about a ritual with some crackers and juice. It's about remembering that we have a covenant with God that He has sealed with the blood of Jesus Christ, and because of that blood we can believe His promises of healing and prosperity. Communion is a time of miracles.

When Peter said, "You are the Christ, the Anointed One of God who removes burdens and breaks every yoke," Jesus said, "I will bless you. I will give you power, and I will also give you the keys to the kingdom of God. Now whatever you bind (forbid or lock up) on earth, I'll do the same in heaven, and whatever you loosen (allow or unlock) on earth, I'll back it up with all My power in heaven."

When Jesus defeated Satan and fulfilled the prophecy in Genesis 3:15 that He would crush Satan's head, He stomped on

Satan's head and took back everything the devil had stolen. He not only has the keys of life; He has the keys of death and hell. (See Revelation 1:18.) Just as Jesus gave Peter the keys of the kingdom, He has given us the keys of the kingdom. No longer will the gates of hell prevail over us! No longer will drugs, alcohol, anger, poverty, divorce, etc. have power in our lives. Jesus, the Christ, has removed the burden and broken the yoke!

In the beginning, God the Father had all the authority. He had all the keys of the kingdom. When He created Adam, He gave him the keys of authority and dominion. But Adam and Eve disobeyed God and followed Satan. At that moment Satan obtained the keys and became the god of this world.

Then Jesus died on the cross, shed His blood for our redemption, and descended into hell to defeat Satan. He took back the keys for you and me. But standing around holding the keys won't open or close anything. There's no power in that! So Jesus is asking you, "Who do you say I am?" When you answer, "You're the burden-removing and the yoke-destroying One. You are the Christ. You are the One who will forgive me of my sin and break this curse off my life," then you are shouting, "I've got the keys!" It's time to bind the curse and loose the blessing!

Blessings and Iniquities through Generations

In the Bible we see people whose lives blessed their families and their nations. We also see people whose actions brought a curse to their households, their cities, and their nations. You and I are no different. We are reaping the results of Adam's sin. We are also reaping the results of God's promise to Abraham that all the families of the earth would be blessed through him. It was through Abraham and his descendants, Isaac and Jacob, that there were twelve tribes of Israel that eventually became the nation of Israel. Through the nation of Israel came Jesus, and through Jesus the curse was broken.

> *I will make you a great nation; I will bless you and make your name great; and you shall be a blessing. I will bless those who bless you, and I will curse him who curses you; and in you all the families of the earth shall be blessed.* (Genesis 12:2–3)

69

It doesn't matter whether you are suffering from a curse as a result of what you have done or as a result of what your ancestors have done. The burden-removing and yoke-destroying Christ came to set you free. No longer do you have to pay the consequences of that curse. You can live in the blessings and freedom of God's redemption and restoration.

Discussion Questions

1. *Christ* literally means "The Anointed One." What does Isaiah 10:27 say will happen because of the anointing?

2. What does Romans 6:23 say is the wages of sin?

3. Look at Isaiah 53:5 and fill in the blanks.

   But He was wounded for our _____. He was bruised for our _____; the chastisement for our peace was upon Him, and by His _____ we are healed.

4. What does Isaiah 1:18 say about our sin?

5. After Peter proclaimed Jesus to be the Christ, what did Jesus say to him in Matthew 16:17?

6. According to Matthew 16:19, after Jesus blessed Peter with power and authority, He backed it up by giving him what?

Chapter Six

The Curse on a Nation

J UST RECENTLY I was in California for a TBN program. Paul Crouch asked me, "Larry, after all these years and all the teachings we have, why is it that God has given you this revelation at this time in history?" I had never thought about it before, but immediately the Holy Spirit gave me the answer. I replied, "Because it's Jubilee."

> *Consecrate the fiftieth year and proclaim liberty throughout the land to all its inhabitants. It shall be a jubilee for you.*
> (Leviticus 25:10 NIV)

One of the promises of Jubilee is to set the captives free. (See Leviticus 25:39–41.) God wants to set us free so we can handle all that He is getting ready to do in these last days. He wants to set individuals free, but He also wants to set nations free.

I remember watching the Olympic games on television as a child. Every entrant was competing intensely for the gold medal in their event. The citizens of each country were pulling for the athletes representing their nation, including the Americans, who were shouting, "We're number one! We're number one!" We are still number one as a nation, but I don't think it is anything we want to be shouting about. There are some areas in which I wish we weren't number one.

Of all the industrialized nations, the United States is number one or close to number one in murders, number one in violent crimes, number one in juvenile crimes, number one in crimes committed by elementary-age children, number one in abortion, and number one in single-parent families. We are probably number one in divorce, pornography, and drug abuse. We are probably number one in getting women pregnant, then dumping them and leaving them to raise their babies by themselves. We are number one in things we don't want to shout about! America needs a touch from God.

We all know what happened in the schools in Pearl, Mississippi; West Paducah, Kentucky; Jonesboro, Arkansas; Springfield, Oregon; and Littleton, Colorado. The magazines on our newsstands showed us the little boys who shot down their teachers and classmates. In Arkansas, two boys, eleven and thirteen years old, schemed a deadly plot to open fire on fellow students and systematically shot and killed or wounded fifteen students and teachers. Twelve students and a teacher were fatally wounded and others seriously injured when two high school students targeted certain groups of students in Colorado.

We're shocked by the violence erupting in our schools, but in 1996 students between the ages of twelve and eighteen were victims of 255,000 incidents of non-fatal, violent crimes. This is not just an inner-city problem; it's happening all over in both rural and urban, affluent and poor neighborhoods.

Then, just when we felt like we had adequately beefed up security in schools throughout the nation, a man entered a church service in Fort Worth, Texas, and started shooting, killing seven and wounding others. Violence occurred in the one place where we thought our kids were safe—at church.

The blood-stained schoolyards, playgrounds, and churches of America are on the covers of every major news magazine in this country, and those magazines prompt Americans to ask two questions:

- Why is this happening in America?
- What do we do to change the course on which America and our young people are traveling?

In the first chapter of Isaiah, we read a description of what Israel was like during the time of Isaiah. When I read this, I thought to myself, *This is true of America today.*

Alas, sinful nation, a people laden with iniquity, a brood of evil-doers, children who are corrupters! They have forsaken the LORD, they have provoked to anger the Holy One of Israel, they have turned away backward. (Isaiah 1:4)

When a nation turns from God, even the children become corrupt. The answer to America's problems is not necessarily more gun control, more metal detectors in our schools, or more police on our streets. The rage and violence in this country result from our nation shutting God out and allowing the devil in. There is a real God and there is a real devil. The devil is not a harmless, little fat man in long red underwear with pointed horns. The devil is an evil spiritual being who comes to kill our babies, destroy our children, and divide our families. We must answer a spiritual problem with a spiritual answer. *"The weapons of our warfare are not carnal"* (2 Corinthians 10:4). We're fighting a spiritual battle, not a worldly battle, therefore we need spiritual answers.

Sowing and Reaping

Be not deceived; God is not mocked: for whatsoever a man soweth, that shall he also reap. For he that soweth to his flesh shall of the flesh reap corruption; but he that soweth to the Spirit shall of the Spirit reap life everlasting. (Galatians 6:7–8 KJV)

Recently, the mayor of Portland asked for a meeting with all the religious leaders of our city. She said to us, "If you will tell me the answer to the violence in our schools, I promise you, whatever the answer is, I will back it and do it."

Everyone in the room began giving responses, trying to be savvy and politically correct. Tiz was sitting next to me and whispering, "Behave yourself. Behave yourself."

Finally, I couldn't take it anymore and I said, "Ma'am, I'll tell you what the answer is. We have hundreds of kids down at our church. They are not carrying dope anymore. They are not carrying guns anymore. However, when they go to school, they are not allowed to carry a Bible. They are not allowed to go in and pray. They can't talk about Jesus. It doesn't take a rocket scientist to figure this out. We are reaping what we have sown.

"If we really care about our kids, if we really care about our nation, if we really care about anything but ourselves, and if we really care about each other, we have to start doing what is biblically correct instead of what is politically correct. We have to start doing what the Word of God says."

Contrary to her promise, she did not back up the solution. Instead, she referred to the law of separation of church and state—a law that was intended to keep the state out of the church's business, not to keep the church out of our schools and government buildings.

What has happened to our kids? Here's what has happened: Many have quit going to church. They have turned from worshipping God to worshipping self-gratification at any cost. Morality and absolutes have been declared outdated and have been replaced with situational ethics. Our nation has allowed the morals of our country to collapse.

> What has happened to our kids? We have turned from worshipping God to worshipping self-gratification at any cost.

These are the seeds that have been planted, nurtured, and harvested in this generation.

It isn't an accident that we have become the number-one nation in abortion. It's not an accident that we have become the number-one nation in juvenile crime and juvenile pregnancies. There is a reason for the bloodshed and violence in our schools and in our nation.

Why is our nation number one in unwed-teen pregnancy? Because every seed produces after its own kind and we are sowing that seed in our television shows, magazines, and movies. We are promoting premarital sex, pregnancies out-of-wedlock, and teen pregnancies on our nation's airwaves.

If we look at what we are harvesting in our nation, we will find out what kind of seeds we have sown. Don't blame guns, don't blame the devil, and don't blame God. If we sow bad seed, we'll reap a bad harvest. But if we sow good seed, we will reap a good harvest.

If we plant apple seeds, we'll get apples. If we plant orange seeds, we'll get oranges. If we plant seeds of immorality, we'll harvest immorality. We're seeing pre-teenagers having babies. We're seeing pregnant single women with no one to support them. We are harvesting an epidemic of immorality because of the seeds we have planted. And not only will every seed produce after its own kind, but every seed will also multiply. (See Genesis 1:11.)

In the 1973 Supreme Court decision of *Roe v. Wade*, America said that it was okay for an adult to make the decision to abort an unwanted child. I don't say this to sound self-righteous or to make anyone feel condemned, but the taking of an innocent life is not a free choice. It's murder. I know that sounds hard, but we need to open our eyes to what spirit is being passed on to our children. Not long after adults were given the right to murder the unborn, the babies who managed to be born to that generation began murdering also. Without spiritual understanding, people cannot understand why children are murdering children today.

When we talk about family curses or iniquities, a family can be as small as those with our same last name or as large as the country we live in. In our American "family," the spirit working in our adults makes it easy to take a life by calling it abortion. The Bible calls it murder. This same spirit has been passed on and is growing in our children.

Iniquity Abounds

It's been said you can count the seeds in an apple, but you can't count the apples in a seed. In other words, you can cut open an apple and count ten to fifteen seeds, but each seed contains orchards of apples because they are capable of multiplying and reproducing.

Matthew 24:12 tells us that not only will iniquity pass from generation to generation, but that iniquity will abound. That word *"abound"* is translated from the Greek word, *pluthuno*, which means "to increase."[4] So not only does this force pass on from generation to generation, but it gets much worse in each generation.

> *Now Judah did evil in the sight of the LORD, and they provoked Him to jealousy with their sins which they committed, **more than all that their fathers had done.***
> (1 Kings 14:22 emphasis added)

The iniquity that caused the sins to be passed on and multiplied resulted in greater sins than their fathers committed. This kills the theory, "It's my life and I can do whatever I want to as long as I'm not hurting anyone." It's not just your life. We don't live independent of others—what we do as a people and as a nation passes on and multiplies to the next generation.

> *Behold, I was brought forth in iniquity, and in sin my mother conceived me.* (Psalm 51:5 NASB)

Although David was speaking of iniquity being passed from one individual to another, we must understand that iniquity can also be passed from one generation to the next generation. My generation was doing drugs when we were eighteen, nineteen, and twenty years old. Iniquity has abounded, and now children are doing drugs at eight, ten, and twelve years old. We were sleeping around and having premarital sex when we were eighteen, nineteen, and twenty years old. Now, children are sleeping around at eleven, twelve, and thirteen years old—and they are having babies.

> We don't live independent of others—what we do as a people and as a nation passes on and multiplies to the next generation.

We can't carry Bibles in our schools anymore, so now kids carry condoms, drugs, and guns. We can't pray aloud in the classroom, but our teachers can teach that it's okay to adopt an alternative lifestyle of homosexuality. In some states, a fourteen-year-old girl can't get her ears pierced without parental permission, but she can get an abortion without parental consent. Iniquity is not just passing on, it's abounding! Sooner or later it will affect every one of our lives—including the lives of our children and grandchildren.

A generation ago, if an elected official said, "If a mother doesn't want her baby, let's just kill it. We'll call it abortion. We'll make it legal, and we'll support it with America's tax dollars," that person would have been an outcast. They would have been thrown out of office. They would have committed political suicide by promoting something so insane as killing unborn children. But today the opposite is true. If a politician takes a pro-life stand, they face the chance of losing the election. What has happened to America?

Years ago I heard that the theaters and drive-ins would show flashing or blinking pictures of popcorn or soft drinks during the movies. These pictures were called subliminal blips. They would pass so quickly that the mind couldn't even detect them, but the subconscious mind would, and the viewers had a sudden desire for popcorn or soda. If these flashes were so powerful that they could affect a person's decisions in life, how much more powerful would hours of easily perceivable violence and immorality be, especially on young impressionable children?

Our minds are powerful spiritual tools. When I speak of the mind, I'm not talking about the brain. Our brains are physical substances of blood and tissue. But our minds are not physical; they're spiritual. Ephesians 4:23 calls it *the spirit of your mind."* We all know that we're body, soul, and spirit. We are spiritual beings, living in the shell of a body, and we function through our soul, or our emotions, feelings, and thinking.

Proverbs 23:7 says, *"As he thinks in his heart, so is he."* I heard years ago, "Sow a thought, reap an act; sow an act, reap a habit; sow a habit, reap a destiny." That's why in 3 John 1:2, John prayed that our health and our prosperity would flourish in direct proportion to how our souls prosper, or according to the way we think and how our emotions function.

I recently read a newspaper article entitled, "The End of an Era." It was talking about the television show, *Home Improvement,* which was coming to an end. Media moguls in Hollywood have basically closed the door to shows and movies that portray a traditional family. They say that a household with a mom, dad, and kids is no longer the *norm* or the only acceptable pattern for a "family." People now want to see shows with unmarried couples living together, a group of co-ed friends living together, or with a straight girl and a homosexual guy living together. The days of *Leave It to Beaver* television shows are officially over—it's the end of an era. A new acceptable pattern has emerged.

Twenty-five years ago evangelist David Wilkerson of New York City gave a prophecy that men and women would be having sexual relations on television. No one thought that would ever happen, but it did. Most of the weeknight sitcoms consist of subject matter that we used to get our mouths washed out with soap just for talking about. Now it is on for all ages to see and hear. When the entertainment industry tells our kids that it is okay for a man and a woman to sleep together even though they are not married, to have a child even though they're not married, to have an abortion or kill that child, or to engage in homosexual acts, do we expect this *not* to affect them?

We are accountable for how we use our influence as politicians, as television producers, as actors or singers, and as businessmen or businesswomen. When the money that is made on movies, TV, and records is worth more than the lives of our children, could it be that we are selling out for thirty pieces of silver? America is betraying her children for money. Jesus has a sobering word about this:

> *But whoever causes one of these little ones who believe in Me to sin, it would be better for him if a millstone were hung around his neck, and he were drowned in the depth of the sea.*
>
> (Matthew 18:6)

A few years ago, I was in Nashville teaching on family curses for TBN. Tiz and I were listening to the news. The nation was reeling from yet another school shooting. During that same news program, there was a report about a certain college professor and some politicians who were debating when human life really begins. Two college students had just delivered a baby in a hotel room, killed the baby, and put the baby in a dumpster. Should they or shouldn't they be tried for murder? Had they aborted the baby a day or two before, they could have received government funding. But waiting those few extra days until the baby was born was reason to be tried by the government for first-degree murder. The college professor argued that a baby isn't really human until it's thirty days old because until then it's what he called a *neophyte*. He said that parents should have the right to choose whether the child should live or die during that period. It was no coincidence that my teaching that night consisted of the material we will discuss in the next chapter, "Reversing the Curse of a Nation."

When I tell that story in churches, people are shocked. But we're no longer shocked at four-, six-, and eight-month abortions because we've become used to it. It's the old story of the frog in the kettle. If you put a frog in a kettle of boiling water, it will jump out. But if you put a frog in a kettle of lukewarm water and slowly turn the heat up, the frog will adjust to it and sit in there until it boils to death. This is what's happening in America. We didn't start off killing babies as they were being born. At first it was okay to abort only during the first trimester, then we stretched it to include the second trimester. Now, in partial-birth abortions, we can snuff out an innocent life as it is leaving the safety of the mother's womb. We're getting used to abortion. We're getting used to crime. We're getting used to immorality. Have our hearts become callused? And has the iniquity of abortion—or taking innocent life—passed to the next generation?

In the United States alone, there are 1.8 million adults behind bars today. The number of people in jail has more than doubled in the last twelve years. Prisons in the U.S. have added 26,000 beds in the last year.[5] Taxpayers pay billions of dollars a year just to operate the prison system, yet it seems that no matter what we do to try to fix this problem, it still keeps growing. Why is this? Because iniquity doesn't just pass on; iniquity abounds.

Is this a hopeless situation? Although it may seem that way, it is not hopeless if our hope is in Jesus Christ.

But where sin abounded, grace abounded much more.
(Romans 5:20)

Jesus Christ is the same yesterday, today, and forever.
(Hebrews 13:8)

If He could deliver the children of Israel from Egypt, He can deliver us from whatever situation we are in. He not only wants to *break* the curse, He also wants to *reverse* the curse.

Discussion Questions

1. In Isaiah 1:4, we read a description of what Israel was like during the time of Isaiah. How is the condition of the United States like Israel in this verse?

2. What does 2 Corinthians 10:4 say are the weapons of our warfare?

3. Describe God's principles of sowing and reaping according to Galatians 6:7–8.

4. What does Genesis 1:11–12 say about seed?

5. What does Matthew 24:12 tell us about iniquity?

6. When iniquity passes from one generation to the next, what happens? Read 1 Kings 14:22.

7. What does Jesus say about the responsibility each of us has regarding children? Read Matthew 18:6.

8. Iniquity abounds in the United States today. Is this a hopeless situation? What does God's Word say about this in Romans 5:20 and Hebrews 13:8?

Chapter Seven

Reversing the Curse on a Nation

BECAUSE GOD HAS called me to teach on breaking generational curses, from time to time I will watch television programs or read articles in magazines that deal with juvenile crime. So many of these children are found to be reenacting, in a bigger way, something that happened to them earlier. Most have been physically or sexually abused. The stories of these children are tragic. I remember one child had a homosexual father and had been molested by the father's lover. Many of the children come from broken homes. They have inherited the iniquity of past generations and have become abusers, molesters, and criminals themselves.

Just as we discussed earlier about confessing our faults to one another (see James 5:16 KJV), we can confess the faults of our nation.

> *That if you confess with your mouth Jesus as Lord, and believe in your heart that God raised Him from the dead, you shall be saved; for with the heart man believes, resulting in righteousness, and with the mouth he confesses, resulting in salvation.*
> (Romans 10:9–10 NASB)

We live in a day and age when many believe there is no such thing as right and wrong. Anything can be right as long as you believe it to be so. We're not teaching absolutes in many of our schools. Children receive math grades based on their efforts instead of whether or not they gave the correct answers. A child commits a crime at school, and the parents sue the school for not having sufficient supervision or for allowing an environment that may have provoked that crime. Instead of teaching our children to accept responsibility for their actions, we're teaching them how to conceal them, how to cover them up, and how to blame others.

Righteousness and salvation are ours through the shed blood of Jesus, but they can also belong to us as a nation. Just as individuals can be set free, our nation can be set free. Our nation can experience God's deliverance, blessing, prosperity, and healing.

> *If My people who are called by My name will humble themselves, and pray and seek My face, and turn from their wicked ways, then I will hear from heaven, and will forgive their sin and heal their land.* (2 Chronicles 7:14)

God is saying, "If My people will repent for the iniquity and the sins of their nation, I will set their nation free."

> *He who covers his sins will not prosper, but whoever confesses and forsakes them will have mercy.* (Proverbs 28:13)

We need to quit playing games, get serious about the claims and cause of Jesus Christ, and go to battle. We need to address spiritual problems with spiritual solutions. We have spiritual answers available that will cause us to win every time. We must get to the root cause. Of course, I thank God for anyone trying to help solve the world's problems, but the answer will not come from a political association, lobby group, or television program. The government will tell us the

> Just as individuals can be set free, our nation can experience God's deliverance, blessing, prosperity, and healing.

problem is with guns. The anti-abortion people will tell us the problem is the abortionist. However, the solution to our nation's problems is not people—*"we do not wrestle against flesh and blood"* (Ephesians 6:12). The solution, like the problem, is spiritual. The problem is that the iniquity of the fathers is passed down from generation to generation.

> *Our fathers sinned and are no more, but we bear their iniquities.* (Lamentations 5:7)

If we let ourselves get talked into looking only for carnal answers—stricter gun control, self-esteem workshops, sex education classes, distribution of birth control devices at schools, and so forth—we're simply treating the symptoms rather than the causes. Spiritual problems require spiritual answers, and that means spiritual warfare.

Repent for America

Daniel stood in the gap for an entire nation. When he repented for Israel's iniquities, those people were set free and they began to ask themselves, "Why aren't we serving God? Why are we doing these things that are not pleasing to God? How have we gotten so far from the blessings of God that we once enjoyed?"

America is spiritually at the same place Israel was when they were taken into captivity, and if God heard Daniel's prayers and delivered Israel, He will hear our prayers and deliver America. All we have to do is call on God again. He is not a mean God or a harsh task master. He is a good God, a great and loving Father who wants to bring us back into His blessing. We need to say, "God, we confess our sins before You and we repent. Have mercy on us." When we do this, God promises to heal our land. (See 2 Chronicles 7:14.)

Daniel's prayer for Jerusalem can be our prayer for America:

We have sinned and done wrong. We have been wicked and have rebelled; we have turned away from your commands and laws....O Lord, in keeping with all your righteous acts, turn away your anger and your wrath from Jerusalem, your city, your holy hill. Our sins and the iniquities of our fathers have made Jerusalem and your people an object of scorn to all those around us.
(Daniel 9:5, 16 NIV)

This was God's answer to Daniel, and I believe it can be His answer to us:

As soon as you began to pray, an answer was given, which I have come to tell you, for you are highly esteemed. (Daniel 9:23 NIV)

Israel is a type and shadow of all who are the children of God. They were in captivity, and the vision Daniel interpreted was that in the seventieth year of their captivity they would be set free. (See Daniel 9:24–27.) At the time of his vision, they were in their sixty-ninth year. Daniel knew their redemption was near, but he was afraid because he understood that even if they were set free, the iniquity of the people would draw them back into their sinful ways.

Yes, Jesus Christ is the burden-removing, yoke-destroying Christ. He was wounded for our transgressions. His blood has set us free. But unless we understand that His blood will also break the iniquity, or the curse, we will continue to fall into sin. Like the Jewish people in Daniel's day, through the power of Jesus' blood we can enter our year of deliverance, our year of Jubilee.

> **If Christians will begin to repent for the iniquity of our nation, God will pour out His covenant blessings on America.**

In this new millennium, God is saying to us as a nation, "Repent." We can repent for the evil our nation has committed against God. We can repent for what those who have gone before us brought into our nation. We can repent for the iniquity that's holding our nation in bondage. Jesus wants to set *all* the captives free.

If they shall confess their iniquity, and the iniquity of their fathers, with their trespass which they trespassed against me,...then will I remember my covenant. (Leviticus 26:40, 42 KJV)

God has a covenant with all nations and all His people who call on His name. If we as Christians will begin to repent for the iniquity that has crept into our nation, God will cause the minds of our people to become right again, and He will pour out His covenant blessings on America.

Our generation's death, destruction, and lack of purpose are not just the media's fault. It's the church's fault. We have lost the power that Jesus meant for us to have. If we are honest, most of us would admit that when we bind the powers of darkness or loose the anointing of God, we're just spouting words—not much is happening.

We have let the walls down and given an opening to the enemy. That enemy is not people—it's the devil. The Bible says our battle is not against flesh and blood. Until we learn this, we can't win because we're fighting the wrong enemy or maybe even not fighting at all. Proverbs 6:31 says that when we discover who the thief is, then he has to return everything that he's stolen, multiplied by seven. The unsaved and non-Christian are not the enemy. They are our goal! Jesus said these words, *"Greater love has no one than this, than to lay down one's life for his friends"* (John 15:13). Now you might say, "Well, that drug addict is not a friend to Jesus." When I was drug addict, Jesus loved me so much that He died to pay for my sins. And don't forget, He died for your sins too.

It always amazes me how judgmental we who are saved by grace can become. Another thing God's people need to repent of is fighting among ourselves. Isn't it amazing how divided the body of Christ is, even when we all know the verse, *"Every kingdom divided against itself is brought to desolation, and every city or house divided against itself will not stand"* (Matthew 12:25)? When we take communion, we're to wait until we have judged ourselves. (See 1 Corinthians 11:23–33.) We're to judge our character and our conduct toward the Lord, but we're also supposed to judge how we treat each other. Verse 29 says that if we don't, the judgment of God comes upon us. In verse 30, the Bible says our neglect in this area is the reason many are weak, sick, and dying. Our churches and ministries are weak, our marriages and families are sick, and our communities and nation are dying.

Why is this happening? Verse 29 tells us that we are not treating the body of Christ properly. When Paul talked about Christ's body, He wasn't talking about a little cracker or wafer. We know this because in 1 Corinthians 10:16–17 the Bible says that we are the bread and we are one body. When I first got saved, I thought all Christians loved God and loved each other. Sometime after I received Jesus, I went to work and told everyone what happened to me. I was born again! Most were excited for me, but one woman, instead of just praising God and being happy, asked in what denomination I got saved. "Christian," I answered, not trying to be a wiseguy. But I was new, and I thought everybody in Jesus was one family.

Have you ever met a mean, gossiping, backbiting, divisive Christian? How can we, who are to be like Christ, accept being mean, argumentative, and gossiping? Being a mean Christian is like being a tall short man or a fat skinny man or a long-haired bald man. It just doesn't work. We say, "Well, that other church just doesn't believe the right things!" Neither do you! Neither do I! None of us understands the Word of God 100 percent correctly.

The Bible says we're all looking through a glass darkly. (See 1 Corinthians 13:12 KJV.) I know when we get to heaven we'll be walking down the streets of gold with Jesus and He'll say, "As long as I've got some time with you, let Me show you something." Then He'll open His Word to us. We'll exclaim, "Wow, Lord! We weren't even close on that one were we?" "No," He'll say, "but you did your best." So before we start shouting too loud for the evil world to repent, pointing the finger of accusation and telling them it's all their fault, we should remember that repentance begins at home. Unity brought the outpouring of the Holy Spirit in the early church, and I know that it will bring God's outpouring and anointing on the last church.

The Bible says "they out there" will know that "we in here" belong to "Him up there" by one thing: They will know that we're His disciples because we love one another. (See John 13:35.) They will know that we belong to Him, not because we're perfect, but because we love one another. Do you know what that means? When we get our act together and love one another as we should, more people will just walk into the church and get saved than ever before because the anointing will come back on our music, singing, teaching, and preaching. The Bible says that if we say we love God and we don't love the person next to us, then we are liars. (See 1 John 4:20–21.) We must be certain that when we speak the truth, we are speaking in love and not from a wrong spirit. The letter of the law will kill or destroy faith in God, but the Spirit brings life to the Word we're teaching and preaching.

> The Bible says that others will know we are His disciples because we love one another.

The church needs to check its fruit production! Believers should speak the truth to one another according to the fruit of the Spirit, which is love, peace, joy, gentleness, kindness, goodness, patience, diligence, and self-control. (See Galatians 5:22–23.) I really think that the owner (God) of the vineyard (the church) is checking for fruit (through the Spirit). When He finds fruit in the church—when the church starts loving and being kind again—the Spirit of God will begin to flow as never before. We need to remember that this Jesus stuff, this church stuff, this Bible stuff is the *Good* News!

Giving It All

God says, "I'll not only break the curse, but I'll reverse the curse and bring all those Abraham and Mosaic covenant blessings back into your lives." Can we really do this? To answer that question, let me give you an example of something we did in our church. Knowing what Luke 6:38 says about giving and it being given back to us, *"good measure, pressed down, shaken together, and running over,"* I wondered why someone would not tithe. The reason the devil doesn't want someone tithing is so they won't be blessed and the church won't be blessed. Therefore, in one of our church services we repented for not giving.

Then we repented from the iniquity that held people in bondage, that kept them from seeing what the Word of God said about tithing and giving unto the Lord—giving whatever the Lord asked us to give.

The praise reports and financial miracles came pouring in, but one in particular stands out to Tiz and me. Todd and Kathy had tried to adopt a baby for over four years and had always been faithful tithers and givers. However, something was blocking their miracle. On several occasions they nearly had a baby in their hands only to have the child given to someone else at the last moment. When I was preaching on giving to God, the Holy Spirit gave me a word for Todd. "Todd, if you give God your spirit of anger, God will give you a daughter." Anger had been in Todd and some of his family members for generations, but that day Todd gave God his anger and was set free! The very next day they received a call from the adoption agency. "We have your baby!"

When we give all we have to God—the good, the bad, and the ugly—He gives us exceedingly great blessings beyond what we can ask or think! (See Ephesians 3:20.) And the same principle holds true for every area of our lives, including our cities and nations. When we give our time to pray and intercede for our family, friends, communities, and countries, God can change things.

How many people are serving God today as a result of their grandmother or mother praying for them? How many times do we hear stories of a child coming back home after his parents prayed and interceded on his behalf for years? Any person can do this for his family, and as Christians, we can do it for our nation.

God places the solitary in families and gives the desolate a home in which to dwell; He leads the prisoners out to prosperity; but the rebellious dwell in a parched land. (Psalm 68:6 AMP)

Just like Daniel repented for the sin of Israel—even though he himself had not turned from God and become corrupt—one person can repent for the iniquity of a nation, church, or family. Then those who are bound by chains and rebellion can be set free. Remember in Leviticus 16:22 when the priest placed the blood on the scapegoat, pronounced the sins of Israel over it, and sent it in to the desert? The iniquity, that spirit that holds people in bondage, was sent to a desert place. Jesus said it goes to a desert place, but then it comes back. Although it finds the house swept and garnished, a door has been left open and more spirits enter. That person is worse than they were before. (See Matthew 12:43–45.) Well, we're going to not only send the curse to a desert place, but we're going to destroy it by understanding, through the blood of Jesus, so that whatever we bind on earth is bound in heaven. (See Matthew 16:17–19.) Our house will be swept and every door will be locked tight.

I have set before you life and death, blessings and curses. Now choose life, so that you and your children may live.
(Deuteronomy 30:19 NIV)

We have the ability to choose life or death. That's not something God does for us.

Know therefore that the LORD your God is God; he is the faithful God, keeping his covenant of love to a thousand generations of

those who love him and keep his commands.
(Deuteronomy 7:9 NIV)

I don't believe we have a thousand generations yet to go because I believe we are in the evening of the sixth day. We are in the eleventh hour. We are in the sixty-ninth year of Babylonian captivity. We're about to go into the millennial reign of Jesus, which will occur after the rapture and the tribulation, and we're going to be ruling and reigning here on earth with Jesus.

This is a prophetic message that we're going into the Sabbath millennium with the blessing for a thousand years on us and our children. Can we really break the curse off our family? Do we have that authority? Who do we say Jesus is? Do we say He is the Christ—the burden-removing, yoke-destroying power of God? If so, He says to us, "Now I give you power and the keys to the kingdom. Blessed art thou."

These are the keys that bind and loosen. Whatever you forbid on earth is forbidden in heaven. "I forbid this curse in my life. I forbid this curse from taking root in my family. I forbid this curse on my church. I forbid this curse on my city. I forbid this curse on my nation." And whatsoever you loose or allow on earth is loosed in heaven. "I loose blessings, healing, joy, and prosperity on my family, city, and nation by the Spirit of God." This is the authority we have when we know who we are in Christ Jesus.

> Who do we say Jesus is? Do we say He is the Christ–the burden-removing, yoke-destroying power of God?

We Have Been Given Authority

I was at a Christian bookseller's convention when a man from Ireland came up to me and said, "Please come teach this in Ireland. We have been at war for hundreds of years. We heard your message on breaking family and national curses, and this is the answer to our nation being free. We're fighting and we don't even understand why we're fighting anymore."

Reversing the Curse on a Nation

How can anyone enter the strong man's house and carry off his property, unless he first binds the strong man? And then he will plunder his house. (Matthew 12:29 NASB)

We can bind the enemy in our lives, families, churches, cities, and nations because of the blood of Jesus Christ. He is the Christ—the burden-removing and yoke-destroying one who can break that spirit of iniquity and set America, Ireland, or any nation, free once again. We have the keys to take back what the strong man has stolen.

And these signs will accompany those who believe: in my name they will drive out demons. (Mark 16:17 NIV)

You have been given the authority to cast out the forces that are attacking your family, home, and nation if you believe in Jesus Christ.

I was recently on an airplane on my way to do a men's conference in Hawaii. Two of my associates were with me, and the man sitting behind me tapped me on the shoulder and said, "Pastor, I'd like to introduce this man to you."

He was sitting next to a pastor from Hawaii. The Hawaiian pastor said to me, "This is a miracle that we're here on the same plane." He pulled out a beautiful, handmade wooden pen set with my name on it. He said, "I was going to send this to you as soon as I got home." He continued, "I listened to your teachings on breaking the curse, and it set me free. But it not only set me free, I taught it for five weeks in my church, and my church has been totally set free. I wanted to give this gift to you to let you know how invaluable your teaching is."

At the men's conference in Hawaii, a man came up to me after I preached and said, "Pastor, this is the answer I've been looking for. My great grandfather was given a name that meant in his language, 'a fiery, demonic deity.' My great-great-grandfather also had that name and ended up losing everything. They had gained land from the king but lost it all. He eventually began abusing alcohol and drugs and ended up in prison. Since then, the strongest male of each generation has been given that name. Every person who carried that name ended up losing everything, turning to drugs and alcohol, and ending up in jail. It's been passed down from generation to generation, and now my son has just been given that name. I'm going home and I'm going to change his name and break that curse so the things that happened to my ancestors will not happen to my son."

Is there a curse on your family? Is there a curse on your church? Is there a curse on your city's inhabitants that keeps repeating itself? Are you tired of living in a nation that is cursed? In order to reverse the curse on your family, city, and nation, you must first have the keys to the kingdom of heaven. You must first have Jesus Christ as Lord of your life.

If you have never asked Jesus to come into your heart and save you, pray this prayer so you can be a child of God, take back what the enemy has stolen, and begin to live the abundant life God has planned for you.

> *Father, I come before You right now in the name of Jesus. I know I've sinned because we've all sinned. But I know You love me so much that You sent Jesus Christ to pay the price in full for all my sin. I ask You to forgive me for all my sins. I give my life to You. Right now, I receive Jesus Christ as my Lord and my Savior.*
>
> *Now, Satan, in the name of Jesus, by the blood of Jesus, and through the power of the cross, I bind you and command you to get out of my life. Get out of my home. Get out of my family. Get out of my body. Get out of my mind. Get out of my spirit. Get out of my finances. I declare every family curse and every generational curse broken and reversed in the name of Jesus. Forgiveness is mine. Joy is mine. Peace is mine. Salvation is mine. Health is mine. Prosperity is mine. It's all mine. Not someday, but today, right now in the name and by the blood of Jesus Christ. Amen.*

You can pray this prayer over your family, church, city, and nation:

> *Lord, I repent for the iniquity that is on our family, church, city, and nation, which has been passed down from generation to generation. Right now, through the blood and by the name of Jesus Christ, I reverse those curses. In the name of Jesus I pray. Amen.*

Discussion Questions

1. According to 2 Chronicles 7:14, is it possible for us to repent for our country?

2. Why is the foundational solution to our nation's problems not people? Read Ephesians 6:12.

3. According to Lamentations 5:7, what is the real problem in our nation?

4. Turn to Daniel's prayer for Israel found in Daniel 9:5, 16 NIV. Write his prayer down and pray it for the United States.

   Now turn to Daniel 9:23. What was God's answer to Daniel? This is also His answer to us as we pray for our country.

5. What will Jesus do when we repent for the iniquity that is holding our nation in bondage? See Leviticus 26:40, 42.

6. Read 1 Corinthians 11:23–33. According to verse 28, who are we to examine? Why are there so many weak and sick among us according to verses 29–30?

7. John 13:35 says "they out there" will know that "we in here" belong to "Him up there" by one thing. What is that one thing?

8. What does the Bible say we are if we say we love God and we don't love one another? See 1 John 4:20–21.

9. List the fruit of the Spirit according to Galatians 5:22–23.

10. What keys has God given you? Look again in Matthew 16:19.

11. According to Matthew 12:29, what are we to do to the strong man (or enemy)?

12. In Mark 16:17, what signs does Jesus say accompany those who believe in His name?

Chapter Eight

The Blood of Jesus Has More Power Than You Know

WEEK AFTER WEEK we receive letters from believers expressing a need to be set free. We also receive many letters from people who are not born-again Christians but who are desperate for answers to their problems. There are people all over this nation who battle generational curses on their own life or on their family's lives—depression, suicide, illnesses of all kinds, uncontrolled lust, promiscuity, anxiety, failure, poverty, abandonment, witchcraft, fear, rebellion, abuse, and addictions of every kind. The list goes on.

One letter came from a man who said that he wept uncontrollably as he listened to my testimony. He told us that my story could have been his story, except that he had already lost his wife and kids because of his raging, out-of-control anger. He had become hopeless as he tried everything he could think of to change his life. He failed every time. He even said he would rather be the victim, the person who was abused, than be the abuser, because as an abuser he had to live with the horrible shame and guilt.

There is a lot of attention focused on the victims of abuse, and rightly so, but this man pleaded, "I'm an abuser, but I'm a victim too, a victim of my own rage. Please help me to change." My heart broke as memories and feelings from my past flooded over me. I saw how desperately people need to know how they can be set free.

Free at Last

When I hear these stories and read these letters, I weep before God. I am reminded of what Hosea the prophet said: *"My people are destroyed for lack of knowledge"* (Hosea 4:6). As a result, I am determined to get the Word of God to those who are being trampled underfoot by Satan, to those who are worn-out and ready to give up in defeat. The enemy does not spare any tactics in trying to defeat God's people. Nothing is beyond demonic assault. Nothing, that is, except the blood of Jesus.

The Power of the Blood

The blood of Jesus is the power source for our salvation and our freedom. The moment we receive Jesus Christ into our hearts and lives, we are forgiven for our sins. Jesus then becomes *Jehovah-Tsidkenu*, our righteousness; and *Jehovah-M'kaddesh*, our ongoing sanctification.

We are made righteous by the blood of Jesus that washes away every sin we ever committed. That means we are no longer enemies of God; instead we are in right relationship with Him. The blood of Jesus does not simply cover up our sin. The good news of Jesus Christ is far better than that! I don't care if the sin is drug addiction, abortion, lying, or stealing, when we claim the blood of Jesus, His blood washes that sin away.

> The blood of Jesus cleanses us so we appear before Him as if we had never sinned.

Though your sins are like scarlet, they shall be as white as snow; though they are red like crimson, they shall be as wool.

(Isaiah 1:18)

Our sins are like a deep-dyed stain that can't come out in a normal washing. But though our sins are deep-dyed stains, the blood of Jesus makes us whiter than snow. From God's perspective, the blood of Jesus cleanses us so we appear before Him as if we had never sinned. (See Acts 3:19.)

As good as that is—and that news is great because it is the hope for our lives—it is not the whole story of our salvation. What many Christians do not know is that their salvation is not

1

96

limited to forgiveness of sins. The God who said to me many years ago, "Larry, your sins are forgiven," is the same God who said, "Cocaine, be gone. Alcohol, be gone. Poverty, be gone. Disease, anger, and violence, be gone." *He is the same God!*

God's plan for our lives is not turmoil, strife, and pain. His plan for our lives is joy, peace, and happiness. Today in my personal life, my marriage, and my family, I am living dreams I never thought possible. I couldn't stop doing drugs by my own determination or by the strength of my own willpower, but Jesus delivered me. Methadone couldn't cure me. Acupuncture couldn't cure me. Hypnosis couldn't cure me. But the blood of Jesus did the work, and it was a complete work!

More Than Conquerors

As Christians, we are grateful that God redeemed us, washing away the sin and destruction in our lives. But our salvation involves more than forgiveness of sins.

> *If you confess with your mouth the Lord Jesus and believe in your heart that God has raised Him from the dead, you will be saved.* (Romans 10:9)

I believe this is the greatest promise in the Bible. The word *"saved"* in the Greek language, in which the New Testament was originally written, is the word *sozo.* It means to be completely whole. When Jesus talked about our being saved, He was not just talking about being forgiven and becoming a Christian. Salvation means receiving everything that is ours—everything that was paid for by the blood of Jesus. That means we are forgiven, but it also means we are healed, delivered, prosperous, blessed, and set free. The salvation Jesus Christ has for us is *forgiveness, healing, deliverance, prosperity, freedom, authority,* and *power.*[6]

Romans 8:37 says, *"We are more than conquerors through Him who loved us."* When we realistically assess everything we are facing and take stock of our own resources (our own strength and power and our own ability to work things out) and see that the odds are stacked against us, then we need to turn to God and find out what He has for us. We need to know the truth that will set us free. And the truth is that, by the power of the shed blood of Jesus Christ, we are not going under—we are going over. No matter how big the giant is that we are facing, in Jesus Christ we are more than conquerors.

When all the circumstances of your life spell defeat, when it seems like people want to keep you down, when everything says you are going to lose, remember, *you are not going to lose because you were born to win.* You are going to win if you don't faint, if you take a stand, and if you rise up like a warrior and say, "In the name of Jesus Christ and in the power of His blood, I am not going under; I am going over. Victory is mine!"

It doesn't matter what you are facing—marriage problems, health problems, financial problems, spiritual problems, alcohol, drugs, cigarettes—Jesus is right here and is your salvation, your redemption, and your deliverance right now. Your *sozo*—your salvation, healing, and deliverance—is here, not in the sweet by and by, but *right now.* I like to say it this way: Not in the sweet by and by when I die, but down on the ground while I'm still around!

> "In the name of Jesus Christ and in the power of His blood, I am not going under; I am going over. Victory is mine!"

The enemy never gives up. He never rests in his battle to defeat us. When we are made righteous by the blood of Jesus, we haven't fought the last battle, but we are now on the winning side. The enemy will continue his assaults, attempting to capture our minds and control our emotions, but we can defeat the enemy and live in victory every day.

The devil comes to you and says, "You know what, you still have that anger problem. You'll never change. You still have that depression problem. You'll never change. You still have that alcohol or drug problem. You'll never change." Your accuser says, "You've been born again, but you're a hypocrite because you are going through your second divorce, and you will never change." You are standing before the throne of grace, but the devil is still accusing you day and night. The Father leans down and asks, "How do you plead?" You know the accusations are true because you really have these faults.

You look up at the Father and say, "Guilty." Then the Father leans down and says, "Don't plead guilty, son. Don't plead guilty, daughter. Plead the blood of Jesus. Don't plead alcohol; plead the blood. Don't plead failure; plead the blood. Don't plead poverty; plead the blood. You have been redeemed by the blood of Jesus."

Experts and streetwise friends told my mom and dad, "Your son will never change." And I could not change on my own. I was born again and couldn't change. I was Spirit-filled, and I couldn't change. Then I found out about the power of the blood of Jesus for my life, and I stood up and said, "Devil, you are already defeated. I am set free by the blood of Jesus." When Jesus hung on the cross, He said, *"It is finished!"* (John 19:30). The blood covenant between God and man has been completed. Everything you need has been paid in full by the blood of Jesus.

People used to tell me, "You'll never change. You will never be free." The world says, "Once a junkie, always a junkie." That may be what the world says, but the Word says something else: *"If the Son makes you free, you shall be free indeed"* (John 8:36).

We can tell the kids in our schools, "You know what? When you say "no" to drugs, there is a power that will give you strength on the inside. You don't have to be drawn back into drugs and alcohol."

We can go into our prisons with the message of hope and overcoming. One of our prison ministries at New Beginnings Christian Center had to go to double services because of the revival that occurred. One of the inmates with whom we minister in the prison is a "lifer" and is helping to lead one of our Bible studies. He was brought before the members of the state legislature who said to him, "Eighty-two percent of the convicts return to prison on another conviction after being released from a previous sentence. Now after six years, only two guys from your group have gone back to prison. The rest of them are out working at their jobs and supporting their families. What's the difference? Tell us why that happens."

He told the legislators, "Number one, Jesus Christ has taken the burden of our sin, and He has washed us clean. He's given us a new beginning. We are born again and we are here to tell you that

He's not only the burden-remover, He is also the yoke-destroyer. We don't have to go back to jail. We don't have to rob again. We don't have to steal again. We don't have to batter our wives anymore. We don't have to do dope anymore. We don't have to have alcohol anymore. Jesus is alive in us. He rose again. He paid the price for us."

These inmates are being set free and are staying free by the blood of Jesus Christ.

The Jewish people understood the teaching of the blood. When they needed forgiveness, they put blood on the altar of the temple. When they needed mercy, they put blood on the mercy seat. When they needed to hear from God, they put blood on the veil so they could enter into the Holy of Holies and be in the presence of God. When they needed peace, they brought a blood sacrifice. When they needed healing, they brought a blood sacrifice. Every time they needed a miracle, they offered a blood sacrifice. (See Leviticus 1–7.)

For you and me, there is a river that never runs dry. It is the source of all God wants to do in our lives and through our lives. It is the ongoing river of the blood of Jesus. Under the new covenant, we don't have to apply it every single time we need a miracle, every time we need to enter into God's presence, and every time we need healing. All we have to do is realize that the powerful blood of Jesus Christ is there for us to call upon any and every time we need a touch from God.

> The powerful blood of Jesus Christ is there for us to call upon any and every time we need a touch from God.

Law or Grace?

After Jesus ascended and returned to heaven, there was a debate by His followers about whether we are saved by obeying the requirements of the law or by accepting the grace of Jesus Christ.

For as many as are of the works of the law are under the curse; for it is written, "Cursed is everyone who does not continue in all

things which are written in the book of the law, to do them." But that no one is justified by the law in the sight of God is evident, for "the just shall live by faith." Yet the law is not of faith, but "the man who does them shall live by them." Christ has redeemed us from the curse of the law, having become a curse for us (for it is written, "Cursed is everyone who hangs on a tree"), that the blessing of Abraham might come upon the Gentiles in Christ Jesus, that we might receive the promise of the Spirit through faith.
(Galatians 3:10–14)

The person who believes he is saved by his own righteousness has to be perfectly righteous in every single matter. If a person thinks he is saved by following the rules and requirements of the law, then he is going to have to follow the law in everything he does or the curse of the law will come upon him.

People often say we are redeemed from the law, therefore we are free from moral obligations or requirements. But what Galatians 3:13 says is that we are redeemed from the *curse* of the law because Christ Jesus became the curse for us. Every sin that anyone ever committed has a curse on it. Jesus not only took our sins on Himself, but He also took our curse for the sin. *Jesus has redeemed us from the curse of our sin.*

Our finances, marriages, homes, emotions, and minds have been kidnapped by the devil. But Jesus came and paid the ransom for every area of our lives in full and has brought us back to the way we are supposed to be.

I have set before you life and death, blessing and cursing; therefore choose life, that both you and your descendants may live.
(Deuteronomy 30:19)

The Law of Moses contained both a blessing and a curse. If you followed the commandments of God, doing all that God says, then there would be blessings on you, your family, your city, and your nation. If you didn't honor God or follow His instruction, then a curse would come on you, your family, your city, your state, and your nation. If you did what was right, you would be blessed. If you did what was wrong, then a curse would come upon you.

But believers in Jesus Christ aren't bound by the Law of Moses. By Jesus' death on the cross, Jesus became the curse so that we can be delivered from the curse and be a blessing to our family, church, city, and nation. Poverty is a curse. Sickness is a curse. Disease is a curse. Divorce is a curse. Drugs, alcohol, and abuse are all part of the curse. When we are under the blood of Jesus, we are redeemed from the curse. As He hung dying on the cross, Jesus said, *"It is finished"* (John 19:30). Our redemption through the new blood covenant was made complete at the cross.

Knowing that you were not redeemed with corruptible things, like silver or gold, from your aimless conduct received by tradition from your fathers, but with the precious blood of Christ, as of a lamb without blemish and without spot. (1 Peter 1:18–19)

Our redemption is total and it covers everything that Jesus shed His blood for, which is every part of us and every one of us. The only way redemption can fall short is if we don't know it and we don't apply it. The devil does not want you to get knowledge of the blood of the Lamb, because if you do not have knowledge of the overcoming power of the blood, then the devil can overcome you. However, by gaining that knowledge and applying it to your life, you can overcome the devil.

> **We are not told to be neutral or to do okay. We can overcome through the blood of Jesus.**

There is nothing defeated about Christianity. There is nothing unvictorious in Christianity. When Jesus hung on the cross, instead of defeat, He shouted with the voice of victory, *"It is finished!"* (John 19:30).

For the message of the cross is foolishness to those who are perishing, but to us who are being saved it is the power of God. (1 Corinthians 1:18)

Christianity is not a weak religion. It's not a just-get-by religion, or a run-and-hide religion. Christianity is a strong religion because greater is He who is in us than he who is in the world. (See 1 John 4:4.) Our accuser, Satan, has been cast down and defeated by the shed blood of Jesus Christ.

Then I heard a loud voice saying in heaven, "Now salvation, and strength, and the kingdom of our God, and the power of His Christ have come, for the accuser of our brethren, who accused them before our God day and night, has been cast down. And they overcame him by the blood of the Lamb and by the word of their testimony, and they did not love their lives to the death."
(Revelation 12:10–11)

The way we overcome the enemy is by the blood of the Lamb. We are not going to overcome the devil through methadone. We are not going to overcome the devil through hypnosis. We are not going to overcome the devil by a year or even a lifetime of professional counseling. The word *overcome* does not mean they "got by." It does not mean they escaped. It does not mean they hid. You can't say, "I'll just hide from the devil." The devil knows where you live. He's got your house number, phone number, Social Security number, credit card number, and bank account number!

The word *"overcame"* in Revelation 12:11 means to conquer, to prevail, and to get the victory.[7] I have realized through the Word of God that it is not by my own might, by my own rights, because I pray and fast, or don't smoke, cuss, chew, or go out with those who do that I can overcome. No, we overcome by the blood of the Lamb.

Not only is the devil *not* going to get me, but *I* am going to get *him!* We are not called to stay in the land we are in now—we are called to take the Promised Land. We can take the streets. We can take back our schools. We can take our judicial system. We can take back the government through the blood of Jesus. We are told to overcome, not to be neutral and not to do okay. We can do better than okay. We can overcome through the blood of Jesus!

We received this letter from a man who recently experienced the fullness of his blood-bought salvation.

Dear Pastor Larry Huch,

I thank God for your anointing to bring deliverance to God's children. I've been saved and filled with the Holy Spirit since 1983, but I still carried addictions, anger, and deep hurts. God is still at work in my life "cleaning up my mess," so to speak.

Recently, I listened to a cassette tape series of your message, "Breaking Family Curses." I felt burdened greatly as I jotted down notes and listened to every word. I got to the last tape of the set and you prayed and bound the powers of darkness, but I didn't think or feel I was delivered.

I stopped the last tape, and as I walked toward my bedroom door, "Pow!" it hit me like a great rainstorm from heaven. I felt God's hand and the power of the Holy Spirit engulf me. I tried to remain standing, but I could not. I dropped to my hands and knees, but my arms could not support me. I yielded to this power and lay prostrate on the floor. I tried to get back up, but the power and electricity going through me kept me on the floor. When I did get back up, I felt totally different—I felt free for the first time in my Christian life! Since that day I have not had to struggle as in the past but am walking in total victory and freedom!

I thank God for ministers like you who not only speak about God, but have experiences such as you have had. This gives you a hands-on ability to know that what God did for you, He can do for others like me.

Grateful and blessed through you,
Jay

There is power in the blood of the Lamb. It is available to me, and it is available to you. You can be free in every part of your life and in everything that concerns you because of the blood of Jesus.

Discussion Questions

1. Read Hosea 4:6. What does the prophet Hosea say about why people are destroyed?

2. What does Isaiah 1:18 say about our sins?

3. From God's perspective, what does the blood of Jesus do to our sin? See Acts 3:19.

4. Read Romans 10:9 to discover the greatest promise in the Bible. Write it here:

5. According to Romans 8:37, we are more than _____ through Him who loved us.

6. After Jesus ascended and returned to heaven, there was a debate by His followers about whether we are saved by obeying the requirements of the law or by accepting the grace of Jesus Christ. After reading Galatians 3:10–14, write down your thoughts concerning this matter.

7. Read Deuteronomy 30:19 and fill in the blanks below.

   I have set before you _____ and _____, blessing and cursing; therefore choose _____, that both you and your descendants may live.

8. When Jesus hung on the cross, what did He shout in victory? Read John 19:30.

9. What is the message of the cross to those who are saved? See 1 Corinthians 1:18.

10. According to 1 John 4:4, how are Christians reassured of God's greatness and His ability to win in our lives?

11. Read Revelation 12:10–11 and answer the following questions: What has become of our accuser, the devil?

    How do believers overcome the devil and his plans?

Part Two

Seven Places Jesus Shed His Blood

Chapter Nine

In Gethsemane, Jesus Won Back Our Willpower

Knowing that you were not redeemed with perishable things like silver or gold from your futile way of life inherited from your forefathers, but with precious blood, as of a lamb unblemished and spotless, the blood of Christ.
—1 Peter 1:18–19 NASB

IN THE LORD'S Prayer, Jesus taught us how to pray. I believe we can identify seven places of power in the Lord's Prayer. Furthermore, in the Old Testament tabernacle, which housed the presence of God, there were seven places of power and anointing. Now we are the new tabernacle of God. We house the presence of God with a new covenant—a seven-fold blood covenant.

In chapter two of this book, we referred to Leviticus 16, where the people brought two goats to the tabernacle. One goat was for the atonement of sin. The second goat was to have the blood of the first goat placed on its head and be released into the desert.

Before the mercy seat he shall sprinkle some of the blood with his finger seven times....Then he shall sprinkle some of the blood on it with his finger seven times, cleanse it, and consecrate it.
(Leviticus 16:14, 19)

At two different times, the high priest would sprinkle the blood with his finger seven times. When I preach this, I'll often ask, "How many know that we're redeemed by the blood?" Everyone answers yes. Then I'll ask, "Do you know where the blood was shed?" And everyone always says, "At the cross." That's true; Jesus' blood was shed at the cross, but His blood was not shed just one time, but seven different times. The source of the power of God for every area of our lives is in the shed blood of Jesus Christ. Jesus shed His blood in seven places that you and I might be made whole, forgiven of our sins, and set free from the bondage of sin and the iniquity that has entered into our families.

The power of Christ's blood flows from His complete work in giving His life and rising again, but we can look at the individual stages to glean insight into what His sacrifice gives us.

> The source of the power of God for every area of our lives is the shed blood of Jesus Christ.

The first place Jesus shed His blood was in the Garden of Gethsemane on the night of the Last Supper with His disciples. It's not a coincidence that the first place Jesus ransomed us or shed His redemptive blood was in a garden, because the first place we lost the power of God's blessing was in another garden, the Garden of Eden.

The word *redeemed* means that we are ransomed or brought back to the original place.[8] That original place and the original blessing is everything we had in the Garden of Eden.

I've heard people say, "I have no willpower. I want to stop overeating, smoking, losing my temper (or whatever it is in their life that is out of control), but I have no willpower." We lost our willpower to do what is right, to do what is best for us, to do what is healthy, and to do what will bring benefit and blessing when Adam disobeyed God in the Garden of Eden. Eve was deceived by the serpent, but Adam willfully disobeyed God. In other words, Eve was deceived by Satan, but Adam made a choice to disobey God.

God had told Adam and Eve, "All in the garden is yours except the Tree of the Knowledge of Good and Evil." (See Genesis 3:17.) In essence, Adam said, "Father, not Your will, but mine be done," and at that moment, Adam sacrificed man's willpower in every area. With Adam's disobedience, we gave our will over to the enemy and lost our ability to say "yes" to all the good God has for us and "no" to all the bad the enemy wants to do to us. The willpower we lost in the Garden of Eden was won back in the Garden of Gethsemane when Jesus said, "Not My will, but Thy will be done." (See Matthew 26:39.)

Jesus Made the Choice—Knowing Everything

Jesus was both God and man. Being God, He knew what His accusers were going to do to Him. He knew they were going to rip the beard from His face. He knew they were going to take Him to the whipping post and beat Him until the organs of His body showed out His back. He knew they were going to strip Him, hang Him naked, and spit on Him. He knew they were going to put that tree on His back.

He knew they were going to take the crown of thorns and jam those three-and-a-half-inch thorns down into His skull. He knew they were going to take those spikes and pound them into His hands and into His feet. He knew they were going to take that spear and jam it into His side. He was God, and He knew what was about to happen to Him.

Being man, He knew He was going to feel the whip on His back. He knew He would feel the beard being pulled from His face. He knew He would feel the nails being pounded into His hands. He would not escape the pain and the humiliation. In the Garden of Gethsemane, Jesus knew what was going to happen to Him. His spirit was willing to do what God wanted Him to do, but His flesh was weak and wanted to escape the agony and the torture He was about to face. Jesus faced the same battle that Adam faced—whether to follow His will or the will of the Father.

O My Father, if it is possible, let this cup pass from Me; nevertheless, not as I will, but as You will. (Matthew 26:39)

The Bible says Jesus got up from praying, went to speak to His disciples, came back to His place of prayer, and prayed the same prayer a second and a third time. (See Matthew 26:40–44.)

In Gethsemane, Jesus Won Back Our Willpower

There was a struggle going on inside Jesus—the will of the Father versus the will of the man.

> *Then an angel appeared to Him from heaven, strengthening Him. And being in agony, He prayed more earnestly. Then His sweat became like great drops of blood falling down to the ground. When He rose up from prayer, and had come to His disciples, He found them sleeping from sorrow. Then He said to them, "Why do you sleep? Rise and pray, lest you enter into temptation."*
> (Luke 22:43–46)

This is how Jesus shed His blood in the Garden. Medical doctors confirm that at times of intense fear or agony, a person's blood vessels can literally break beneath the skin and blood will begin to come out of their pores like sweat. Out of Jesus' pores came sweat and blood because of the anxiety, the fear, and the turmoil He was experiencing. Why is this significant? We must keep in mind that we've been redeemed by the blood. The first Adam surrendered our willpower to Satan. The second Adam, Jesus, redeemed our willpower by saying, "Father not My will, but Thy will," and sweating great drops of blood. This is where we gain back our willpower to overcome the drug problems, the alcohol problems, the anger problems, and the depression problems.

> Because Jesus shed His blood, you can say yes to the will of God for your life and no to the enemy of your life.

Jesus knew what was going to happen to Him. His spirit and His flesh were battling, but He won the victory when He submitted to the will of the Father. Jesus won the battle, broke the curse, redeemed us, and gave us back our willpower.

Willpower Restored

When the devil comes against us to say, "You cannot change. You're not strong enough," we have the willpower to rise in victory because Jesus said, "Not My will, but Thine be done." Because Jesus shed His blood in the Garden of Gethsemane, you can say "yes" to the will of God for your life and "no" to the enemy of your life.

Free at Last

Before I knew the Lord, I was desperate to quit drugs. I would take that needle, stick it in my arm, get high, and throw up. Then I would say, "I'm not going to do this anymore. I am going to quit now and quit forever." I would stand on the front porch of my cabin out in the woods where I lived and throw that needle as far as I could possibly throw it. But within two hours, I would be out in the woods, crawling on my hands and knees, going through the leaves and brush trying to find that needle so I could mainline again.

I couldn't quit.

I used to be full of hate, violence, and anger, and I would say, "I don't want to explode in this anger anymore. I don't want to be like this anymore." I tried to quit. I wanted to, but I couldn't. I had no willpower. My spirit was willing, but my flesh was weak.

How is it that Jesus can set us free when we cannot do it on our own? Because when Jesus sweat drops of blood in the Garden of Gethsemane, our willpower was redeemed and given back to us. What Adam lost in the Garden of Eden was restored in the Garden of Gethsemane. All we have to do is say, "I plead the blood of Jesus."

Surrender Control

But Moses said to God, "Who am I, that I should go to Pharaoh and bring the Israelites out of Egypt?" And God said, "I will be with you. And this will be the sign to you that it is I who have sent you: When you have brought the people out of Egypt, you will worship God on this mountain." Moses said to God, "Suppose I go to the Israelites and say to them, 'The God of your fathers has sent me to you,' and they ask me, 'What is his name?' Then what shall I tell them?" God said to Moses, "I AM WHO I AM. This is what you are to say to the Israelites: 'I AM has sent me to you.' "God also said to Moses, "Say to the Israelites, 'The LORD, the God of your fathers—the God of Abraham, the God of Isaac and the God of Jacob—has sent me to you.' This is my name forever, the name by which I am to be remembered from generation to generation."

(Exodus 3:11–15 NIV)

In Gethsemane, Jesus Won Back Our Willpower

"I Am" in these verses is translated from *Yahweh*, and can be translated, "I will be everything you need Me to be whenever you need Me to be it."[9] God told Moses, "Tell My children I Am has sent you. I will be their everything." He is the same I Am for us today as He was for the children of Israel. God delivered the Israelites from bondage and captivity, and He is wanting to deliver you from whatever bondage you are in through the power of the blood of Jesus Christ.

> *Jesus therefore, knowing all things that should come upon him, went forth, and said unto them, Whom seek ye? They answered him, Jesus of Nazareth. Jesus saith unto them, I am he. And Judas also, which betrayed him, stood with them. As soon then as he had said unto them, I am he, they went backward, and fell to the ground. Then asked he them again, Whom seek ye? And they said, Jesus of Nazareth. Jesus answered, I have told you that I am he: if therefore ye seek me, let these go their way.*
>
> (John 18:4–8 KJV)

The King James Version italicizes the word *"he,"* which means we put it there. When they asked for Jesus of Nazareth, He really responded, "I Am." Immediately they fell to the ground because of the anointing of God. Jesus is I Am for us today. He is the source for everything we need. If you need strength, Jesus is your strength. If you need wisdom, Jesus is your wisdom. If you are ready to submit your will to Him, He is there to give you the power to do that. You can choose to do the will of God.

> God told Moses, "I will be everything you need Me to be whenever you need Me to be it."

Until I gave God control of my desires and surrendered my will to Him, I was out of control. Even as a Christian, I was out of control until I yielded complete control to Him and allowed Him to direct my desires and change my will. I had to resist the devil. I said, "I am *not* going to let this anger control me. I am *not* going to let these things control me. I am *not.*" I had to yield control of my will to God's will. I prayed, "Father, I give You my will. I submit to the great I Am." When I did that, Jesus Christ strengthened my will to do His will.

Each of us has to make up our own mind and choose God's will or our will. We can pray the prayer of Jesus by the power of the blood of Jesus: "Father, not my will, but Thine be done."

Knowing Who You Are

For if anyone is a hearer of the word and not a doer, he is like a man observing his natural face in a mirror; for he observes himself, goes away, and immediately forgets what kind of man he was. But he who looks into the perfect law of liberty and continues in it, and is not a forgetful hearer but a doer of the work, this one will be blessed in what he does. (James 1:23–25)

This passage of Scripture says that we go to the mirror (the Word of God) and see what the Bible says we are, but when we walk away, we forget who we are in Jesus. I heard a man preaching on this one time, and his theory was that the Word of God reminds us how sinful and worthless we are, but as soon as we walk away we forget all about it. Now that may be one way of looking at it, but I believe God is showing us something completely different.

> The Word of God is like a mirror. When we look in it, we don't see ourselves the way the devil says we are, but the way God says we are.

The devil doesn't want us to experience all the power and blessing that is ours through Jesus Christ, so he does everything he can to make us feel like we'll never win or accomplish anything. The Word of God is like a mirror. When we look in it, we don't see ourselves the way the devil says we are but the way God says we are. He doesn't see our failures and sin; He sees the blood of Jesus.

When you look in the mirror of God's Word, see yourself the way your heavenly Father sees you. He sees you healed, without sickness. He sees you free, without bondage. He sees you full of joy, not sorrow. He sees you a winner, not a loser.

The Lord asks us, "How do you plead?" We take a look at ourselves, forget what we saw in the mirror of God's Word, and say, "I plead guilty. I'm a drug addict, I'm an angry person, I'm depressed, and I'm no good." But the Lord whispers in our ear, "Don't plead guilty; plead the blood." When the Son sets us free, we are free indeed! We can tell every drug addict, every alcoholic, and every person with any problem that God has redeemed us and bought back our willpower.

The government has spent millions of dollars trying to help in the "Just Say No" program. Drug addicts, alcoholics, and people with depression and anger say "no" a hundred times a week to no avail. Most people can't "just say no" in their own strength and willpower because they go back and do it again and again. They might have no willpower in themselves, but in Jesus Christ their willpower has been ransomed and redeemed by the blood of the Lamb.

We recently received this testimony from a man who had given his life to the Lord but was still bound by uncontrollable habits until he claimed the blood of Jesus for his life.

Hello Pastor Huch,

I want to write to you about the miracles and freedom that have taken place in my life after listening to your tape series, "Breaking Family Curses." I have recently come to know Jesus Christ as my Savior and Redeemer. When the Holy Spirit came upon me, I saw my sins and the shame of what I had done. I was so ashamed that I wept. Until I found Jesus, I was truly on my way to hell.

My father was a preacher who left his calling to become a hair stylist. He was drunk and on drugs all of the time and had many sexual relationships with both men and women. He would move out of the house for several months and then want to come back home. As a child I said, "I will never be like my father, I will never drink, never cheat on my wife, and never abandon my wife or child. I will never hit anyone and I will never lie." My father was indeed a sinner, and the bondage he lived in was passed on to his five children.

I married the love of my heart, we had a child, and I became a deputy sheriff. I had fulfilled my childhood dream of becoming a law officer. I promised myself that I would be different from my father.

When I completed my year of job probation, my friends took me out to a bar for a celebration party. As soon as I took my first drink, something happened—the drink took me! I began to drink with the guys every day after my shift. I stayed away from home and began to have affairs with other women. I had become my father.

My wife, Julie, was diagnosed with breast cancer. She went through surgery, radiation, and chemotherapy to try to slow down the spread of this disease. Julie was an angel and loved God. In spite of her horrible cancer, she never complained or turned away from God. The day before she died, we sat together in the living room. She could not lift her head but kept looking up in the corners of the room. I asked her what she was looking at, and she said, "These angels are taking me to Jesus tonight." When she died later that night, I was out with another woman.

My life continued this horrible decline. All that my father was, I was, but worse. In 1998 the Holy Spirit of God knocked on the door of my soul and Jesus made Himself real to me. I was baptized in water, paid my tithes without failure, and read the Word of God. However, I was still in bondage.

Some friends told me they wanted me to hear your sermon on breaking the curse. The Holy Spirit of God came upon me as I listened, and I began to understand the blood of Jesus breaking the yokes of bondage of my father's sins and my sins. I had been redeemed, but I was not free. I claimed the blood of Jesus for my freedom just as God revealed to you. God broke the generational curse that had controlled my life!

I am free indeed. My child is free. The Holy Spirit of God is moving through my sister, and my brothers are calling to Jesus and asking to be free. My father is looking to God, and we are fighting in prayer for him daily.

All that I was is dead; all that I did is dead. I am no longer just living, but I am living for God. Jesus is my King. The Holy Spirit is my comforter and my driver. Your message revealed the true Word of God. I took back my freedom by the blood of Jesus, who paid the price and set me free on Calvary.

Pastor, thank you for teaching the Word of God and obeying God our Father.

Respectfully,
Your brother in Christ,
John

If you want to quit alcohol, drugs, or your violent anger and haven't been able to in the past, know that you can now. The blood of Jesus has bought back your willpower and that curse on you is broken in the name of Jesus. You can quit drinking. You can quit smoking. You can quit doing those things you know God does not want you to do. Jesus has broken the curse of the past that keeps you from being free.

When you *choose* to break the curses on your life, the power of the blood of Jesus will strengthen you, and you will no longer be bound. You will be set free to do God's good work.

> *And I heard a loud voice saying in heaven, Now is come salvation, and strength, and the kingdom of our God, and the power of his Christ: for the accuser of our brethren is cast down, which accused them before our God day and night. And they overcame him by the blood of the Lamb.* (Revelation 12:10–11 KJV)

Discussion Questions

1. Where was the first place Jesus shed His blood? Read Luke 22:44.

   This is no coincidence. What did God tell Adam and Eve in Genesis 3:17?

2. The willpower we lost in the Garden of Eden was won back in the Garden of Gethsemane when Jesus said, "_____

   _____." (See the last part of Matthew 26:39.)

3. The Bible says that Jesus prayed the same prayer three times in Garden. What was the struggle going on inside Jesus? See Luke 22:43–46.

4. In Exodus 3:11–15, Moses questioned God about being chosen as the man who would lead the Israelites out of their captivity in Egypt. In verse 13, what did Moses ask God?

   In verse 14, what name does God call Himself?

   Why do you think God called Himself by this name?

5. Read John 18:4–8 KJV and fill in the blanks.

In Gethsemane, Jesus Won Back Our Willpower

Jesus therefore, knowing all things that should come upon him, went forth, and said unto them, Whom seek ye? They answered him, Jesus of Nazareth. Jesus saith unto them, _____ _____ _____. And Judas also, which betrayed him, stood with them. As soon then as he had said unto them, _____ _____ _____, they went backward, and fell to the ground. Then asked he them again, Whom seek ye? And they said, Jesus of Nazareth. Jesus answered, I have told you that _____ _____ _____: if therefore ye seek me, let these go their way.

6. What does James 1:23–25 say we sometimes do after going to the mirror (the Word of God) and seeing who we are?

Chapter Ten

The Stripes on Jesus' Back Won Back Our Health

But He was wounded for our transgressions, He was bruised for our iniquities; the chastisement for our peace was upon Him, and by His stripes we are healed.
—Isaiah 53:5

THE SECOND PLACE JESUS shed His blood was at the whipping post. It is believed that Jesus was scourged, or flogged, thirty-nine times. (See Matthew 27:26.) Under Jewish punishment, a prisoner could be given forty lashes; however, they usually only received thirty-nine, because forty was often fatal. (See Deuteronomy 25:3.)

I heard a missionary doctor preach that the thirty-nine lashes represent all the diseases known to all mankind. We need to remember that this is God's plan of redemption. It's not an accident or a coincidence, but it's His divine plan. Every time they laid the whip on Jesus' back—splitting His skin and ripping His muscles and tissue—healing was provided for every disease. AIDS, cancer, diabetes, muscular dystrophy, and every disease on this earth has been defeated and conquered by the blood of Jesus Christ. This shows God's willingness to heal everyone.

Some people say, "God doesn't heal anymore." But the Bible tells us, *"Jesus Christ is the same yesterday, today, and forever"* (Hebrews 13:8). Because He made a blood covenant, He doesn't change, and the blood covenant includes healing. Salvation doesn't just mean to be *forgiven*; it also means to be *healed*. Salvation means to be made whole in every way.

Others say, "We know God can heal, but does God *desire* to heal?" Keep in mind that Jesus willingly surrendered Himself to the whip! And many asked Jesus the same question while He walked the earth:

> *A man with leprosy came to him and begged him on his knees, "If you are willing, you can make me clean." Filled with compassion, Jesus reached out his hand and touched the man. "I am willing," he said. "Be clean!"* (Mark 1:40–41 NIV)

This man knew Jesus could heal him, but he wondered if He would heal him. One of the worst prayers we can pray is "If it be Thy will, please heal me." The Bible tells us what the will of God is! If Jesus suffered the whip for our healing, of course it is His will we be healed. When we pray, *"if* it be Thy will," we're saying that we're not sure it's the will of God for us to be healed. But the Bible tells us to ask in rock-solid faith:

> *Let him ask in faith, nothing wavering. For he that wavereth is like a wave of the sea driven with the wind and tossed. For let not that man think that he shall receive any thing of the Lord.* (James 1:6–7 KJV)

To come boldly and confidently to God for healing is the opposite of saying, "If it be Thy will." If we question God's will for us when we ask Him for something, we are double minded, cannot ask in faith, and He cannot heal us. Therefore, we must settle the question, "Can God heal?" Yes! Absolutely! Not only can God do anything, but our healing is so important to Him that He made a covenant with us in the blood of His Son. The price for your healing was paid over two thousand years ago. All you have to do is reach out and touch Jesus and receive your miracle.

> The price for your healing was paid over two thousand years ago. All you have to do is reach out and touch Jesus to receive your miracle.

I've preached in the Philippines many times, and word would get around when we arrived that the men of God were in town. We would get up in the morning, and the sick, the blind, and the lame would already be lined up along the street. We are just normal human beings. We don't have the power to heal ourselves, but people would come because they heard the Word of God and they believed when they heard, *"By His stripes we are healed"* (Isaiah 53:5). We would walk along the long lines of sick people, touch them, lay hands on them, and pray for them in the name of Jesus and by the power of His blood. Then we would watch them get up and walk. God still heals, saves, and delivers. We overcome the devil and his infirmities by the blood of Jesus.

I'm often asked, "Pastor why do we see so many more miracles overseas than we do in the United States or Europe?" Someone once said it's because they have greater needs. I tend to disagree. If someone is blind or lame or diseased, it doesn't matter if we're in South Carolina or South Africa: We need a miracle. Jesus taught us to come to Him as a little child in order to see the kingdom of God—not just after we die—but now. Remember, Jesus told us to pray that His kingdom would come and His will would be done on earth as it is in heaven now.

The apostle Paul declared in Romans 14:17 that the kingdom of God is righteousness, peace, and joy in the Holy Spirit. The apostle John declared in 3 John 1:2 that he wished we would prosper and be in health above everything else. When we get to heaven, we won't need any miracles. We need them now! We must trust God and believe for our healing now, when we need it. Other people on earth may fail us, even leave us, but our heavenly Father never will. When I get on an airplane, I have to have faith and trust in the pilot, crew, and everyone else involved in that flight. How much more can we trust the One who owns the sky, the earth, and the sea? We must not waver or be double minded but trust God at His Word like little children and believe in the power of the blood of Jesus.

We received this letter from a woman who is still alive because of the healing stripes of Jesus Christ. The doctors gave her no chance to live after being diagnosed with a terminal illness. We prayed for deliverance from the curse of infirmity that has been in her family, and she was miraculously healed.

Pastor Larry and Tiz,

I went to the doctor on January 18, and he said I was dying of Lou Gehrig's disease. I wrote you a letter to pray for me. I went back to the doctor on February 26, and he said the disease is gone. I am now healed!

God has done this great miracle for me. I thank Him and praise Him now, today, tomorrow, forever, until He comes. He is my Father. Thank You, Jesus!

> *God bless you,*
> *Sarah*

A Spirit of Infirmity

Our salvation starts with the forgiveness of our sin, but it doesn't stop there. It goes on to healing, deliverance, and freedom.

Now He was teaching in one of the synagogues on the Sabbath. And behold, there was a woman who had a spirit of infirmity eighteen years, and was bent over and could in no way raise herself up. But when Jesus saw her, He called her to Him and said to her, "Woman, you are loosed from your infirmity."
(Luke 13:10–12)

Here's a woman who, for eighteen years, walked around all bent over with a crippling disease. Jesus looked at her and said, "This woman has a spirit of sickness on her."

All sickness, no matter where it comes from—birth, inheritance, injury—is from the devil. Some people have told me they believe God will give a person cancer to test their love for Him. What God are you talking about? That is not my God! God can certainly use the circumstances of your sickness to accomplish His purposes, but He does not make you sick.

We read in Luke 12:32 that Jesus said, *"It is your Father's good pleasure to give you the kingdom."* It is the devil who steals, kills, and destroys. God gets pleasure by blessing those who believe in Him, not by sending sickness into their lives. There wasn't sickness or injury in the Garden of Eden. When Adam sinned, Satan entered the Garden, the curse came in, and that curse is an evil spirit.

Infirmity is a spirit that is a result of the curse, but everyone who is born again is redeemed from the curse. The price for your healing has been paid. If you are sick, injured, or diseased, Satan is trespassing on paid-for property. We don't need to say, "I need more faith to get my miracle." Instead, we can say, "By the blood of Jesus Christ I have already received my miracle. And Satan, I bind you from my life. Get out of my life! Leave me in the name of Jesus."

I was at a Bible conference some years ago, and people who wanted to be prayed for were standing in a line. We prayed for each person in the line, "In the name of Jesus, be healed." When I finished praying, I went back to a man I had already prayed for and I asked him, "What's wrong with you?" He said that his hip socket was dissolving. He had been to the doctor earlier that day to have his hip X-rayed and tests done. Without thinking or even fully understanding what I was saying, I said, "That's a spirit of cancer. That's a demon of cancer." And we prayed for his deliverance.

A couple of weeks later I was in Mexico with this man's pastor doing a miracle crusade. The pastor told me that after we had prayed for the man, he went back to get the results of his tests. The pastor then showed me a copy of the X-ray they took of this man's hip. As plain and as clear as a photo, we saw a complete face of a demonic-looking creature where the man's hipbone was supposed to be. Obviously startled by this, the man had asked the doctors about it. They told him that it was not totally uncommon to see something like this! In the end, however, the devil lost. The man was completely healed and his hip was restored, praise God!

When we were in Australia, there was a Samoan woman in our church in Melbourne who had a tumor on her head the size of two golf balls. The doctors brought me into their office to talk to me because I was her pastor. Then I was to go and talk with her. I asked her doctor, "Where does cancer come from?"

He said, "Well, some will say one thing and some another. Some say it has to do with the red blood cells, and others will say it has to do with the white blood cells. To be honest with you, if we knew, we could fix it."

I told him, "Doctor, do you know what I think? I think it is a demonic spirit."

They looked at each other, and her doctor looked at me and said, "I wouldn't doubt it." That cancer was not just a sickness; it was alive.

One of the greatest miracles we've ever seen was when we prayed for this woman and God completely healed her. The tumors disappeared, the symptoms disappeared, and the doctors and nurses were astounded. Instead of sending her home to die, they sent her home to live!

When Jesus saw the woman who was bent over, He said, "You spirit...." Jesus spoke directly to the spirit. When I pray for healing from cancer, I don't say, "You sickness, be healed." I speak directly to the demon and I say, "You come out of him right now in the name of Jesus." We see people healed of cancer all the time.

Then one of the crowd answered and said, "Teacher, I brought You my son, who has a mute spirit. And wherever it seizes him, it throws him down; he foams at the mouth, gnashes his teeth, and becomes rigid. So I spoke to Your disciples, that they should cast it out, but they could not." He answered him and said, "O faithless generation, how long shall I be with you? How long shall I bear with you? Bring him to Me." Then they brought him to Him. And when he saw Him, immediately the spirit convulsed him, and he fell on the ground and wallowed, foaming at the mouth. So He asked his father, "How long has this been happening to him?" And he said, "From childhood. And often he has thrown him both into the fire and into the water to destroy him. But if You can do anything, have compassion on us and help us." Jesus said to him, "If you can believe, all things are possible to him who believes." Immediately the father of the child cried out and said with tears, "Lord, I believe; help my unbelief!" When Jesus saw that the people came running together, He rebuked the unclean spirit, saying to it, "Deaf and dumb spirit, I command you, come out of him and enter him no more!" Then the spirit cried out, convulsed him greatly, and came out of him. And he became as one dead, so that many said, "He is dead." But Jesus took him by the hand and lifted him up, and he arose. (Mark 9:17–27)

Jesus didn't offer up some eloquent prayer for the child. He spoke directly to the demon. Jesus called that spirit by name and commanded it to leave that boy.

In Mark 5:25–34 we find the story about a certain woman who had an issue of blood for twelve years. *"She had suffered a great deal under the care of many doctors and had spent all she had, yet instead of getting better she grew worse"* (Mark 5:26 NIV). This woman had seen every doctor available and had spent all her money on medical care, yet she was worse than when this infirmity began. When she heard about Jesus coming to town, *"she thought, 'If I just touch his clothes, I will be healed'"* (Mark 5:28 NIV). And when she touched the hem of his garment, immediately the bleeding stopped and she was healed.

Jesus knew right away that power had gone out of Him. He looked around him and asked His disciples, *"Who touched me?"* (Mark 5:31 NIV). Now there was a large crowd that had gathered around and people all around Him were touching Him. But Jesus knew that one particular person had touched Him in faith, causing power and anointing to be released. Fearfully, the woman fell at Jesus' feet and admitted that it was she who had touched His cloak.

> **Is it the will of God for you to be healed? Yes, because by His stripes we are healed.**

He said to her, "Daughter, your faith has healed you. Go in peace and be freed from your suffering." (Mark 5:34 NIV)

Remember that this illness had stolen her health and all of her living. When she touched Jesus and was made whole, I believe that not only was she healed physically, but through her faith, God restored everything financially that the disease had taken from her. Is it the will of God for you to be healed? Yes, because by His stripes we are healed. (See Isaiah 53:5.) The word *stripe* means "the blow that cuts."[10] The suffering for sickness and disease has already been paid by the shed blood of Jesus Christ.

God Still Heals Today

Don't be discouraged if someone you know isn't healed yet. Be motivated. There are people in my family who need to be saved. I'm not condemned or discouraged by that; I am motivated because I know God is still working. He is not finished.

Just a couple of days ago in our church here in Portland, the presence of God was absolutely marvelous. As we were worshipping the Lord, I began to weep from the presence of God. I knew God was doing something very, very special. In our second service, I never even got to preach. Instead, I began to call people through the word of wisdom and the word of knowledge. In one case, the Lord showed me there was a woman who had a lump on her breast and that she was not to worry because He had just healed her.

We received a phone call a couple of days later from a woman who lived in California. As she was watching our television program, God spoke to her to come to our church that Sunday, and she would get the miracle that she'd been seeking. On Monday she was to have her breast operated on because of cancer. She told us that before they operated they needed to take one more X-ray. When they did, they found nothing! They x-rayed her two more times and said, "Get up and get dressed. There is no reason to operate." Glory to God, the Great Physician worked again!

A couple of days after that, a lady in our church who also had a lump in her breast told us that when I said God was healing that problem, the lump in her breast completely dissolved. God is still a miracle-working God!

After the Garden of Gethsemane where Jesus shed His blood, He went to the whipping post. When they tied Jesus to the whipping post, they whipped Him thirty-nine times with a whip consisting of several leather thongs, each loaded with jagged pieces of metal or bone and weighted at the end with lead. With each strike of the whip, flesh was torn and blood came out of the back of our Savior. Every single time the devil put the whip to Jesus' back, blood was shed and we overcame one disease, two diseases, three diseases, until the point that every sickness brought on mankind was conquered by the blood of Jesus. No longer do you have to live under the curse of sickness and disease. You have been set free by the precious blood of Jesus!

Discussion Questions

1. Some people say God doesn't heal any more and that He only healed people during biblical times. But what does the Bible say about Jesus Christ in Hebrews 13:8?

2. Others believe God can heal but question His desire to heal. Many people asked Jesus about His willingness to heal. What did He answer the man with leprosy in Mark 1:40–41 NIV?

3. How does the Bible say we should ask in James 1:6–7 KJV?

4. What does Isaiah 53:5 say about our healing?

   What does the apostle John declare in 3 John 1:2 about healing?

5. Read Luke 13:10–12 and answer the following questions: What kind of spirit did the woman have on her?

   What did Jesus say to the woman?

6. Another dramatic healing took place in Mark 9:17–27. What kind of spirit was on the boy?

Could Jesus' disciples cast the spirit out of the boy?

What did Jesus say about the importance of belief in verse 23?

7. Read Mark 5:25–34. What do verses 27–28 say the woman with the issue of blood did when Jesus came to town?

What happened to her?

Chapter Eleven

Jesus' Crown of Thorns Won Back Our Prosperity

WE ARE REDEEMED by the precious blood of Jesus. Through His blood, we have been brought back to the state Adam and Eve enjoyed in the Garden of Eden. They lived in the blessing and the presence of God. There was no sickness or poverty. When Adam was obeying God, he had everything he needed. Adam and Eve literally lived in the land that flowed with milk and honey. But when Adam disobeyed God, God declared the curse that came upon the land through Adam's sin.

> *Because you have heeded the voice of your wife, and have eaten from the tree of which I commanded you, saying, "You shall not eat of it": Cursed is the ground for your sake; in toil you shall eat of it all the days of your life. Both thorns and thistles it shall bring forth for you, and you shall eat the herb of the field. In the sweat of your face you shall eat bread till you return to the ground.* (Genesis 3:17–19)

God cursed the ground with thorns and thistles. If we don't understand that we've been redeemed from the curse by the blood of Jesus, then the land we go to work in, the land we build our businesses in, and the land we live in is still under a curse. When Adam sinned, no longer could he live in God's abundance and splendor. The land was cursed, and by the sweat of his brow, man would eke out an existence. Since that day, mankind has sweated for everything it has gotten. But the third place Jesus shed His blood broke the curse of poverty.

Thousands of years after Adam sinned, Jesus Christ, the second Adam, was taken before the religious and political authorities to stand trial as a fraud and a heretic. On the way to Pilate, as they were mocking Jesus, "All hail, King of the Jews," they saw a thorn bush—the symbol of the curse of poverty on the land. They took some of the thorn branches, wove them into a crown, and placed them on the brow of Jesus until the blood flowed from His head. (See Matthew 27:29.)

The symbol of poverty was placed on the brow of Jesus, the second Adam. When those thorns pierced His brow, He shed His blood for our redemption from poverty. We were cursed with poverty by the sweat of Adam's brow, but we were redeemed from the curse of poverty by the blood on Jesus' brow.

> We were cursed with poverty by the sweat of Adam's brow, but we are redeemed from the curse of poverty by the blood on Jesus' brow.

What Satan means for evil, God will use for good. (See Genesis 50:20.) The soldiers took that crown of thorns and placed it on Jesus' head. Instead of sweat, out poured the blood of Jesus. Now, by the power of the blood of Jesus, not only is the curse of poverty broken, but those who take the name of Jesus and claim His blood are anointed to prosper.

> *For you know the grace of our Lord Jesus Christ, that though He was rich, yet for your sakes He became poor, that you through His poverty might become rich.*   (2 Corinthians 8:9)

Jesus was never poor. When the Bible says Jesus became poor, it means He was poor in comparison to what He had in His heavenly home. In heaven the streets are made of pure gold, walls and gates are made of precious gems, and there's not one poverty bone in all of God's body. When someone reads that Jesus became poor, He was poor in relationship to how He lived in heaven. If you were to take all the money in the world and give it to one man, that one man would be a poor man in comparison to what

Jesus had in heaven before He became a human being on earth. Even on earth, Jesus may have refused material goods while He was preaching, but He could have called down the angels at any time to provide for His needs.

A man said to me one time, "Jesus was poor, and I want to be just like Jesus." I asked him why he thought Jesus was poor. He said Jesus was poor because He was born in a manger, and this was to show us that we don't need worldly comfort. Yes, Jesus was born in a manger, but not to teach us poverty. He was showing us that we were not making room for the Savior to be born in our lives.

Before Mary and Joseph went to the barn, they first went to the inn to get a room. I doubt if Mary was going to put the room on one of her credit cards or that she intended to sneak out of the window in the morning without paying the bill. Mary and Joseph had plenty of money to get a room at the inn. The problem was that the inn had no room for the Savior.

Nevertheless, we have religiously and traditionally taught that Jesus was poor, so Christians should be poor. Christmas programs usually show three wise men around the manger with their little gifts: small boxes of frankincense, myrrh, and gold. A friend of mine researched the three wise men and their gifts. He discovered that gold was not the only priceless gift they offered Christ. Frankincense and myrrh are also precious substances. Furthermore, according to Matthew 2:1, there could have been many wise men. These gifts could have ensured that Jesus and His family lived in comfort.

When I teach this, I always ask people, "How many know that the Word of God is the most powerful thing on earth?" Everybody always shouts, "Amen!" Then I shock them by saying, "But it's not. The Bible says that man's religious traditions make the Word of God of no effect." (See Mark 7:13.) So in order to avoid making the Word of God powerless and impotent in our lives, we must beware not to fall into lifeless, religious thinking and traditions—which is one of the wiles of the devil.

Paul taught us to beware of the wiles of the devil, which means we must understand his strategies, the ways he will attempt to ambush us. One of his greatest wiles is used to keep us poor. If he can get us to believe that Jesus lived in poverty and that to be like Jesus we must live in poverty, then he has trapped us and the Word of God—*"I have come that they may have life, and that they may have it more abundantly"* (John 10:10)— becomes ineffective in our lives. The devil's strategy is to make us speak the tradition of men so that we should be poor and shut our mouths to the Word of God that in Christ Jesus we are rich.

There are a couple of times in the Bible when Jesus would touch someone and say, "Now don't tell anybody." And what would they do? Immediately they would run off and tell everybody. I have to believe that Jesus would just laugh to Himself. He knew they couldn't keep their mouths shut. They are like my brother Norm when he got saved—I mean really saved—a couple of months ago. Now all he wants to talk about is Jesus. He tells everybody what Jesus did for him and has already started a Bible study in his home. Norm didn't get a religion; he got a relationship with the Son of God. Norm is just like these people in the Bible. When Jesus touched them, they couldn't stop talking about Him. The

> No matter what we're going through, no matter what we need, Jesus will meet that need.

devil knows this too! He knows we're going to tell as many as we can that no matter what we're going through, no matter what we need, Jesus will meet that need. So the devil's strategy is to get us to believe the lie that we're supposed to be poor. Then we can't afford to get the Good News out.

I used to believe in the poverty doctrine. I believed it, I preached it, and believe me, it worked! But one day Tiz and I met John Avanzini, a man of God who changed our lives. God was stirring us about prosperity, but our traditions were battling with the Word of God. Finally I said to John, "I really want to know the truth. So if I say anything that's wrong, just tell me and show it to me in the Word." Then I began to tell him why I thought it was wrong for us to prosper and have nice things. Immediately John said, "Larry, you're wrong."

"Why?" I asked.

"You think that instead of Christians having a nice home or a nice car or a nice church that this money ought to be used to win the world to Jesus."

"Yes," I said, "exactly."

What John told me then, has changed my life, my ministry, and my family forever. He said, "Larry, God's not on a budget; He owns it all. He has enough money to win the world a thousand times over and still see all of His children blessed above anything they could ask or think."

Proverbs 13:22 says, *"A good man leaves an inheritance to his children's children, but the wealth of the sinner is stored up for the righteous."* Do you know what that verse means? Not only are we supposed to be so wealthy that we leave an inheritance to our grandchildren, but God is trying to get the wealth of the world into the hands of the church. Every good thing comes from our Father above, including the wisdom and provision for houses, cars, clothing— and for preaching the Gospel to every creature on the earth. The wealth of this earth is for God's children.

We have a blood covenant with Jesus to move us from poverty into prosperity, but look at the abundance that is out in the world. Unbelievers have got our stuff! God knows we have need of all these things. So we must rise up and tell our Father, "We're ready for our stuff now!"

We must realize that acquiring goods is not the goal. True riches are not material. However, if we ask God to provide salvation, healing, or help in times of trouble, can we not rely on Him to provide us with the means to pay our bills? Then we can take good care of our families and bless the world with the Gospel of Jesus Christ.

Is Poverty of God or the Devil?

Some people believe that wealth is of the devil and that God wants Christians to be poor, but James 1:13 tells us that God can tempt no man with evil. If money and prosperity were evil, then God never would have given us promises of blessings when we give Him our tithes.

> *"Bring all the tithes into the storehouse, that there may be food in My house, and try Me now in this," says the LORD of hosts, "If I will not open for you the windows of heaven and pour out for you such blessing that there will not be room enough to receive it. And I will rebuke the devourer for your sakes, so that he will not destroy the fruit of your ground, nor shall the vine fail to bear fruit for you in the field," says the LORD of hosts; and all nations will call you blessed, for you will be a delightful land," says the LORD of hosts.* (Malachi 3:10–12)

The New International Version translates *"windows"* as *"floodgates."* The floodgates hold back the flood. If we believe that prosperity is not of God and rob Him of our tithes and offerings, the floodgates remain closed and we are unable to experience the blessings He has for us. I don't know about you, but I like the idea of God pouring out so much blessing on me that I don't have enough room to contain it!

The word *"windows"* also is derived from the word *ambush.*[11] God wants to ambush us with prosperity! I believe He has to ambush us, or sneak up on us, because we have taught that poverty and Christianity are synonymous.

Tiz and I have never missed giving of our tithes in all the years we've been saved. We have never made a pledge and not paid it. But we never saw the financial blessing and prosperity of God until we realized that poverty is part of a curse from which we've been redeemed. Poverty is not God's will; prosperity is God's will.

> *Give, and it will be given to you: good measure, pressed down, shaken together, and running over will be put into your bosom. For with the same measure that you use, it will be measured back to you.* (Luke 6:38)

God doesn't want us to live out of the bottom of the barrel. He wants our houses paid for, our cars paid for, our churches paid for, and enough money to evangelize the world. God is not broke. He owns the cattle on a thousand hills. (See Psalm 50:10.) The earth is the Lord's and the fullness thereof, and we are heirs to that covenant promise. (See Psalm 50:12.)

Let's see what else the Word of God has to say about prosperity.

> *The wealth of the sinner is stored up for the righteous.*
> (Proverbs 13:22)

> *You shall remember the LORD your God, for it is He who gives you power to get wealth, that He may establish His covenant.*
> (Deuteronomy 8:18)

> *And God is able to make all grace abound toward you, that you, always having all sufficiency in all things, may have an abundance for every good work.* (2 Corinthians 9:8)

Poverty is not part of Christianity. *Prosperity* is part of Christianity. Prosperity is part of God's redemption plan for His people. We need to remember that we are spirits who live in bodies and we function through our souls—our emotions and intellect. As a man *"thinks in his heart, so is he"* (Proverbs 23:7). So if we think poverty is part of Christianity, then poverty stays with us. But when we understand that we are redeemed from poverty by the blood of Jesus, we can be set free and receive the prosperity God has for us.

There are teachings in pulpits across the nation that prosperity is not of God, but don't forget that money turns on the lights! Money feeds kids in Cambodia. Money supports our foreign missionaries as they present the Gospel to the lost. Money supports the orphanages. Money means we can reach the kids on the streets.

Don't listen to anyone who teaches that God wants you to be poor and needy. If you listen to it, you're going to absorb it, and it is scripturally wrong. God has reversed the curse.

> *Blessed is the man who walks not in the counsel of the ungodly.*
> (Psalm 1:1)

Be careful who you listen to. The blood that Jesus shed when they pressed the crown of thorns on His head has reversed the curse of poverty. All you have to do to move out of poverty and into prosperity is believe that the blood of Jesus has reversed the curse, accept His promise of prosperity for your life, and obey God in giving.

I was teaching this in the Philippines and a pastor said to me, "Well, that's okay for you guys, but we're not in America." The Bible is not a book written solely for Americans. The Word of God is not exclusive to a certain race or a certain nation. The Bible was written for *all* people. So I said to this pastor, "How can you say prosperity is not for you? You can see prosperity at work when your cows have two calves instead of one. You see your fishermen bring in an abundance like Peter did when he fished and the nets were full and the fish were large yet the nets didn't break. And you've seen your rice crops yield double the amount of what was expected."

Our idea of prosperity can be so limited. Don't limit God! Recognize the prosperity of God in your life and be thankful.

Work Is Not a Curse

Do we have to work? Yes, we have to work. In this world, it is a day's work for a day's wage. However, God multiplies our work. The work it takes the world to bring in a year of harvest, God can bring to His children in a month. What takes the world ten years to earn, God can bring to us in six months. The world functions by the law of poverty, by the sweat of their brow, but you and I function by the law of redemption, by the blood of His brow, and that curse of poverty has been broken.

> Living by faith does not mean you don't have to work. Living by faith is working and believing God will bless your labor.

Work itself is not the curse because Adam worked before the curse. The Bible says that if you don't work, you don't eat. (See 2 Thessalonians 3:10.) You can't be saying, "Oh, God, meet my need," and your relatives and friends are asking, "Why aren't you working?"

"Well, I'm living by faith," you answer.

No, if you are able to work and are not working, you are living by mooch, not by faith! Living by faith does not mean you don't have to work. *Living by faith is working and believing God will bless your labor.* Don't tell people, "Well, I don't work because I live by faith and I know God will provide." That is *not* God's faith.

Welfare may provide, but welfare is for people who *can't* work, not for people who *won't* work. Seek God's wisdom, delight yourself in the Lord, meditate in His Word day and night, and whatever you do will prosper. (See Psalm 1:1–3.)

Fruitless Labor

Adam was living in abundance when he was tending the Garden, and God multiplied Adam's abundance through his labor. Things were growing and flourishing. But when Adam disobeyed God, the ground was cursed and instead of bubbling with provision, Adam had to work to pry out that provision. Instead of automatically yielding fruit, herbs, and trees, the ground yielded thorns and thistles. Hard work, labor, and sweat became a way of life just to survive.

Before the curse, Adam was blessed as he toiled. God blessed his work and it yielded great abundance. However, when the curse came, the ground that once yielded abundance was cursed and Adam had to work hard in order to barely get by.

This is where most of us live. We have to pry out an existence because the earth we live on is cursed. *But we have been redeemed from that curse by the blood of the Lamb.* God has provided a way for us to break the curse of poverty.

A woman wrote to us after watching our television program and hearing that curses are broken by the blood of Jesus Christ. She found hope for her family who had been afflicted by poverty for five generations.

Dear Pastor Huch,

We are a hard-working people, but we can never get any further than working hard. No matter how many jobs I have at one time, I cannot seem to save that "nest egg." Something always seems to come up, whereby I have to use that little money saved to pay for something else. I would like to see my entire family with property of their own and money for retirement years, instead of working until the body grows old and becomes ready for the grave.

To my knowledge, there have been five generations of terrible marriages, divorce, and lack. I hate the poverty in my life, in my family's life, and in this city. When I heard your message on TBN,

I was thrilled. Although I did not have a label for the problems, I have always known there must be something terribly wrong because of the poverty, divorces, and single parents in our family.

Pastor Huch, I grieve for my family, for myself, and for the city in which I live. It doesn't have to continue this way, and I rejoice in the knowledge that it can and will change.

I was watching your program one Sunday afternoon on TBN. The Lord gave me that moment to view your program, so I know He wanted me to seek your ministry. Please pray for me and all that I have shared with you.

Sincerely yours,
Sonja

I've heard a lot of people say, "I believe God will bless us in the sweet by-and-by and give us the pie in the sky when we die." But God also wants us to have it here on the ground while we're still around! You can't bless the world if your prosperity is in the sky. Prosperity means that as you're doing your work, as you're doing your job, as you're running your business, or building your church, you are doing it all for God. God said, "I get involved and I don't move by the world's ways; I move by supernatural ways, and I prosper you in the journey."

We sometimes limit God because our idea of prosperity conforms to the world's idea of prosperity. A person may give up everything to become a missionary in a third-world country yet still be prosperous. How is this possible? Because God will provide the plane ticket to get there, will supply Bibles and medical supplies for the people, and will multiply your work so that a whole village can be saved. God may not give you a Rolls Royce, but He will make sure your clothes don't run out, as He did for the Israelites as they wandered in the desert, until you get that raise you've been asking for. Prosperity is manna in the desert because a priceless ruby isn't going to feed your empty belly. God knows what you need.

A lady in our church ran up to me the other day and said, "Pastor, thank you for teaching on breaking the curse of poverty and living in prosperity! I want you to know I'm the first person in the history of our family to purchase a house. The spirit of poverty is broken off my life and my children's lives, and I am a proud homeowner. Praise be to God!"

A couple came and told me they had been $14,000 in debt with a hospital bill from an unexpected illness and were close to losing their home. Their mother heard the message of God's supernatural debt cancellation and said to God, "You mean You can get my kids out of debt?" So she began to pray. Shortly afterwards, the hospital called this couple and said, "We're going to cancel your debt. It's paid in full." They are blessed, and the kingdom of God is blessed through them because they obeyed God and gave their tithes and offerings out of the money that was restored to them.

Don't Lose What You Already Have

The blessing from God is not just what is out in front of you but also what is not overtaking you from behind. Part of the curse of poverty is that the devourer tries to overtake you from behind. Being devoured means you start to get ahead and your car breaks down; you start to get ahead and your kids get sick and you have a hospital bill; you start to get ahead and some other bill comes along and drains your reserve.

If you are paying your tithes and giving offerings, God *"will rebuke the devourer for your sakes"* (Malachi 3:11). There are times when the devil is going to try to cause your car to break down and your engine to blow up. Then God intervenes and says, "No, don't touch that because he's paid his tithe and that curse of poverty is reversed."

God said, "All the world will see you and say, 'They are blessed of the Lord.'" (See Malachi 3:11–12.) When you have a nice home and car, and your wife and children are dressed nicely, the world says, "They are blessed." Your life reflects the nature of God. You represent His goodness and blessing.

For fifteen years, Tiz and I witnessed to our family about the Lord, but they wouldn't listen to a word we said. We had sold out for God, were buying our clothes at thrift stores, driving pieces of junk, and just barely able to make ends meet. They would ask us, "If you're working for God so much, why doesn't He take care of you?" That made sense! We were preaching the

Gospel while living in poverty and bragging about it! "C'mon, join us, lose everything. C'mon. Where is everyone? C'mon. What's wrong with you? Don't you want to be in constant need like us?" Then we learned that God wants to bless His children.

> *Let them shout for joy and be glad, who favor my righteous cause; and let them say continually, "Let the LORD be magnified, who has pleasure in the prosperity of His servant."* (Psalm 35:27)

My giving has quadrupled because God prospers everything I put my hands to. If you are already tithing, all you have to do is accept what the blood has done and say, "I apply the blood of the Lamb to my job, my finances, and my family."

There is a lot of controversy over the prosperity message. I agree that there has been misuse and abuse by some, but that doesn't change the Word of God. I know some people say, "Well, we've seen people backslide once they gained money and material things." So have I. But I've seen a lot more backslide because they were sick and tired of "paying the price," and "suffering for Jesus," and working year after year with nothing to show for it.

Poverty is part of the curse. God never intended for His children to live in poverty. God never intended for His children to be the "scourge of society." From the beginning, God's intention for His beloved children has been blessing and prosperity. In Deuteronomy 28:1–14, God tells His people the results of serving Him wholeheartedly—blessing, blessing, blessing!

Probably the greatest lie that Satan has ever pulled off was that poverty is an indicator of godliness. If Christians are bound financially, they have very little to give to their church. If the churches are bound financially, they have very little to do their work. Consequently, the work of God is slowed down or stopped completely. Missionaries can't be sent out. Bibles can't be printed. People say the Gospel is free. Yes, the message is free, but it takes lots of money to accomplish God's vision. The Good News is that He is our source and our provider.

I taught this message in a foreign church that had been supported by American mission money for fifty-three years. They accepted the fact that Jesus shed His blood for our prosperity and the curse of poverty on them was broken. Not only did they not need missionary money any longer, but within a year they launched three of their own churches.

There is an end-time harvest of souls that is beginning to take place. God is bringing an end-time transfer of wealth to His people so we can fulfill His plans. We need to get positioned to move from poverty to prosperity. We've got to get positioned in our minds, in our spirits, and in our actions to receive what God wants to do in our lives.

God is not against us having money. He is against money having us. If we keep God and His work first priority in our lives, there's no end to the prosperity He'll pour through us and to us. God is not asking us to take a *vow of poverty*, but He is asking us to take a *vow of priorities*. As we are faithful in our finances in the natural realm, God will multiply and pour out finances in the supernatural realm.

> **We have to get in a position in our minds, our spirits, and our actions to receive what God wants to do in our lives.**

Read this testimony from Suzanne, one of our members at New Beginnings Christian Center, who broke the curse of poverty in her life and is living in God's prosperity.

Pastor Huch and Tiz,

The teaching I have received in the last six years of attending New Beginnings has had a large part in the person I am today.

When I arrived in Portland six years ago, I was homeless. Six years of a very physically and emotionally abusive marriage left me fearful and with little self-esteem. I lived in shelters for battered women and started attending New Beginnings.

I was put in "the system" on welfare and low-income housing. I got off welfare and my children and I lived on child support of $423 a month. I had no job skills, had never finished high school, and had not worked in six years. I had my talent as an artist, and I tithed, even when I lived in poverty.

In November 1996, I asked God to be my business partner. I said my life was His—I would do whatever He asked. All of this time I have been reading His Word, listening to tapes, and *growing. In 1996 my gross income from my art was under $8,000. In 1997 I started praying "specifically," just as you taught us to do. In January I prayed I would make $6,000 and it happened! Then I prayed that I could double it. In March I grossed $12,000.*

I lived in low-income housing and wanted to move, so I prayed God would give me enough money to buy a house. In September, I grossed over $20,000 in a thirty-five-day period and bought a home on a contract.

Then I said, "God, I need a new van. This one is no longer safe." A week later, I had a new van. I now have a successful business where I can gross $10,000 plus a month. I now make $500 plus a day—more than I used to live on in a month. I believe this year my tithe will be more than I used to live on in a year.

My mind-set has been changed through the messages I have received in church and through tapes and books. Everything you are teaching works, if people would just do it. I'm working very hard, but I'm also faithful to attend and stay involved in church. I know I have to stay connected to my source.

"He raiseth up the poor out of the dust, and lifteth the needy out of the dunghill; that he may set him with princes, even with the princes of his people" *(Psalm 113:7–8 KJV). My clients are some of the most powerful, wealthy people in the state, and they are willing to wait in line for me to work for them. I just turned thirty years old the other day, and my life has only just begun.*

Thank you.

God bless,
Suzanne

Our God is the Lord of the harvest! What He has done for Suzanne, He can and wants to do for you! Poverty no longer has a place in your life because that curse has been broken. It was broken when the crown of thorns pierced Jesus' sinless head and His sinless blood poured down His body. If you are needing a job, seek the Lord. I believe you will receive a job that you will not only love but that will also pay you above and beyond what you need. And as you receive God's blessings, you can turn around and be a blessing to others. You cannot outgive God!

Discussion Questions

1. In Genesis 3:17–19, what did God tell Adam would happen because of his disobedience?

2. On the way to Pilate, as the soldiers were mocking Jesus, what did they place on His head? See Matthew 27:29.

3. What does Genesis 50:20 say about Satan's plans?

4. In 2 Corinthians 8:9, what does it say you become as a result of Christ taking your poverty on himself?

5. What does Mark 7:13 say about religious traditions?

6. When it comes to the devil, Paul taught us to be aware of what? See Ephesians 6:11.

7. Proverbs 13:22 says, *"A good man leaves an inheritance to his children's children, but the wealth of a sinner is stored up for the righteous."* What do you think this verse means?

8. Some people believe that wealth is of the devil and that God wants Christians to be poor. What does James 1:13 tell us?

9. Read Malachi 3:10–12 and fill in the blanks below:

    "Bring all the _____ into the storehouse, that there may be food in My house, and try Me now in this," says the LORD of hosts, "If I will not open for you the _____ of heaven and pour out for you such blessing that there will not be room enough to receive it. And I will rebuke the _____ for your sakes, so that he will not destroy the fruit of your ground, nor shall the vine fail to bear fruit for you in the field," says the LORD of hosts; "And all nations will call you _____, for you will be a delightful land," says the LORD of hosts.

10. What do the following Scriptures tell you about prosperity?

    Luke 6:38

    Proverbs 13:22

    Deuteronomy 8:18

    2 Corinthians 9:8

11. Have you ever wondered why we need to work and how work fits into the prosperity God has for His people? Do you believe that work itself is part of the curse Adam brought on the world?

12. What does God say in Deuteronomy 28:1–14 are the results of serving Him wholeheartedly?

13. Turn again to Deuteronomy 28:1–14 and pray the verses out loud, inserting your own name every place it says, *"thee,"* *"thou,"* or *"thine."*

Chapter Twelve

Jesus' Pierced Hands Won Dominion over What We Touch

THE FOURTH PLACE Jesus' blood was shed was from His hands, where the soldiers pounded spikes to nail Him to the cross. I believe that through the blood shed from His nail-pierced hands, God says everything we put our hands to He will cause to prosper. (See Genesis 39:3.)

Before the fall of Adam, you and I were created by God to be in charge of and to have dominion over all the earth.

> *Then God said, "Let Us make man in Our image, according to Our likeness; let them have dominion over the fish of the sea, over the birds of the air, and over the cattle, over all the earth and over every creeping thing that creeps on the earth." So God cre-ated man in His own image; in the image of God He created him; male and female He created them. Then God blessed them, and God said to them, "Be fruitful and multiply; fill the earth and subdue it; have dominion over the fish of the sea, over the birds of the air, and over every living thing that moves on the earth."*
> (Genesis 1:26–28)

God placed all authority in the hands of Adam and Eve, but when Adam disobeyed God, that authority was taken from us and Satan became the god of this world. Satan began to take charge. I believe that, when Jesus was crucified, He shed His blood as they drove spikes into His hands so you and I would regain our dominion and become overcomers. Our authority has been redeemed through the shed blood of Jesus' hands.

Many Christians are running away from the devil or trying to hide from him. We think that if we run fast enough and speak in tongues enough, the devil won't get us too badly. Then there are other Christians who are holding ground and think the devil will ignore them if they just keep quiet and don't make too much noise.

As Christians, we are not to be timid, be on the defensive, or operate in neutral. We can overcome the devil. We can defeat the devil. We can have victory over the enemy of our lives who is out to destroy us. We can go after the attacks of Satan and defeat them. We can take the offensive to thwart the enemy's tactics against us.

Lay Hold of What Belongs to God

Even the world notices when the Lord causes His people to prosper. For example, Potiphar observed that although Joseph was a slave, he was successful and prosperous and *"the LORD made all he did to prosper in his hand"* (Genesis 39:3). That is why the devil doesn't want you to lay your hands on things and take authority over what belongs to God and His people.

Once when I was preaching in Michigan, we laid hands on and prayed for a woman who needed a double blessing. This is the testimony she later sent to us.

Dear Pastor Huch,

I came to see you when you were in Detroit. What a wonderful and anointed message on breaking the curse of financial debt you preached. The Lord spoke to me and it was confirmed that I would be doubly blessed. After asking who would like to receive the laying on of hands for the release of the anointing, I ran forward with everyone else. You laid hands on me twice.

Over a month later, I became pregnant, which I have been praying about for over three-and-a-half years. On the very same day I found out I was pregnant, my husband received a $50,000-a-year *job. For the past two years, he had been unemployed. Through it all, the Lord has sustained us and met our every need.*

I will continue to believe that during this Jubilee year, the Lord will take care of all our financial debts we have acquired over these years of unemployment. Thanks to your teaching of breaking generational curses, I am able to receive God's promise for a pain-free delivery of this blessed and healthy baby I am carrying.

God bless,
Jamilla

When Jesus bled from His hands, dominion was returned to God's children. That means that whatever evil we encounter, we have the authority in Jesus' name to render it harmless.

They will take up serpents; and if they drink anything deadly, it will by no means hurt them; they will lay hands on the sick, and they will recover. (Mark 16:18)

You need to lay hands on your children, cover them with the blood of Jesus, and say, "I break the iniquity off my kids. I break the iniquity off my family." You need to lay hands on your child's pillow and declare that they are going to serve God. You need to lay your hands on your children's school and cover it with the blood of Jesus. If you have an unsaved husband, lay your hands on your husband's pillow and release the anointing of the Spirit of God. Take authority over those demons of iniquity and, all of a sudden, Dad is going to start opening the Bible and reading it. He said he would never go to church, but now he's getting the whole family to go. Why? Because the iniquity is broken by the blood of Jesus the moment you take authority over the enemy, and the Holy Spirit is loosed to bring God's promises to pass in your life.

> Whatever evil we encounter, we have the authority in Jesus' name to render it harmless.

Everything you put your hands to, God will cause it to prosper. (See Genesis 39:3.) Why? Not because it's a ritual but because authority has been returned to our hands through the precious blood of Jesus.

When we were pastoring a church in Santa Fe, a large building was being renovated downtown for a homosexual and lesbian disco. We got our church members together, went down there, laid hands on the building, and said, "You foul spirit, we bind you, we take dominion over this place, and we declare that it will not open."

On the day of the grand opening, all the electricity blew up, so it had to be shut down. Repairs were made and another grand opening was scheduled. We went back to the building, laid hands on it, and said, "You foul spirit, in the name of Jesus, we take dominion over you. You are not going to rise up in this city for immoral purposes." They were set to open and something else blew up. This went on for a year-and-a-half while millions of dollars were spent and went down the drain. It never did open. Was this simply a coincidence? Absolutely not!

It's Real!

We are to have authority! God gave us authority in the Garden of Eden, we lost it through Adam's sin, and Jesus redeemed it on the cross. Jesus laid His hands down. He didn't resist His opponents, He just laid His body down, and they drove those spikes into His hands. His blood was shed and dominion came back into the hands of all who believe in Him.

The Word of God says we have been redeemed by the blood of Jesus. Our authority has been redeemed. Our dominion has been redeemed. We need to take our hands, lay them on everything, and claim the blessings of God with authority, by the blood and in the name of Jesus Christ!

Discussion Questions

1. Read Genesis 1:26–28 and list all the things God gave man dominion over.

2. In Genesis 39:3, what did Potiphar observe about the slave Joseph?

3. According to Mark 16:17–18, what signs follow those who believe in Jesus' name?

4. The Word of God says we have been redeemed by the blood of Jesus. Our authority has been redeemed. Our dominion has been redeemed. Take your hands right now, lay them on everything, and claim the blessings of God with authority, by the blood and in the name of Jesus Christ.

Chapter Thirteen

Jesus' Pierced Feet Won Dominion over the Places We Walk

THE FIFTH PLACE where Jesus shed His blood was where they drove the spikes through His feet, nailing Him to the cross. The blood shed from His feet also redeemed us from our loss of dominion and authority. Man was supposed to be the head and not the tail. Man was supposed to be above only and not beneath. (See Deuteronomy 28:13.) That is our place through the shed blood of Jesus. When Adam disobeyed God in the Garden of Eden, he lost dominion and authority, and at that moment, Satan became the god of this world. But through Jesus' shed blood, we don't have to be trampled by Satan. Instead, we are to trample him!

> *Every place on which the sole of your foot treads shall be yours.*
> (Deuteronomy 11:24)

We have been commanded to *"go into all the world and preach the good news to all creation"* (Mark 16:15 NIV). Wherever we go, we're to tell people, *"The kingdom of God is near. Repent and believe the good news!"* (Mark 1:15 NIV). This would be impossible unless we had the authority to take dominion over Satan's earthly kingdom. We are told to *"be strong and courageous. Do not be afraid or terrified... for the LORD your God goes with you; he will never leave you nor forsake you*" (Deuteronomy 31:6 NIV). Dominion over this earth is ours again because of the shed blood of Jesus Christ, and wherever we are, the kingdom of heaven is at hand.

As a believer, you have the authority to walk around your neighborhood and say, "I bind the devil in my neighborhood. I bind the drug addicts and the dope dealers." You can walk through the schools and say, "I bind violence, I bind homosexuality, I bind perversion, and I bind New Age teaching," because wherever you go, God is with you.

The lawless and the gangs will yield to the power of God. You can stand on your front porch and say, "You spirit of violence, I bind you in the name of Jesus. I rebuke you out of my city. I command you to leave my neighborhood. I command you to leave my school. I command you to leave my government."

> You can claim your position in God as His child, washed in the blood of Jesus with your dominion restored.

The enemy will say to you, "Who do you think you are?" And you can claim your position in God as His child, washed in the blood of Jesus with your dominion restored. Every place you put the sole of your feet, you are going to take dominion. God gives to you every place you lay the sole of your foot.

Pleading the Blood over Your Family

At the beginning of this past school year, parents were expressing their concerns to me about the safety of their children during the school day. I told them what Moses told the children of Israel, "Put the blood of Jesus over your doorpost, because when that spirit of iniquity and destruction tries to come in, it will see the blood and flee." How do you put Jesus' blood on your doorpost? You speak the Word over your children. Believe His promises of protection for your family. Command the enemy to leave your children alone. Pray for your children, plead the blood of Jesus over them, and know that the angel of death and destruction cannot cross the blood. Go to the school when no one is there, lay hands on the front doors, and pray over that school. Walk around the school and claim it for the kingdom of God, because *"every place where you set your foot will be yours"* (Deuteronomy 11:24 NIV).

There are things in the natural you can do also. Be there for your children. Talk to them. Get to know their friends. Get involved in their school activities. Volunteer at their school. Be the parent that goes the extra mile. Make your children your passion.

The devil has been occupying our schools long enough. It is time to take back what the enemy has stolen and consecrate it for God's work. But don't stop there. Put the blood of Jesus over the tabernacle doors of your own life. Then, when that spirit of iniquity, death, and destruction comes, it understands that it cannot cross that blood line. It doesn't matter whether it is guns, divorce, poverty, or sickness, because *"He who is in you is greater than he who is in the world"* (1 John 4:4).

For the unbelieving husband has been sanctified through his wife, and the unbelieving wife has been sanctified through her believing husband. Otherwise your children would be unclean, but as it is, they are holy. (1 Corinthians 7:14 NIV)

Your spouse may not be saved, but you can plead the blood over them and your children and break that family curse. When we learned this years ago, we encouraged all the wives in our church who had unsaved husbands to start pleading the blood over their husbands. At first, the husbands were mad at their wives because they were going to church, but within two weeks, every one of those husbands came in and got saved. Thirty women were faithfully praying and thirty husbands gave their lives to Jesus. Why? Because the prayers of their wives broke the iniquity that was holding them in bondage. This will also work for your children. Through the power of the blood of Jesus, you can see your children turn their face to God and live for Him. You can see your children rise up and make a godly impact on their schools. You can see your child stand against the wiles of the evil one and stand for righteousness.

When we were looking at a piece of property for the church, we went to the mayor and the mayor said, "This is industrial, commercial property. No church can be allowed to be built here." That didn't stop us because we knew by the Spirit of God this was the land God had for us. We went out there, walked around that land, and claimed it for our church. Later, we met with the city council, who had already decided they were going to turn us down. They said, "We don't know why we're doing this, but we're going to 'grandfather' you in. You're the only church that's going to be able to build on this commercial property." God gave us dominion, and I knew that wherever I put the sole of my feet was blood-bought property.

We were originally planning to purchase fifty acres, but it ended up being eighty-four acres. Today, that land is worth more than five or six times the amount we paid for it. Not only does God give us dominion over the places we walk, He prospers the places we walk.

Rise Up and Take Dominion

But one testified in a certain place, saying: "What is man that You are mindful of him, or the son of man that You take care of him? You have made him a little lower than the angels; You have crowned him with glory and honor, and set him over the works of Your hands. You have put all things in subjection under his feet." For in that He put all in subjection under him, He left nothing that is not put under him. But now we do not yet see all things put under him. (Hebrews 2:6–8)

We are not simply God's little boys and girls. You and I are heirs of salvation. That means that the angels are under us; we are not under them. We are joint heirs with Christ Jesus. (See Romans 8:17.) When we go where He tells us to go, He goes with us, and we are able to take dominion by His authority.

> When we go where He tells us, He goes with us, and we are able to take dominion by His authority.

We don't serve a Savior who is dead or a Lord who is still in the tomb. We serve a resurrected Savior full of life, full of power, and full of anointing! Our burden-removing, yoke-destroying Savior says, "As my Father sent me, now I am sending you. Wherever you go, tell them the kingdom of heaven is at hand." (See John 20:21 and Matthew 10:7.)

Years ago, people used to do "Jericho marches." Now understand that there is no power in *religious ritual*, but there is life-changing power in *revelation*. The original Jericho march happened because Joshua received a revelation from the Lord that everywhere his feet trod would come under his God-given authority. (See Joshua 1:3.) Get concerned about your children's schools and walk around the school grounds and say, "Every place I put the soul of my feet is blood-bought ground for the kingdom of God. He gives it to us for an inheritance." Don't do this in a way that makes you look ridiculous, but you can march around that school and the spirits of violence, anger, depression, and disease will crumble.

When the children of Israel put the blood of the lamb on their doorposts, the spirit of death could not cross. (See Exodus 12:22–28.) You need to put the blood around your house, your church, and your children's schools, and understand that God restored dominion to you by the blood that flowed from Jesus' feet.

When we bind the devil, our next step is to loose the peace of Jesus in our streets. Loose the righteousness of Jesus in our cities.

> *Truly I say to you, whatever you shall bind on earth shall be bound in heaven; and whatever you loose on earth shall be loosed in heaven.* (Matthew 18:18 NASB)

We can bind the enemy and kick him out of our cities and nation, but to keep him out we must release the power of God to transform lives. We must preach the Good News and make disciples of all people to really walk in dominion.

We say, "Well, God ought to do something about this mess."

He says, "I already did."

"God ought to send someone."

He says, "I'm trying! Are you listening?"

> *And he said unto them, Go ye into all the world, and preach the gospel to every creature....And these signs shall follow them that*

believe; in my name shall they cast out devils; they shall speak with new tongues; they shall take up serpents; and if they drink any deadly thing, it shall not hurt them; they shall lay hands on the sick, and they shall recover. (Mark 16:15, 17–18 KJV)

Are you ready to take dominion? Are you ready to take your town for Jesus? Are you ready to turn your nation back to God? It's time to go into the enemy's camp and take back what he has stolen!

Jesus' Feet Won Dominion over the Places We Walk

Discussion Questions

1. What does Deuteronomy 28:13 say the Lord will make you?

2. According to Deuteronomy 11:24, what places will you have dominion over?

   In Mark 16:15 NIV, what are we commanded to do?

   Mark 1:15 says wherever we go, we're to tell people what?

3. What are we told to be in Deuteronomy 31:6 NIV?

4. You can put the blood of Jesus over the tabernacle doors of your life because, according to 1 John 4:4:

   He who is in _____ *is* _____ *than he who is in the world.*

5. According to Romans 8:17, we are not simply God's little boys and girls. We are "_____ *of* _____."

6. In Matthew 18:18, what does Jesus say to us about binding and loosing?

Chapter Fourteen

Jesus' Pierced Heart Won Back Our Joy

The Jews therefore, because it was the preparation, that the bodies should not remain upon the cross on the sabbath day, (for that sabbath day was an high day,) besought Pilate that their legs might be broken, and that they might be taken away. Then came the soldiers, and brake the legs of the first, and of the other which was crucified with him. But when they came to Jesus, and saw that he was dead already, they brake not his legs: but one of the soldiers with a spear pierced his side, and forthwith came there out blood and water.
—John 19:31–34 KJV

THE SIXTH PLACE Jesus shed His blood was where a soldier shoved a spear into His side and blood and water poured out. Jesus died so that we could be forgiven. He was heartbroken from the weight of our sins. We have all heard it said that the nails in His hands and feet didn't hold him on the cross; His love for us did. As He hung on the cross, Jesus' heart broke for us. When the Roman soldier pierced his side, that blood from His broken heart flowed forth for us.

It was the rule of the observance of the Sabbath that there could not be anyone on the cross when the Sabbath began. Jesus was crucified on a Friday and the Sabbath began at sunset that day. To comply with Jewish law, the soldiers went to each of the crucified to break their legs. This was to hasten their death so that they would be dead before the Sabbath began.

When someone died on the cross, he didn't die from the pain of the crucifixion in a few moments or an hour or so—it could take days. Eventually he couldn't hold himself up any longer and the weight of his own body caused his lungs to collapse. He died a slow and horrible death from suffocation. However, according to the Jewish law, the body was not to remain on the cross overnight, so it was taken down and buried, lest the curse be transferred to the land. (See Deuteronomy 21:22–23.)

Scripture had prophesied that no bone in the Messiah's body would be broken. (See John 19:36 and Psalm 34:20.) When they got to Jesus to break His legs, they found there was no need, for He was already dead.

When Jesus announced His ministry in the synagogue, He read from the scroll.

The Spirit of the LORD is upon Me, because He has anointed Me to preach the gospel to the poor; He has sent Me to heal the brokenhearted, to proclaim liberty to the captives and recovery of sight to the blind, to set at liberty those who are oppressed. (Luke 4:18)

Jesus was anointed with the burden-removing, yoke-destroying power of God to heal the brokenhearted. Why the brokenhearted? Because God desires for His people to live in joy. When we are filled with joy, we have the strength to fight the good fight of faith.

> Jesus was anointed with the burden-removing, yoke-destroying power of God to heal the brokenhearted.

The joy of the LORD is your strength. (Nehemiah 8:10)

Jesus will not only take your sin, but He'll also take the pain of that sin. As the old saying goes, "He'll turn our hurts into halos and our scars into stars."

People do not despise a thief if he steals to satisfy himself when he is starving. Yet when he is found, he must restore sevenfold; he

may have to give up all the substance of his house.
(Proverbs 6:30–31)

The devil is the one who comes to steal, kill, and destroy. When you discover that we battle not with flesh and blood, you'll realize that it's not people who steal life from you. The thief is not your ex-wife, your ex-husband, or your ex-boss. The thief is the devil. The Bible says so, and now he has to pay you back sevenfold. Knowing that, you can say with confidence, *"We know that all things work together for good to those who love God, to those who are the called according to His purpose"* (Romans 8:28).

Romans 8:28 is one of my favorite Scriptures in the Bible, because it is the only way we can carry out God's instruction to rejoice in the Lord always. You may say, "How can I rejoice after all I've been through?" Because God says that He can take even the worst things that happen to you and turn them to good. No matter what it is, the power of Jesus' blood will reverse it to your prosperity and your blessing.

> God can take even the worst things that happen to you and turn them to good.

Remember the story of Joseph? When he shared his dreams with his brothers, instead of rejoicing with him, they threw him into a pit and sold him. They told his father that he had died. Joseph went through incredible hardships, but eventually he ended up in the very place God had intended for him to be: the second most powerful man in all of Egypt. When famine hit the land, Joseph's brothers came to him for food. As he forgave his brothers and provided for them, Joseph gave us one of the greatest faith teachings in the Bible:

> *But as for you, you meant evil against me; but God meant it for good, in order to bring it about as it is this day, to save many people alive.* (Genesis 50:20)

Christians must get a revelation that what the devil means for evil in our lives, God will use it for our good. Why? Because Romans 8:28 says that all things work together for good for God's children, who love Him and are fulfilling His purpose in their lives. Now that's something to give us joy!

The joy the enemy has stolen from you must be returned to you sevenfold. It's payday! Jesus said, "I've come to give you joy, I've come to give you life, and I've come to give you good cheer." (See John 10:10.) Joy is to be the centerpiece of the Christian life. As a matter of fact, after we get saved and are baptized in the Holy Spirit, if we don't have joy, we have no strength. Jesus came to heal the brokenhearted, to restore our joy, and to renew our strength.

A woman in our church had suffered for over thirty years with bipolar disorder, also known as manic depression, an incurable genetic disease with a suicide rate of 20 percent because of the extreme depression it causes. She had been through everything medically possible, including psychiatric confinement and medication, to cure her wild and uncontrollable mood swings. Since she was ten years old, she suffered not only her own debilitating depression, but also the misunderstanding and rejection of people who didn't understand her extreme mood fluctuations. After praying with her, this is what she wrote to us:

> *Dear Pastor Huch,*
>
> *Since being set free from generational curses, my moods are more stable than they have ever been in my whole life! My mental function is far beyond what I ever experienced or thought was possible. I'm claiming a sevenfold restoration in all areas that Satan has tried to destroy.*
>
> *Shelly*

For over two years now, she has been living a life of joy and freedom that she never thought possible. The joy of life is being restored back to her because of the broken heart that Jesus suffered on the cross.

The Broken Heart of Jesus

Jesus knows what it is to suffer a broken heart, not just physically in His death on the cross but also through the betrayal and rejection by the very ones He came to love and call His friends. Many of those He ministered to cried, "Crucify Him!"

When Jesus stood before Pilate, the Roman governor in Israel, Pilate felt the conviction of the Holy Spirit. He wanted to release

Jesus because he knew Jesus was without fault. Pilate's own wife even warned him, *"Have nothing to do with that just Man, for I have suffered many things today in a dream because of Him"* (Matthew 27:19). Pilate was looking for a way out, but he also wanted to please the people who were calling for Jesus' execution. In observance of the custom of Passover, a prisoner could be released, so Pilate suggested to the people that they choose Jesus.

> *Now at the feast he was accustomed to releasing one prisoner to them, whomever they requested. And there was one named Barabbas, who was chained with his fellow rebels; they had committed murder in the rebellion. Then the multitude, crying aloud, began to ask him to do just as he had always done for them. But Pilate answered them, saying, "Do you want me to release to you the King of the Jews?" For he knew that the chief priests had handed Him over because of envy. But the chief priests stirred up the crowd, so that he should rather release Barabbas to them. Pilate answered and said to them again, "What then do you want me to do with Him whom you call the King of the Jews?" So they cried out again, "Crucify Him!" Then Pilate said to them, "Why, what evil has He done?" But they cried out all the more, "Crucify Him!" So Pilate, wanting to gratify the crowd, released Barabbas to them; and he delivered Jesus, after he had scourged Him, to be crucified.* (Mark 15:6–15)

Jesus was the Son of God. He had the Spirit of God. But He was also flesh and blood, a man who felt the same way you and I feel. Jesus grew up in a family and lived and walked among people for thirty years. Then he walked among the people for three years of ministry. He loved people. He blessed people. Children ran up to Him and hugged Him. Then He was betrayed by Judas, one of the disciples whom He loved.

Jesus knew what it was to have a broken heart. First, one of His close friends betrayed Him and turned Him over to Roman authorities. Second, the very people He loved, the very people He ate with, healed, delivered, and blessed began to cry out, "Give us the murderer Barabbas. Crucify Jesus." These very people whom He loved and who had walked with Him were striking Him, spitting on Him, mocking Him, and making a spectacle out of Him.

Then Peter denied Him three times. It would be like your best friend or your spouse looking at you and telling someone, "I don't know him or her." Jesus felt just like we would feel if that happened to us.

Jesus hung on the cross naked in front of His mother. They had ripped the beard from His face. They had put a cruel crown of thorns on His head to mock Him. Spit was running down His hair. On top of it all, every sin that had ever been committed— every lie, every murder, every rape, every pornographic picture, every drug addiction, every holocaust of terror—came on Him, the One who had never sinned. He took our sins upon Himself, and at that moment, God, His own Father, had no choice but to turn His back on Him.

And at the ninth hour Jesus cried out with a loud voice, saying, "Eloi, Eloi, lama sabachthani?" which is translated, "My God, My God, why have You forsaken Me?"   (Mark 15:34)

His heart was broken so your heart and my heart could be made whole. We overcome the wounds of broken hearts by the blood of the Lamb. Jesus became our sin so we wouldn't have to sin. He became our sickness so we wouldn't have to be sick. He became our broken heart so we wouldn't have to have a broken heart. Jesus came to restore our joy.

And God will wipe away every tear from their eyes; there shall be no more death, nor sorrow, nor crying. There shall be no more pain, for the former things have passed away.
                              (Revelation 21:4)

He heals the brokenhearted and binds up their wounds [curing their pains and their sorrows].   (Psalm 147:3 AMP)

Give God Your Hurts

If you don't allow God to heal your hurt, your untended hurt turns to bitterness. Jesus taught His disciples in Matthew 6:12 to pray, *"Forgive us our debts, as we forgive our debtors."* He then told them, *"If you forgive men when they sin against you, your heavenly Father will also forgive you. But if you do not forgive men their sins, your Father will not forgive your sins*" (Matthew 6:14–15 NIV).

This is how I learned how to forgive: I discovered who the thief is, and it isn't a person; it's the devil. I also realized that I battle not with flesh and blood. I refuse to battle with people; I battle with principalities and powers and rulers of darkness in high places. (See Ephesians 6:12.)

People are nothing more than tools of either God or the devil. If I lay my hands on a person and bless them, or I touch them and they're healed, who has blessed them? We know it is Jesus. But if I lay my hands on a person and destroy them or try to hurt what they're doing, who has hurt them? Most people will say I did, but I just chose to let the devil use me so that he could hurt someone. We've been trained to give God the *glory*, but we've got to be trained to give the devil the ultimate *blame*.

Now don't misunderstand me. I'm not saying that people shouldn't be held accountable for their actions! If a man comes into my house and steals all I have, he must take responsibility for his actions. No court of law will excuse a crime because the criminal says, "The devil made me do it!" But as Christians, we must look beyond the person to the power behind their actions. And it also forces us to ask ourselves the question, "Just who is using me right now? Jesus or Satan?"

> If we're in the hands of the Carpenter, He uses us to build people up. If we're in the hands of the destroyer, we are used to tear people down.

People are simply tools. If we're in the hands of the Carpenter, Jesus, He uses us to build people up. If we're in the hands the destroyer, Satan, we are used to tear people down. Let me give you an example. A hammer is simply a tool. That hammer can build a wall or tear it down. If you see a wall, you don't give the hammer the glory. If you see a wall with holes punched in it, you don't blame the hammer. The hammer is just a tool in someone's hands. This is why Jesus said we battle not with flesh and blood but with evil spirits. Unfortunately, we've all been hammering on each other one minute and trying to build each other up the next.

In dealing with forgiveness, we must forgive in order to be forgiven, and in order to forgive, we must realize who the thief is. When we do, he has to return the joy of the Lord to us sevenfold. We must forgive those who hurt us, knowing that the one behind their actions against us is the devil.

Then Jesus said, "Father, forgive them, for they do not know what they do." (Luke 23:34)

Jesus understood it was the devil, not the people, who was trying to destroy Him.

And they stoned Stephen as he was calling on God and saying, "Lord Jesus, receive my spirit." Then he knelt down and cried out with a loud voice, "Lord, do not charge them with this sin." And when he had said this, he fell asleep. (Acts 7:59–60)

Steven understood that our battle is not against flesh and blood.

Jesus will stop the curse and He will reverse the curse. He will heal your pain, and once the healing has taken place, you won't be bitter anymore. Resentment and hatred will no longer be part of your life. Receiving the joy of the Lord will open the windows of heaven over your life.

- When you get your joy back, you become strong in faith.
- When you are set free, you're not bitter; you are better.
- When you are happy, your light shines to others who are hurting.

The Bible tells us to put our hands to the plow and not look back. We should not look at what could have been, what might have been. We must look forward! Our harvest of joy, blessing, and prosperity is not behind us but in front of us. The plow is the blood, and Jesus is the Lord of the harvest!

We received this letter from a woman who experienced brokenness and great sorrow stemming from the hardships of her young life. However, the Lord had more for her than she ever thought possible.

Dear Pastor Tiz,

I spent my teenage years in foster homes. I was lost and bitter, and for me, drugs and alcohol were the "good life" I didn't have. Most of my adult life I was a late-stage alcoholic and drug abuser. Due to fear and addictions, I was unable to work and lived on welfare for many years.

My alcoholism put me in situations where I was raped twice and beaten more times than I can count. It caused my children to be taken away from me. I lived in vileness, poverty, sickness, and sin. My life was utter despair and depravity.

In 1981, on my second round of treatment for chemical abuse, I managed to stay sober in Alcoholics Anonymous for one year. Then I became suicidal and wanted to end my life. I believed I was the worst sinner in the world and that God couldn't possibly love me.

One night I was listening to a Christian album and I surrendered my life to Jesus. My life has been radically changed since that time. I have now been sober for fifteen years due to the precious mercy and grace of my Savior.

When I had been sober for six years, I learned how to drive, because I wanted to go to college. In 1993 I graduated from Portland State University with high honors, and was accepted to medical school on a state grant. I am on the Dean's List at my medical school and was nominated for Who's Who Among Students in Universities and Colleges in America for 1996. All to the glory of God.

I believe the Lord has brought me to New Beginnings for a divine purpose. I praise God for all you and your staff are doing for those who lived as I had and for others who are lost and helpless.

I thank God every day for what He has done. What would I have done without my Savior? Jesus is truly "able to do exceedingly abundantly above all that we ask or think" *(Ephesians 3:20).*

Nicole

Healing broken hearts is not something we can do ourselves; it is something God has already done. We must claim it. Even if you have walked for years with a broken heart, Jesus Christ will make you every bit whole. Today, allow the healing power of Jesus Christ to deliver you from all pain, sorrow, and grief. Let Him fill you with the joy of the Lord, and let that joy become your strength, not just for today, but for the rest of your life.

> *The LORD's lovingkindnesses indeed never cease, for His compassions never fail. They are new every morning; great is Thy faithfulness.* (Lamentations 3:22–23 NASB)

Discussion Questions

1. According to Jewish law, why was a body not to remain on the cross overnight? See Deuteronomy 21:22–23.

    Scripture had prophesied that no bone in the Messiah's body would be broken. When the soldiers got to Jesus to break His legs, what did they discover? See John 19:36 and Psalm 34:20.

2. What did Jesus say He came to do? Read Luke 4:18, and list the things the Spirit anointed Him to do.

3. What does Proverbs 6:30–31 say the devil must restore to you?

4. It's not people who steal life from you. The thief is the devil, and now he has to pay you back sevenfold. Knowing this, what can you say with confidence according to Romans 8:28?

5. As Joseph forgave his brothers and provided for them, what great faith teaching did he give us in Genesis 50:20?

6. Jesus knew what it was to have a broken heart. Read each of the following Scriptures, and list the heartbreaking circumstances surrounding His death:

Mark 14:10–11

Mark 14:72

Mark 15:11–14

7. What did Jesus cry out in Mark 15:34?

8. Jesus' heart was broken so your heart can be make whole. How does Psalm 147:3 prove this statement?

9. What did Jesus teach His disciples to pray in Matthew 6:12, 14–15?

10. We must forgive those who hurt us, knowing that the one behind their actions against us is the devil. What did Jesus say in Luke 23:34 that demonstrates this principle?

Chapter Fifteen

Jesus' Bruises Won Our Deliverance from Inner Hurts and Iniquities

But He was wounded for our transgressions, He was bruised for our iniquities; the chastisement for our peace was upon Him, and by His stripes we are healed.
—Isaiah 53:5

THE SEVENTH PLACE Jesus shed his blood was in His bruises. He went to the gates of hell and took back the keys to the kingdom to break every curse of iniquity. Not only was He wounded for our transgressions; this verse says, *"He was bruised for our iniquities."* As we discussed before, *iniquity* means "a wicked act or sin," but the Holy Spirit has shown me that *iniquity* can also be understood as any spirit that tries to break us down. It is a spiritual force on the inside that pressures us to bow or bend under its destructive nature.

If you have a bruise on your body, it means you are bleeding on the *inside*. Some bruises last a long time and go very deep. God said, "Not only will I forgive what they've done on the *outside*, but I'm going to give them power on the *inside* so they can walk in total victory."

Changed from the Inside Out

The Bible says that the iniquities of the father are passed down to the third and fourth generation—from the father, to the children, and to their children's children. The iniquity may be something *in* your family or *on* your family. But it is the driving demonic force within a person that causes that person harm in some way. Jesus said, "Not only was I wounded to forgive you for your sins, but I was also bruised on the inside to do a miracle within you, allowing you to go from an angry man to a godly man. You'll go from an addicted child to a child who is set free. You'll go from a woman who was suicidal to a woman full of joy because My blood is greater than any demonic force that comes against you."

When I talk about breaking a generational curse, I am not talking about struggling against a character weakness or family curse for the rest of your life. I am talking about being redeemed by the blood of Jesus. I am talking about being healed, both physically, emotionally, and spiritually. We can plead the blood of Jesus to wipe away our sin and to set us free from the iniquity that drives us to do the very thing we do not want to do.

> *And He died for all, that those who live should live no longer for themselves, but for Him who died for them and rose again.... Therefore, if anyone is in Christ, he is a new creation; old things have passed away; behold, all things have become new.*
> (2 Corinthians 5:15, 17)

When someone has suffered a physical strike or a blow, they develop a discolored bruise. Yet a person who has been bruised on the inside often doesn't show that hurt on the outside. We go around to one another saying, "How are you doing?" We reply, "Great, man!" but on the inside we are saying to ourselves, "Horrible." We say on the outside that things are tremendous, but on the inside we are saying, "I'm dying."

A woman might be sitting in the pew singing, "What a Mighty God We Serve," and clapping her hands with everyone else around her, but inside she's grieving. She feels lonely and doesn't know how to have friends. She was molested as a child, and she is bruised. When a part of our body gets bruised, that area gets tender and we don't want anyone touching it. It hurts too much!

Our bruises don't always show. We put on a good face and cover it up well because we are people of faith and we believe we are to rejoice in the Lord always. However, on the inside we are desperately hurting. We have been knocked down, ground down, and beaten down, and we think that because we are "overcoming" Christians, we are never to let anyone know about this.

A member at New Beginnings Christian Center shared her testimony of God healing her on the inside.

Dear Pastor Huch,

I am an ex-drug addict and an ex-prostitute. I am one of those people no one wanted. I attended church until the age of five. I never forgot about God, even though for most of my life I did not live for Him.

When I first got born again, I started attending New Beginnings Church. I believe Pastor Huch and I believe in his ministry. I am happy to be in the church and I am so happy to be alive and serving God.

Laura

We prayed for Laura and God broke the curses of poverty, addictions, and low self-esteem that were on her life. She earned her GED, went to college, got a good job, and became one of the greatest givers in the church. She is also a regular soulwinner and a mentor to young girls coming off the streets.

> Through His shed blood, we are not just free; we are free indeed!

When someone is bruised, it means they are bleeding not on the outside but on the inside. God said, "Not only will I forgive what they've done on the outside, but I'm going to change that person on the inside." Jesus shed His blood on the inside as well as on the outside. He was bruised inside to change the person on the inside, to change the nature that causes them hurt or suffering. Through His shed blood, we are not just free; we are free indeed!

> *For He made Him who knew no sin to be sin for us, that we might become the righteousness of God in Him.*
>
> (2 Corinthians 5:21)

Discussion Questions

1. Read Isaiah 53:5 and fill in the blanks below.

   But He was _____ for our _____, He was _____ for our _____; the chastisement of our peace was upon Him, and by His _____ we are healed.

2. Larry writes,

   When I talk about breaking a generational curse, I am not talking about struggling against a character weakness or family curse for the rest of your life. I am talking about being redeemed by the blood of Jesus. I am talking about being healed, both physically, emotionally, and spiritually. We can plead the blood of Jesus to wipe away our sin and to set us free from the iniquity that drives us to do the very thing we do not want to do. The key to receiving the blessing of God is not just getting saved, but getting changed—transferred from the old creature to the new!

   How does 2 Corinthians 5:15, 17 support his comment?

3. What assurance did Jesus give us in John 8:30 that through His shed blood we are free?

Part Three

Eight Steps to Be Set Free and Stay Free

Chapter Sixteen

Step One: Recognize the Curse

IN ORDER TO get set free and stay free, you have to admit you have a problem. That sounds simple, but we live in a day and age of denial. In today's world, people are conditioned to blame everyone but themselves for who or what they are—their mother, their dad, their neighbor, their school teacher, and ultimately, their society and government.

The key to finding your freedom is this—the buck stops with you!

This may seem like a contradiction to the foundations we've already laid about curses coming upon you through no fault of your own. It is vital that you understand how and why you are doing what you don't want to do, but this does not dismiss you from being accountable for your actions. No matter what has happened to us in our lifetime, we are each responsible for the choices and decisions we make. If you really want to be free, you will accept that responsibility.

You Are That Man!

In 2 Samuel 12, we read about the prophet Nathan confronting King David about his sin. David had committed adultery with Bathsheba, and when she became pregnant with his child, he arranged the murder of her husband, Uriah. Nathan told David a story about two men who lived in the same city. One man was rich, having many flocks and herds. The other man was poor and owned nothing but a small ewe lamb, which he cherished and fed from his own table.

One day, a traveler came to the rich man. The rich man was obligated to show the stranger hospitality, take him into his house, and feed him. The rich man had great herds of livestock from which to take an animal to prepare dinner for the traveler, but instead of taking from his own flock to feed the stranger, the wealthy man took the poor man's only ewe lamb.

When Nathan told David this story, it angered David.

Then David's anger was greatly kindled against the man, and he said to Nathan, As the Lord lives, the man who has done this is a son [worthy] of death. He shall restore the lamb fourfold, because he did this thing and had no pity. Then Nathan said to David, You are the man! (2 Samuel 12:5–7 AMP)

David was the man who had done the deed, but he could not see his own sin until he saw the sin in the man in Nathan's story. Then he immediately accepted responsibility for his sin and repented to God.

Do you remember the account of Jesus' Last Supper with His disciples? (See Matthew 26:20–25.) During their meal together, Jesus said one of them at the table would betray Him. One by one, each asked, "Is it I? Is it I?" It's easy to imagine Judas asking Jesus, "Is it I?" as though he were innocent and knew nothing about the traitorous plot he had already schemed. Judas knew he was the one. He had already received the thirty pieces of silver to betray Jesus! (See Matthew 26:14–15.) Within hours of the Last Supper, after eating and fellowshipping with Jesus, Judas betrayed Jesus to His accusers with a kiss. What would have happened if Judas had confessed his sin at the Last Supper and said, "I am that man"?

I've been in ministry for more than twenty years, and when I'm preaching, I look out at the crowd and I know there are people who really need to hear the message. I see people nodding their heads, and I can almost see their thoughts: *That's right, Pastor, tell those folks what's wrong with them.* I want to stop and say, like the prophet Nathan, "No, I'm talking to you! You're the one I'm talking to. There are many other people here, but *you* are the one who needs to hear this."

The first step toward freedom is to quit ignoring the problem and admit it.

When we lived in Australia, there was a nationwide fitness movement to encourage the Australians to get off their couches and get out and exercise by walking, jogging, and playing sports. The fitness campaign was publicized by a cartoon character named Norm, who was always sitting on the couch. Norm's wife would come by dressed in her jogging clothes and say, "Come on, Norm. Come on, let's go play tennis. Let's go walking. Let's go do something."

Norm sat on the couch with a big belly hanging over his belt and a half-eaten bag of potato chips nearby. She'd say, "Norm, it's not healthy to be overweight." Norm would reply, "I'm not fat. I just have big bones." She would continue, "Look at your stomach." Without missing a beat, he'd reply, "I have big stomach bones."

It's easy to be like Norm, not wanting to admit to having a problem or having a need to change our behavior. This tendency seems to be true of all kinds of people. But also like Norm, denying that we have a problem primarily hurts ourselves.

Stop Blaming Others

Besides admitting you have a problem, you also have to stop blaming others for your problems. When dealing with family curses, we recognize that the iniquities of the previous generations get passed down to the third and fourth generations. We recognize where the iniquities come from, but we can't excuse our behavior by blaming others for the things we do.

One of the most important keys to walking free and changing your life is not to blame anyone. No matter what happened to you in your past, no matter whose genes or whose curses you inherited or whose tendencies you favor, you have to look at your life and, like King David, say, "You're right. I am the dude who did the deed."

Whenever Tiz and I see a couple for marriage counseling, the husband always knows exactly what the wife must do to change in order to improve the marriage, and the wife knows exactly how the husband must change to improve their lives. To end the finger-pointing and the standoff, we say to the husband, "Now, what must *you* do to make it better?" Then we look at the wife and ask, "And what must *you* do?" In a troubled marriage, people tend to see themselves as the innocent party and the other person as the one who is at fault and causing the problem.

The tendency to pass blame has been with us throughout human history. It is an inherited iniquity. It began with the very first husband and wife in the Garden of Eden, Adam and Eve. God told them they could eat of every tree in the Garden, except the Tree of the Knowledge of Good and Evil. God said, "Don't eat from that tree." (See Genesis 2:16–18, 3:8–13.)

The next thing you know, God came to the Garden in the cool of the day looking for His friends, Adam and Eve. He couldn't find them because they were hiding. "Where are you?" He asked.

"We're here in the bushes hiding, Lord."

God asked, "Why are you hiding? What have you done? Have you eaten of the Tree that I told not to eat?"

Adam replied, "It wasn't me, Lord. It was that woman. And, by the way, it was You who gave her to me." Adam tried to blame the woman and then blame God for what he had done.

Then God asked the woman, "What have you done?"

She responded, "It wasn't me, Lord. It was the snake."

Does that sound familiar? We have all made those same excuses.

The Great Cover

Late one night, years ago, I was studying in my office at home in Australia. My son, Luke, who was about three years old at the time, was supposed to be asleep in his bedroom next to my office, but I could hear him playing with his little cars and trucks. After about fifteen minutes of hearing pretend motors revving and tires screeching, I said to him, "Luke, go to sleep!" After a moment, I heard his little voice say, "I *am* asleep."

Like Adam, each one of us, even a three-year-old child, has a tailor-made excuse to justify our negative behavior and the way we are. We know the excuses that fit us and make us feel really good. Like those old jeans we know we should throw away, our excuses are very comfortable, but they are full of holes. "It's my nationality, you know, my Irish temper," or, "It's my Latin temper." Or we say, "It's a guy thing." Or, "It's the kids." Or, "You drive me to act this way."

Our courts and prisons are filled with people whose defense is that they are a product of society, come from a dysfunctional home, were victims of abuse, or can't help themselves because they were born this way. Many of these factors are legitimate reasons why people behave the way they do. There is a very real truth, both in the natural and spiritual realms, in each of these influences. But we do not have to be *controlled* by these destructive factors that have shaped our lives. Jesus shed His blood to give us freedom from every bondage that keeps us from being the people God created us to be. (See John 8:36.)

> Like those old jeans we know we should throw away, our excuses are very comfortable, but they are full of holes.

The Word of God tells us how to sever those chains that bind us to our past and how to break the driving force behind our negative behaviors, but we must first deal with the issue of *personal accountability*—taking responsibility for our actions and behavior. God is not here to cover up, He is here to clean up!

Today's society has created loopholes and scapegoats for almost every imaginable crime and injustice. We allow our children to be ruled by their emotions and moods because we don't want to discipline them and "warp their psyches." As a result, we are raising our children to become adults who are experts in manipulation, emotional blackmail, and denial of reality.

Step One: Recognize the Curse

No More Excuses

No temptation has overtaken you except such as is common to man; but God is faithful, who will not allow you to be tempted beyond what you are able, but with the temptation will also make the way of escape, that you may be able to bear it.

(1 Corinthians 10:13)

We are partners with God, which means we walk in His power and anointing. He will not allow us to be tempted beyond what we can handle. With every temptation, there will be a way of escape, a way out of our situations without sinning. So the buck stops with us.

We are dealing with family curses, but that doesn't mean we can excuse ourselves because of what's been passed down from generation to generation. It doesn't matter if your great-great-grandfather was a horse thief—you don't need to become a car thief. It doesn't matter if your great-great-grandmother couldn't control her temper—you can control yours by the power of God in you.

What matters is what we are going to do today. How are we going to take responsibility for our actions today? We can't control what has happened to us, but God has given us His power to control what happens in us and through us. If we are ever going to be set free, we have to admit we have a problem and allow God's power to operate in our lives.

> We can't control what has happened to us, but God has given us His power to control what happens in us and through us.

Have you ever read the comic strip *Pogo* in the Sunday papers? Years ago, *Pogo* said these now-famous words: "I have met the enemy and he is us!"

Many Christians have a hard time admitting they have a problem because they fear other Christians will condemn them. *Remember, when God deals with an area of our lives, He never points a finger of accusation; He reaches out a hand of healing and deliverance.* Satan is the one who is our accuser and tells us we don't have a chance. Jesus is the one who came to set us free.

And you shall know the truth, and the truth shall make you free....Therefore if the Son makes you free, you shall be free indeed. (John 8:32, 36)

The following letter came to us from a woman requesting prayer for deliverance from the curses that had been on her family for several generations. By recognizing her problem, Sue was taking the first step toward breaking the family curse off her life and walking in freedom.

Dear Larry,

I am twenty-five years old, and my family has a long history of anger and rage. Through my father, grandfather, and great grandfather, my family is full of anger, hostility, violence, torment, and fear.

Stories are told that my great grandfather beat all of his animals, and when he came home from work, the animals would hide and tremble. His son, my grandfather, was so mean he had to leave the state because the law was looking for him. He is one of the most violent men I ever knew. He said he left many men for dead. He is lucky to be alive.

I have lived with my father off and on for twenty-five years. He is angry and has a very bad temper. The whole family revolves around him, praying we won't make Daddy mad.

I am writing because his anger and temper are in me. I need deliverance. I am a born-again Christian. I have the Holy Spirit and have been baptized. I am trying so hard to live a holy life, but at times, my temper and rage seem to take over.

I watched your program on TBN. My father was watching you too, and he later asked me, "Sue, did you get that man's address?" I know you will be a blessing to us. You already have been.

Please help us.

Your sister in Christ,
Sue

Sue and her father took the first step to deliverance: They took responsibility for their lives.

Our Own Worst Enemy

Please understand, I am in no way ignoring or denying the seriousness of emotional problems, past traumas, or generational abuse. It is because of hurts and injustices in my own past that I have great compassion for wounded people. We are living in a world where many, many people have suffered incredible pain and anguish and have legitimate reasons for being emotionally disturbed and traumatized.

The church needs to realize whose side we are on when we point an accusing finger at someone who has made a mistake. Those who point fingers are not on God's side. Not one of us is flawless, without mistakes or sin.

> *Brethren, if a man is overtaken in any trespass, you who are spiritual restore such a one in a spirit of gentleness, considering yourself lest you also be tempted.* (Galatians 6:1)

This is what our response should be toward one who has fallen into sin. When another Christian falls or makes a mistake, we aren't to kick them and keep them down. We are to reach out and bring them back so they can be healed by the blood and the love of Jesus. Christianity is a "come as you are" party. You don't have to get cleaned up before you come to Jesus. When we go to Jesus, we find rest for our souls, not condemnation.

At some point, however, those who are in pain must begin to accept responsibility for their actions if they are ever going to stop vicious, destructive cycles and go forward to live positive, healthy lives. If we are not held personally accountable for our actions and attitudes, then we are all off the hook and how will the cycle ever stop? When we are out of control in any area of our lives, we are our own worst enemies.

The issue is not where we have come from but where we are going. It's not what happens *to* us but what happens *in* us.

Unfortunately, countless numbers of people have had to face brutal injustices or traumatizing events in their lives. All too often, people allow those hardships to close in around them and rob them not only of their pasts but of their futures as well. Many others, on the other hand, have been able to rise above these hardships, often using these negative events to make them stronger and help build their future. In fact, if you would do the research, you would find that the majority of our world leaders, past and present, were raised in poverty, abused as children, or had some serious physical disability.

Many of God's greatest leaders in the Bible had troubling backgrounds: Moses killed an Egyptian, Peter cut off the ear of a Roman soldier and denied Jesus, and Paul persecuted Christians before he met Jesus on the road to Damascus. (See Exodus 2:11–12; Matthew 26:51; Acts 8:1, 3; Acts 9:1–14.) I could name many others. Their personalities, once powerfully destructive and out of control, had to be sanctified by God. But once that sanctification happened, they became great leaders in God's kingdom.

> Our attitude needs to be, "Change me, Lord."

Many people want to see changes in their lives or their circumstances, but they don't want to change themselves. It's easy to look at others and see all the areas they need to work on. Jesus said we should look first at ourselves.

And why do you look at the speck in your brother's eye, but do not consider the plank in your own eye? (Matthew 7:3)

Our attitude needs to be, "Change me, Lord."

God's Power to Change

I once thought nothing of responding to any difficulty with anger, but when I began to seek the Lord to set me free from the rage and violence that seethed within me, I had some powerful breakthroughs that changed my thinking. I couldn't have changed my thinking on my own. Without God, I was defeated in trying to change the way I was.

God changed things in me that I absolutely could not change by myself. That is the incredible power of God that is available to me and to you! God can set us free from the most degrading lifestyles and deadly addictions if we ask Him and allow Him.

Circumstances may have robbed you of your past. Don't let your circumstances rob you of your future!

God *can* and *will* set you free. Through the power of the blood of Jesus, you can break the chains that have kept you bound. We have established that the first step in changing your life is to confess your sins and admit that you have a problem. Then *you* must learn how to break old, negative thought patterns and destructive habits. You can't do it without God, and God can't do it without you.

If we confess our sins, He is faithful and just to forgive us our sins and to cleanse us from all unrighteousness. (1 John 1:9)

As Christians, we have God's *limitless power* available to us to change our lives once we decide to take responsibility for our own actions.

But if the Spirit of Him who raised Jesus from the dead dwells in you, He who raised Christ from the dead will also give life to your mortal bodies through His Spirit who dwells in you.
(Romans 8:11)

When we are born again, the old excuses don't hold up anymore. It's hard to make excuses when the Lord says that the same power that brought a dead man back to life is working inside of us!

Are you getting the picture? We can't do this without God! When we give up trying to change ourselves and make ourselves over through our own efforts and with our own strength and resources, God takes over and makes our lives new and gives us new possibilities.

Therefore, if anyone is in Christ, he is a new creation; old things have passed away; behold, all things have become new.
(2 Corinthians 5:17)

God gives us a new nature.

As His divine power has given to us all things that pertain to life and godliness, through the knowledge of Him who called us by glory and virtue, by which have been given to us exceedingly great and precious promises, that through these you may be partakers of the divine nature, having escaped the corruption that is in the world through lust. (2 Peter 1:3–4)

Your first step to freedom is recognizing that your need is beyond what you can handle and that you need God's help to change.

This letter is from a woman who was delivered and received great freedom in her marriage after she recognized the source of her problem.

Dear Pastor Huch,

Hallelujah! The first day I watched your program on TBN, I was set free from a generational curse that I had for twenty years. I don't even know what to call it, but I had an ugly spirit, and I used to attack my husband with hate, anger, bitterness, and rage. But as I prayed with you, I saw it come off of me, and I was delivered. God set me free.

Please send me your tapes on "Breaking Family Curses." I hope to share with others this important message. I see so many Christians who are saved but still in torment.

Thank you, thank you! I am one grateful Christian lady. This has changed my whole life. God bless you for this ministry.

In Christ's love,
Linda

The day of blaming others is over. The day of accepting responsibility has begun. The day of covering up and making excuses is over. The day of being set free is here. No longer do you have to rely on your own power, because you are a new creature in Christ and His power resides within you. If you keep your heart open and are honest with yourself, the Lord will come in and change the things you never could change on your own. He will bring you joy and peace you never dreamed possible!

Why don't you pray this prayer with me:

Father,

I come to You in the name of Jesus. I admit that my life is messed up. I know You are not pointing a finger to condemn me, but You are reaching out Your hand to help me. On my own I can't change, but through Your strength and power I can change. I open my heart now to all You want to do in my life. Thank You for a new beginning. Amen.

Step One: Recognize the Curse

Discussion Questions

1. According to 2 Samuel 12:5–7, how did David react to Nathan's story?

2. Who did Nathan say the man in the story represented?

3. Who did Adam blame in Genesis 3:12 for his disobedience?

4. In Genesis 3:13, who did Eve blame for her disobedience?

5. List the excuses you have used in the past, excuses like, "It's just a guy thing" or "My kids make me act this way."

6. What does 1 Corinthians 10:13 say about temptation?

7. According to John 8:32, 36, what and who sets us free?

8. According to Galatians 6:1, how should Christians treat people who have fallen into sin?

9. Many of God's leaders in the Bible had troubling backgrounds. What did Moses do in Exodus 2:11–12?

How did Peter express his fear and anger in Matthew 26:51?

How did Saul (Paul) treat Christians in Acts 8:1, 3 before he met Jesus on the road to Damascus?

10. It's easy to look at others and see all of the areas they need to work on. Who did Jesus say we should look at first in Matthew 7:3?

11. You can't change without God, and God can't do it without you. What reassurance do you have in 1 John 1:9 that this is true?

12. Read 2 Corinthians 5:17, and fill in the blanks.

    Therefore, if anyone is in Christ, he is a _____ creation; behold, _____ things have passed away; behold, all things have become new.

13. What does 2 Peter 1:3–4 say God gives us?

Chapter Seventeen

Step Two: Break the Generational Curse

N O ONE WANTS to be an alcoholic. No one says, "Do you know what? When I get older, I think I'll be a drug addict." No one wants to have an anger problem. No man gets married and wants to hit his children or his wife. No one who suffers from depression or oppression wants to be that way. However, if you look further into the situation, you can usually find out through counseling that their mother was like that, their father was like that, or their grandparents were like that. This is a generational curse.

We recently had a "Freedom Service" in our church. We prayed specifically for people to break the generational curses on their lives. One woman testified that as a child, her mother would beat her and hit her on the head. Now, as a mother, she does the same thing to her child, and her little girl is doing the same thing to her doll.

Maybe you've inherited a family curse or maybe the curse has begun with you. Either way, God has a plan for your freedom that will shatter the chains of that cycle forever! It will stop it in your life and stop it from passing on to your children!

The word of the LORD came to me again, saying, "What do you mean when you use this proverb concerning the land of Israel, saying: 'The fathers have eaten sour grapes, and the children's teeth are set on edge'? As I live," says the LORD GOD, "you shall no longer use this proverb in Israel. Behold, all souls are Mine;

the soul of the father as well as the soul of the son is Mine."
(Ezekiel 18:1–4)

You can be free! John 8:31–36 reminds us that as we abide in Jesus Christ, we receive His freedom. Not only has Jesus set us free from our sins, He has set us free from the penalty, the moral liability, and the ongoing curse of that sin! Jesus Christ is the Anointed One. That means He is the burden-removing, yoke-destroying power of God in our lives.

There's going to come a time when the fathers may eat sour grapes, but the children's teeth will not be set on edge, when the curse will not be passed down from generation to generation. It doesn't have to be "like father, like son." Through the shed blood of Jesus Christ, we have a new and better covenant with God the Father. Through Jesus' blood, He forgives us our sin and delivers us from our iniquity.

God has redeemed us from the curses being passed on from one generation to the next. This redemption comes as we understand that the root of our problems is in the spiritual realm. As we apply God's Word and power to our lives, and as we choose to walk in righteousness and obedience to God, the chains of bondage will be broken. The freedom we have longed for can become reality!

> As we apply God's Word and power to our lives, and as we choose to walk in righteousness and obedience, the chains of bondage will be broken.

Becoming the Very Thing We Hate

There have been many studies conducted to determine why behavior patterns are passed from one generation to the next. As we have discussed earlier, evidence shows that astounding numbers of people with negative behavior patterns produce children with the same negative behavior patterns. The government is trying desperately to determine why and how this happens and to develop ways to break the cycle. Does the answer lie in the study of the genes? Can we find the answer in the study of the environment in which we grow up?

Step Two: Break the Generational Curse

No. The answer lies in the study of the Word of God. The Bible tells us there are generational curses that are passed from one generation to the next. Thank God, Jesus has provided a way to not only break the cycle in our own lives but to stop it from passing on to our children.

How many of you faced things as a child and now, today, your children are facing the same things with *you* as the adult? We swore we would never be like that, but we have become the very thing we hated. We want to change, but we can't. We can relate to Paul when he wrote,

> *For what I am doing, I do not understand. For what I will to do, that I do not practice; but what I hate, that I do.*
>
> (Romans 7:15)

Breaking the Bondage

When I was a drug addict, even though I hated it, I would stick that needle in my arm over and over again. I was bound by drugs and controlled by the needle. I went from being an athlete in college sports to a drug addict living in a deserted shack far out in the woods. Every dollar I could beg, borrow, or steal was spent to put drugs into my veins. My money was gone, my health was gone, my life was gone, and I hated myself. I wanted to change. I had a desire to change. But in myself, I had no power to change.

Many people ask me, "How did you do it, Larry? How did you change your life?" I'll tell you how. There are three steps to breaking a generational curse.

1. BE BORN AGAIN BY THE BLOOD OF JESUS CHRIST.

> *Do not marvel that I said to you, "You must be born again."*
>
> (John 3:7)

The real turning point in my life came when I gave my life to Jesus. I didn't just decide to turn over a new leaf or to be a better person. The Lord changed me from the inside out. Unfortunately the term *"born again"* has been so overused and abused that it has lost its impact. Repeat it to yourself slowly: "born again." Let the meaning sink into your heart and mind as though you were hearing it for the first time.

When we are born again, Jesus gives us a chance to start life all over again. He is not giving us a religion; He is giving us a relationship—a living and vital relationship with the Almighty God of the universe. And that is just the beginning of our miracle! In Genesis 17:1 God told Abraham, *"I am Almighty God."* Think about this for a moment. He is not "partial-mighty," not "somewhat-mighty," but "ALL-mighty." He is God with a capital "G."

We come to God through His Son Jesus, whose name is above all names. His name is greater than any other thing that is named. That means the name of

> When we are born again, Jesus does not just give us a religion; He gives us a relationship.

Jesus is above drugs, violence, alcohol, hatred—anything and everything that torments us. And *all* power is available to us through Jesus Christ to destroy *every* bondage and burden in our lives. That is what God does for us! He forgives us our sins and He sets us free. Jesus died so we could live. He shed His blood so we could be free.

The blood of Jesus removes our sin. When we apply the blood of Jesus to our lives, we are using the weapon God has given us to destroy the power of the enemy. We can now move in victory. One of the truths we need to understand is that the moment we receive Jesus as our Savior, every sin we have ever committed is gone, washed away by the blood Jesus shed on Calvary. I don't care if we were raised in a church pew or raised in a prison cell, it is the same for every person—every sin we have committed is gone as though it was never, ever done.

The sin that is washed away by the blood of Jesus is as if it had never been committed. That is what it means to be born again: to be made new by the power of the blood of Jesus; you are just as if you had never sinned.

2. BREAK THE CURSE ON YOUR LIFE WITH SPIRITUAL WEAPONS.

For the weapons of our warfare are not carnal but mighty in God for pulling down strongholds. (2 Corinthians 10:4)

Step Two: Break the Generational Curse

Most Christians know and can quote this verse, but they do not know what those weapons of spiritual warfare are. Quoting Scripture does no good if we don't understand what it means, but if we do, the Word of God is one of the most powerful weapons we have to fight the enemy. People often say, "The truth will make you free," but that is not the complete Scripture. Read that together with the rest of the verse, *"And you shall **know** the truth, and the truth shall make you free"* (John 8:32, emphasis added).

It is the truth that you *know, understand,* and *believe* that will set you free.

The problems we face are spiritual problems. Anger is a spiritual problem; addiction is a spiritual problem; depression is a spiritual problem; racism is a spiritual problem. Abortion is not a political problem; it is a spiritual problem. It is a sign of the spiritual temperature and condition of our nation. We are in a war that is spiritual and the war won't be won through carnal means but through spiritual means. Be strong in the Lord and in His power.

> *Finally, my brethren, be strong in the Lord and in the power of His might. Put on the whole armor of God, that you may be able to stand against the wiles of the devil.* (Ephesians 6:10–11)

Webster's Dictionary tells us the word *wiles* is from the word *stratagems* from which we get the word *strategies,* as in battle and warfare.[12] In other words, we are to put on God's armor in order to stand against the strategies that the devil brings against our lives.

> *For we do not wrestle against flesh and blood, but against principalities, against powers, against the rulers of the darkness of this age, against spiritual hosts of wickedness in the heavenly places.* (Ephesians 6:12)

The government is not your enemy. The people down the road or across the street aren't your enemies. Your ex-husband or your ex-wife is not your enemy. Your in-laws or your "out-laws" aren't your enemy. Your enemy is a spiritual enemy.

> *Therefore take up the whole armor of God, that you may be able to withstand in the evil day, and having done all, to stand.* (Ephesians 6:13)

Free at Last

The promise to us is that when we have on the armor of God and the devil attacks us, we will be able to defeat him, not in our own power or by our own might, but in the power of God. But how many Christians get up every morning and put on the full armor of God? Did you put on each piece of armor today?

We should begin our day by saying, "I gird my loins with truth. I put on the breastplate of righteousness. I put on the helmet of salvation. I take the shield of faith and hold it before me. I shod my feet with the preparation of the Gospel of peace. I take in my hand the sword of the Spirit, which is the Word of God, so I am fully prepared for the day." (See Ephesians 6:14–17.)

Most Christians go into battle naked. The Word of God says that Christians are at war, yet we don't put on the armor of God every day, and we aren't armed with spiritual weapons for spiritual battle. Imagine a real army in a real war. The enemy's troops have tanks, bombers, and fighters, but we send our troops into battle naked, defenseless, and unarmed. If we are going to win this spiritual war, we must learn how to put on the armor of God and fight.

> Most Christians go into battle naked. They don't put on the full armor of God every day.

We are not given the weapons of warfare so we can draw little Jesus soldiers for the children's Sunday-school room but so we can engage in spiritual warfare and win. You are in a war against the enemy of your soul right now. You will be in a war tomorrow, and you will be in a war the next day. You are in a war until the day you die or until Jesus returns. So prepare yourself with the Word of God, and learn to put on the armor.

3. REGAIN CONTROL OVER THE POWER OF YOUR WILL.

God made each one of us with a free will with which to make decisions and to live up to them. He intends for us to exercise that will for our own good. We are challenged by a society that encourages us to live without restraints. We are urged to do whatever feels good, to walk away from commitments that no longer meet our needs, to develop addictions of every kind, and to please ourselves at any cost.

In our schools today, kids are taught to "just say no" to drugs. Thank God for any attempt to keep kids away from drugs, but in spite of all their efforts, drug use is still on the rise. In their own strength, it's not easy to "just say no."

Our will sets the direction for our lives. If we are influenced by the world's slack standards and a lack of personal accountability, our will is weakened and our ability to make godly decisions is hindered. Every one of us has experienced the inner battle of knowing what is the right thing to do and being unable to do it. We read in Matthew 26:41 the words of Jesus in the Garden of Gethsemane, *"The spirit indeed is willing, but the flesh is weak."* Jesus knows what we are made of.

Our weaknesses are not a surprise or a disappointment to God. He has known it all along, and He made provision for our will in His plan of redemption. As we have seen, through Adam we lost the willpower to say "no" to sin in the Garden of Eden, but through Jesus, what we lost—our willpower to say "no" to sin—was redeemed in the Garden of Gethsemane! No longer do we have to be like puppets on a string, unable to control our own actions. When Jesus shed His blood, He bought back our willpower. Through the blood of Jesus, we can say, "NO!" No to drugs. No to alcohol. No to anger. No to violence. No to whatever has kept us bound. We can be free!

If you will make up your mind that with God's supernatural power you will change your course, change your thinking, and change your habits, then there's nothing you can't do!

Now to Him who is able to do exceedingly abundantly above all that we ask or think, according to the power that works in us.
(Ephesians 3:20)

God has equipped you from within so you have His strength to do what you know is right. The things you never thought you could change, the life you never thought you could have—God will do exceedingly abundantly above all you could ask or think to give you that life! Through Jesus Christ, the generational curse that has held you and your family in bondage can be broken— *today*!

Let's pray together.

Father God,

I come before You in the name and in the power of Your Son, Jesus. I admit that I'm a sinner, and I ask You to forgive me of all my sins. Jesus, come into my heart and make me a new person. Change me from the inside out and mold me into who You want me to be. Father, as You gave Your Son's life for me, I give my life to You.

Right now, I break every family curse and every generational curse on my life. I plead the blood of Jesus Christ over my mind, my spirit, and my body. I break every yoke and every bondage from my past, and I sever those ties through the power of the blood of Jesus.

I declare my freedom right now. I claim my liberty right now. I claim all that has been lost to be restored to me right now. Fill me, Lord, with Your love, Your peace, Your joy, and Your victory. Thank You.

In Jesus' name, amen.

Step Two: Break the Generational Curse

Discussion Questions

1. Read Romans 7:15 and explain how you relate to Paul's statement in this verse.

2. The term "born again" has been so overused that it has lost its impact. Repeat it to yourself: "born again." Let the meaning sink into your heart and mind as though you were hearing it for the first time. Read John 3:7 and write your thoughts below.

3. When you are born again, you have a living, vital relationship with the Almighty God of the universe. And that is just the beginning of your miracle. What did God tell Abraham in Genesis 17:1?

4. What does 2 Corinthians 10:4 say about the weapons of our warfare?

5. John 8:32 says, *"The truth will make you free,"* but that is not the complete Scripture. What does the first part of this verse say?

6. When we put on the whole armor of God, what can we stand against according to Ephesians 6:10–11?

7. If you doubt that the devil has strategies, read Ephesians 6:12 again. What do we wrestle against?

8. Every one of us has experienced the inner battle of knowing the right thing to do but being unable to do it. How do the words Jesus spoke in the Garden of Gethsemane (Matthew 26:41) demonstrate that He knows what we're made of?

9. When Jesus shed His blood, He gave us the power to use His name to resist the devil. What reassurance does God give us in James 4:7 that this message of freedom is true?

Chapter Eighteen

Step Three:
Reverse the Curse

WHEN WE HAVE broken the power of generational curses, we are no longer destined to just outrun the enemy, but to defeat him as well. By the shed blood of Jesus, the power of that bondage is broken forever. We truly became more than conquerors!

> *Yet in all these things we are more than conquerors through Him who loved us.* (Romans 8:37)

I want to show you how to take this even a step further—to actually *reverse* the curse. If all Jesus did was die for us on the cross to pay the price for our sin so we could make heaven our home for eternity, we would still never be able to repay Him. But as I have repeated again and again in this book, this isn't the sum total of what Jesus did for us on the cross. He did more than forgive us of our sin; He broke the curse of sin.

There are three keys we can use to reverse the curse and live in victory.

1. RECOGNIZE THE ENEMY.

We must learn to recognize the enemy for who he is. As Christians, we are to *"fight the good fight"* (1 Timothy 6:12) in *every* area of our lives. It's only a good fight if it's a fight we can win, and we can only win when we're fighting the real enemy.

We have already discussed the fact that people are not our enemies, but I believe this is vitally important and bears repeating. They are simply tools in the hands of the enemy. When something good happens to us, we should give God the glory, and when something bad happens, we should blame the devil and his demons, not human beings. When we blame men for the bad that happens to us, we begin to perceive them as our enemies, as being against us.

For we do not wrestle against flesh and blood, but against principalities, against powers, against the rulers of the darkness of this age, against spiritual hosts of wickedness in the heavenly places.
(Ephesians 6:12)

One of the most powerful revelations I have ever received has to do with recognizing my real enemy. The Lord used this to release me from the cursed spirit of anger and bitterness—we battle not with flesh and blood.

When people pray for you and you are blessed or healed, it is God who uses them and works through them. They are simply tools in the hands of God. The same principle is true if people are used to hurt you. They are still just tools, but instead of being tools in the hands of God, they have become tools in the hands of the devil to do his evil work.

> If all Jesus did was die for us on the cross to pay the price for our sin so we could make heaven our home, we would still never be able to repay Him.

God moves through people to bless people. Satan moves through people to hurt people.

God gets the glory. Satan gets the blame.

When you begin to realize that people are tools, it brings into focus who our real enemy is. Again, it sounds ridiculous to get mad at the hammer, doesn't it?

The key to victory in this area for each one of us is to realize the nature of our warfare. Our enemy is not a person or another human being. Our enemy is Satan. The battle is not with flesh and blood or against enemies we can see. It is spiritual.

2. FORGIVE PEOPLE WHO HAVE HURT YOU.

And forgive us our debts, as we forgive our debtors.
(Matthew 6:12)

Jesus taught His disciples how to pray, and He included forgiveness as a vital part of prayer. We are to ask God to forgive us of our sins as we forgive others who have sinned against us. When we ask God to forgive us, He will forgive, but on the condition that we forgive those who have hurt us or sinned against us. If we want Jesus to forgive us of our sin, then we must forgive others of their sins against us. If we do not forgive, then God will not forgive us.

I was the type of person who would hold a grudge for years. I kept score! But God delivered me of that. Maybe you're that way also. Maybe you think, like I did, that you have every right to remember all the wrongs brought against you, and you're never going to let them or yourself forget it. But that's not what the Bible instructs us to do.

But I say to you, love your enemies, bless those who curse you, do good to those who hate you, and pray for those who spitefully use you and persecute you.   (Matthew 5:44)

We cannot forgive unless we realize that *a person* is not our enemy. Did you ever wonder how Jesus could say, while He was hanging on the cross, *"Father, forgive them, for they do not know what they do"* (Luke 23:34)? What did He mean when He said, "They don't know what they are doing?" Those who crucified Jesus knew *exactly* what they were doing. They had carefully plotted His demise and set Him up. They beat Him and whipped Him. They mocked Him, ridiculed, and slandered Him. They pounded nails into His hands. How could Jesus say they didn't know what they were doing?

Jesus understood what we must come to understand. These people were not His enemies. Satan was His enemy, and Satan is our enemy. Satan is behind every evil thing that happens to us. So we must never go to war with people; we must go to war with our real enemy—Satan. If we are at war with people, we are fighting a losing battle! The weapons of our warfare as Christians are spiritual weapons, and we can only use spiritual weapons on spiritual enemies. We can then forgive those who hurt us and bind the evil that caused them to hurt us.

Forgiveness stops the reruns of pain and reverses the cycle of destructive events.

When we refuse to forgive another person or when we ignore the issue, we deprive ourselves of the healing we need and remain in bondage to the past hurts of life. Problems that are not dealt with do not go away—they go underground. By not forgiving, we continue to fuel the fury within us, reliving the painful events over and over again. We become a prisoner of our past.

Why allow that person who has hurt you in the past continue to hurt you and have power over your life? When you release the wrongdoer from the wrong he or she has done to you, you set a prisoner free—and the prisoner is *you*! Forgiving the person who has hurt you breaks their controlling power over your life.

> **When you release someone from the wrong he has done to you, you set a prisoner free–and the prisoner is YOU!**

We also forgive others because we need forgiveness ourselves.

But if you do not forgive men their trespasses, neither will your Father forgive your trespasses. (Matthew 6:15)

The truth is that if you are holding resentment toward someone who hurt you, you are not hurting them; you are hurting yourself. The other person goes on with their life, but your bitterness will tear you up on the inside and rob you of your destiny. There is too much at stake to wallow in unforgiveness. The devil may have ripped you off in your past, but don't let him rip you off in your future!

3. DO NOT TREAT THE SYMPTOMS, TREAT THE CAUSE.

The third key to reverse and overturn the curse on our lives is to get to the root of our problems. We must not treat the symptoms; we must treat the cause. The pains we suffer in life require more than slapping a bandage on them because our problems go deeper than what we see on the surface. We must look carefully:

> *Looking carefully lest anyone fall short of the grace of God; lest any root of bitterness springing up cause trouble, and by this many become defiled.* (Hebrews 12:15)

Deep down, we all want to love and be loved. We all want to feel good about ourselves, but wounds from the past often prevent us from experiencing love and contentment. The truth is, hurting people hurt people. One of the main reasons for a person's violent, aggressive nature is that somewhere in their past they have been hurt or rejected. When we feel hurt or unloved, we put up emotional walls and barriers in self-defense to protect ourselves. We respond to people out of our own personal insecurities, which affect every area of our lives. We overreact to what we suspect are slights or criticisms, and we are often defensive toward those who never intended to hurt or threaten us.

If we're honest, we have to admit that we all have suffered from low self-esteem at one time or another. When we've been deeply rejected, our self-esteem suffers severely and we usually end up retaliating against someone. We may also end up taking on some form of addictive behavior. Addictions such as alcohol, drugs, food, sex, gambling, and excessive spending are obviously destructive. Many people also throw themselves into their jobs and even their ministries, trying either to escape from their inner feelings or to prove their own self-worth.

A person who is in bondage of any kind usually struggles with one or more of these issues:

- Insecurity—feelings of low self-esteem and inferiority.
- Jealousy and paranoia—difficulty in trusting people.
- Defensiveness—always trying to prove themselves.
- Martyr mentality—"It's me against the world."

- Self-pity—"Poor me."

- Isolation—"I'm the only one; I'm different".

- Chip on your shoulder—"What exactly did they mean by that?"

- Argumentative and contentious—always looking for a fight.

- Anxieties, phobias, and disorders—inner turmoils always stirring.

- Pessimistic—always seeing the "dark side."

- Depression—a cloud of gloom hangs over them.

- Loneliness and fear of intimacy—keeping people at a distance.

- Victim mentality—it becomes their source of attention and identity, and their excuse for their failures and behavior.

- Controlling and domineering—"My way or the highway."

- Fear of failure—no confidence to try to succeed.

- Fear of success—no confidence to hold on to successes.

- Aloof and cold—"I don't need anyone or anything."

- Denial—"Everyone else has the problem, not me."

The pain from hurts and the fear of further rejection sets off a whole chain reaction of defense mechanisms in us. By realizing that these traits are actually the symptoms of a deeper wound, we can get to the root of the problem. When we treat the cause, we find the cure.

Years ago, I had a horse that kicked at an old wooden fence and cut his back leg. I treated the wound with ointment, but it still became infected. I then treated the infection by soaking the horse's leg in hot water and wrapping it, and then finally by giving the horse penicillin injections. The leg would get better, but as soon as I stopped the antibiotics, it would swell up, and I would have to start the process all over again.

As you can imagine, after several months of this, the poor horse hated to see me coming! Finally, one day I was soaking and massaging his leg when I felt a bump I hadn't noticed before. I thought it was a pocket of infection and I began rubbing it, trying to work it out through the cut. All of a sudden, a chunk of wood popped out! All this time, a piece of wood from the fence had been stuck in his leg, causing the infection and swelling. I had been treating the symptoms, not the cause. Once I found the problem and dealt with it, the symptoms naturally disappeared.

So many times when we feel we have been mistreated, our response is way out of proportion to what actually happened. Our overreaction seems to come out of nowhere, but we are actually responding out of past hurts and emotions because an evil root has grown inside of us. We are responding to today's situations out of yesterday's memories, and we end up sabotaging our own futures because we can't shake loose from the past.

We received a letter from a man who had watched us on television. He found God's peace after being freed from a battle with sin in his life.

Dear Pastor Huch,

I watch your program on TBN here in Trinidad, West Indies. Your timely message on breaking family curses touched a chord in my life. I was plagued with the sin of sexual lust and couldn't understand why I always fell back into this area of sin. When I traced back a couple of generations, there it was, coming through the family line from both of my parents and their respective families.

I prayed the prayer, wept before the Lord, and broke that curse and others from my life and from my son's life before it hits him. Since being delivered from the effect of the curses and by reversing the curse, there is a peace in my heart. I am finding out about praise and worship and the marvelous works of God. Hallelujah! God be praised!

Yours in Christ,
Edward

God is completely willing and able to set you free from every emotional bondage you face. As you allow Him to pinpoint the cause and the root of your pain, He can deliver you from the cause, the root, *and* the tormenting symptoms they have produced. You can't change your past, but you can change your future. You have to reach a place of victory over your past before you can move forward into your future.

And we know that all things work together for good to those who love God, to those who are the called according to His purpose.
(Romans 8:28)

Unforgiveness may be the only thing standing between you and your miracle. Someone may have robbed you of your past but don't let them rob you of your future! Forgiveness can release the miraculous intervention of God and unleash all His blessings in your life. But forgiveness begins with a choice. Let go of the past and grab on to God's promises for your future, for it is a glorious one!

> God is completely willing and able to set you free from every emotional bondage you face.

"For I know the plans I have for you," declares the LORD, "plans to prosper you and not to harm you, plans to give you hope and a future." (Jeremiah 29:11 NIV)

Are you ready? Let's pray.

Dear Lord,

You know all the situations I've been through in my life. You know all the wounds and hurts I've carried. And I know You care about everything that has happened to me in my past. But I realize You care more about what happens to me in my future. Today, I am deciding to let go of my past—all the hurts, disappointments, bitterness, hatred, anger, unforgiveness, and vengeance. I repent of it all, and I close the door of my mind to it today. I choose this day to walk only in forgiveness, love, and kindness.

Lord, fill my heart with Your supernatural joy and peace. Give me Your supernatural ability and wisdom to think and act in a godly way. My past is behind me. My future is in front of me. Thank You for all You're going to do in me, for me, and through me.

In Jesus' name, amen.

Step Three: Reverse the Curse

Discussion Questions

1. Look at Matthew 6:12 and fill in the blanks.

   And forgive us our _____ as we forgive our _____.

2. Are you the type of person who can hold a grudge for years? Do you believe you have every right to remember all the wrongs brought against you? What does the Bible instruct us to do if we find ourselves in this position? Read Matthew 5:44.

3. What did Jesus say when He was hanging on the cross? Read Luke 23:34.

4. What does the root of bitterness cause in our lives according to Hebrews 12:15?

5. A person who is in bondage usually struggles with one or more of the following issues. Check the ones you are currently struggling with.

   ☐ Insecurity—feelings of low self-esteem and inferiority.
   ☐ Jealousy and paranoia—difficulty trusting people.
   ☐ Defensiveness—always trying to prove myself.
   ☐ Martyr mentality—"It's me against the world."
   ☐ Self-pity—"Poor me."
   ☐ Isolation—"I'm the only one; I'm different."
   ☐ Chip on my shoulder—"What exactly did they mean by that?"
   ☐ Argumentative and contentious—always looking for a fight.
   ☐ Anxieties, phobias, and disorders—inner turmoils always stirring.

- ☐ Pessimistic—always seeing the "dark side."
- ☐ Depression—a cloud of gloom hangs over them.
- ☐ Loneliness and fear of intimacy—keeping people at a distance.
- ☐ Victim mentality—it becomes their source of attention and identity, and their excuse for their failures and behavior.
- ☐ Controlling and domineering—"My way or the highway."
- ☐ Fear of failure—no confidence to try to succeed.
- ☐ Fear of success—no confidence to hold on to successes.
- ☐ Aloof and cold—"I don't need anyone or anything."
- ☐ Denial—"Everyone else has the problem, not me."

6. What reassurance do you have in God's Word that God has a glorious future planned for you? Read Jeremiah 29:11.

Chapter Nineteen

Step Four: Release the Power of Love

But above all these things put on love,
which is the bond of perfection.
—Colossians 3:14

To become a person whose life is transformed by the love of God, we must not only get rid of what holds us captive and keeps us in bondage, but we must also be filled up with love—for God, for self, and for others.

A vacuum cannot exist in nature—something must fill up an empty space. It is also true that a vacuum cannot exist in your spirit. It is not enough to put an end to bad traits. You must *replace* them with good traits, or else bad traits will come back in. We have discovered in deliverance ministry that it is not enough to "bind" the old nature. We have to "loose" the new nature. (See Matthew 18:18.) We must let go of the hate and bitterness and replace it with the love, joy, and peace of the Holy Spirit.

The greatest release of blessing in my life came when I began to love unconditionally. Once you have been freed of generational bondage, you can release the blessing of God's love in your life by learning to walk in love. It doesn't matter if a person loves you or not, you can love that person with the love God has for them, regardless.

We Are Commanded to Love

Jesus said to him, "'You shall love the LORD your God with all your heart, with all your soul, and with all your mind.' This is the first and great commandment. And the second is like it: 'You shall love your neighbor as yourself.' On these two command-ments hang all the Law and the Prophets."

(Matthew 22:37–40)

God has *commanded* us to love one another, and what God commands us to do, He fully equips us to do. When I grasped this revelation, it literally transformed my life, my family, and my ministry. If you will let God get this truth down into your spirit, He will do the same thing for you.

> God has commanded us to love one another, and what God commands us to do, He fully equips us to do.

Let me show you something so powerful and yet so obvious that most of us totally miss it. Scripture teaches us that one reason we are not living in blessing is because we do not treat others right. The Bible warns us to examine ourselves, espe-cially when we take communion:

But let a man examine himself, and so let him eat of the bread and drink of the cup. For he who eats and drinks in an unworthy manner eats and drinks judgment to himself, not discerning the Lord's body. For this reason many are weak and sick among you, and many sleep. (1 Corinthians 11:28–30)

We all know this passage is relating to the Lord's Supper, and we have probably heard it many times while taking communion, but this Scripture is the key to releasing God's blessing in our lives and in the church. Paul said we are weak, powerless, sick, and dying because we are not *"discerning the Lord's body."* When we "discern" the Lord's body, we give proper treatment to the Lord's body. Now this is not referring to Jesus' physical body or the wafer of bread we eat during communion. To discern the Lord's body means to give proper treatment to *each other,* for *we* are the body of Christ. That proper treatment is to love one another.

Step Four: Release the Power of Love

I was not born and raised in church, so after I became a Christian, I just assumed Christians would try to act like Jesus and be kind to one another. After years of pastoring, I went to my pastor and told him I was quitting the ministry. I told him it had nothing to do with my relationship with God. I am not a "weepy" type of guy; but as I sat there weeping, I told him, "I have found nicer people in the drug business than in the church business." Obviously, I stayed in the ministry, but over the years I have been continually astounded by how mean and vicious God's people can be to one another.

Love Is the Victory

Sometimes we get so intent on experiencing the power of God that we forget the very reason God gives us His power—to demonstrate the love of Jesus to one another. I want to give you three important reasons why we must learn to love one another: Not walking in love is a sin, not walking in love is satanic, and not walking in love is self-destructive.

> God gives us His power—to demonstrate the love of Jesus to one another.

1. NOT WALKING IN LOVE IS SIN.

Not walking in love is sin, and sin separates us from God and brings spiritual death to our lives.

Being filled with all unrighteousness, sexual immorality, wickedness, covetousness, maliciousness; full of envy, murder, strife, deceit, evil-mindedness; they are whisperers, backbiters, haters of God, violent, proud, boasters, inventors of evil things, disobedient to parents, undiscerning, untrustworthy, unloving, unforgiving, unmerciful; who, knowing the righteous judgment of God, that those who practice such things are deserving of death, not only do the same but also approve of those who practice them.
(Romans 1:29–32)

The sinful behavior and attitudes we read about in these verses are worthy of death. When we think of sins that are deserving of death, we think of the biggies, such as murder. But, right next to murderers are whisperers, backbiters, proud, and boasters—all worthy of death! Yet every week, in nearly every church, these attitudes and behaviors are as normal and acceptable as the hymns and praise choruses we sing.

In many churches and teachings today, slandering the brethren is not only acceptable, it is regarded as "spiritual discernment" and "depth." We wouldn't think of acting like this toward Jesus, yet when we hurt others, we also hurt Jesus. If we are fulfilling the first great commandment of loving God with all our heart, soul, and mind, fulfilling the second great commandment of loving our neighbor will be easy. But we cannot love God and at the same time hurt other people!

> *If someone says, "I love God," and hates his brother, he is a liar; for he who does not love his brother whom he has seen, how can he love God whom he has not seen? And this commandment we have from Him: that he who loves God must love his brother also.* (1 John 4:20–21)

When Saul was on the road to Damascus, he heard the voice of God speak to him.

> *Then he fell to the ground, and heard a voice saying to him, "Saul, Saul, why are you persecuting Me?" And he said, "Who are You, Lord?"* (Acts 9:4–5)

Saul had never personally seen Jesus. He had never laid a hand on Him or spoken a hurtful word to His face. But when Saul persecuted God's people, he directly persecuted Jesus! Whatever we do to other people, we do to Jesus. If we hurt people, we are hurting God.

2. NOT WALKING IN LOVE IS SATANIC.

> *Then I heard a loud voice saying in heaven, "Now salvation, and strength, and the kingdom of our God, and the power of His Christ have come, for the accuser of our brethren, who accused them before our God day and night, has been cast down."* (Revelation 12:10)

Satan is the accuser of the brethren, and his job is to point his finger at God's people and stir up strife among them. We had an obvious example of this several months ago at our church. I met a woman who had recently been saved. She confessed that she had been part of a coven of witches and was sent to our church to destroy it. When I asked her how she was going to do this, she said, "It's simple. Through gossip and slander." She had been sent to sow discord among the brethren. What Satan meant for evil God turned to her good and our good!

God makes it very clear how He regards gossips and slanderers:

> *These six things the LORD hates, Yes, seven are an abomination to Him: a proud look, a lying tongue, hands that shed innocent blood, a heart that devises wicked plans, feet that are swift in running to evil, a false witness who speaks lies, and one who sows discord among brethren.* (Proverbs 6:16–19)

When we sow discord among believers, we are taking on the very nature and tactics of Satan himself. That, in itself, should stop this evil practice! Instead, we must encourage and support one another and walk in love at all times.

3. NOT WALKING IN LOVE IS SELF-DESTRUCTIVE.

> *Do not be deceived, God is not mocked; for whatever a man sows, that he will also reap.* (Galatians 6:7)

Un-Christlike behavior chokes off the blessing of God from our lives. Don't fool yourself! If you sow love, you will reap love. If you sow discord, you will reap discord. It's remarkable how so many people live their lives sowing all kinds of negative seeds, and then they can't figure out why all kinds of negative things are happening to them!

The spiritual world reacts according to the law of sowing and reaping just as certainly as the physical world does. That is how the kingdom of God functions. Here are Jesus' words:

> *And He said, "The kingdom of God is as if a man should scatter seed on the ground, and should sleep by night and rise by day,*

and the seed should sprout and grow, he himself does not know how. For the earth yields crops by itself: first the blade, then the head, after that the full grain in the head." (Mark 4:26–28)

We see a clear example of reaping what we sow in how we treat our bodies. In the natural realm if you eat something good for your body, your body will react positively to the vitamins and minerals you have just put into it. If you eat junk food, your body automatically reacts adversely to the toxins you have just taken in. Even if you accidentally ate the junk, your body can't nullify it and say, "Oops! That was an accident." The consequences of our actions are the same whether or not we understand what we are doing.

The same principle applies to the spiritual realm. If we feed our spirit positive things, our spiritual life will have healthy, positive growth. If we feed our spirit negative things, our spiritual life will produce negative, harmful results. If you sow negative seeds, you will reap negative results. If you sow positive seeds, you will reap positive results.

Whatever you sow will grow and multiply back into your life. It doesn't take a rocket scientist to figure this thing out! If you want to stop the curse in your life, stop sowing bad seed. If you want to reverse the curse and release the blessing, start sowing good seed.

Jesus has commanded us to love each other, even our enemies. Most of us respond to this like the gang member in the movie *The Cross and the Switchblade,* who said, "Yeah, I'll love my enemy all right. I'll love him with a sharp blade! Yeah, I'll pray for them. I'll pray that lightning strikes them!" Love and forgiveness are never easy if we attempt to do it in our own strength, but once we have made the decision to obey God and walk in love, He equips us to do it.

To know more of the love of God in our lives, we must love those who have hurt us, those who have opposed us, and those who have sinned against us. That is the kind of love Jesus has for each of us. It is so easy for us to accept God's love for us, but it is so hard for us to love someone else. We were all sinners—thieves, liars, drug addicts, prostitutes, gossips, slanderers, or religious hypocrites. God chose to love us even when we did not love Him in return. All He asks is that we love others with the same love with which He loved us.

To release the blessing of God in your life, sow a blessing in the life of someone else. I say all the time that I have no enemies. People say to me, "What do you mean? There are a lot of people who don't like you."

> It is so easy for us to accept God's love for us, but it is so hard for us to love someone else.

"Yes," I respond, "but I don't have any enemies. They don't have to like me, they don't have to approve of what I do, they don't have to even care about whether I live or die. I have no enemies because I have made a choice to love every person unconditionally, no matter what."

Who Wins? You Win!

No matter what anyone has done to you, through Jesus Christ you can let go of your bitterness and love them. When I need to forgive others who have wronged me, I focus on these promises from the Bible.

So I will restore to you the years that the swarming locust has eaten. (Joel 2:25)

Yet when he [the thief] *is found, he must restore sevenfold; he may have to give up all the substance of his house.*
(Proverbs 6:31)

And we know that all things work together for good to those who love God, to those who are the called according to His purpose.
(Romans 8:28)

Think of the person you are finding difficult to forgive and love. Give them to God and leave the outcome in His hands. God will *always* bring justice and make everything turn out for good. Your part is not to bring vengeance but to keep your own heart right with God. He will take care of the rest. Your responsibility is to love your enemies and to do good to them who despitefully use you.

But love your enemies, do good, and lend, hoping for nothing in return; and your reward will be great, and you will be sons of the Most High. (Luke 6:35)

I like what Abraham Lincoln said when they asked him why he was so kind to his enemies when he had the power to destroy them. He responded, "Sir, don't I destroy my enemies when I make them my friends?"

Love Is the Witness

The Bible does not say they will know we are Christians because we wear crosses around our neck or because we carry Bibles or raise our hands in worship. The evidence of our Christianity is that we *"have love for one another"* (John 13:35). When we mistreat other people, the world has every right to question whether or not we are Christians.

> Every day we have a choice to make—will we or will we not love other people? But keep in mind, God loves us even when we don't deserve it.

I ask myself continually, "Who am I representing today—Jesus, the lover of all mankind, or Satan, the accuser of the brethren?" Every day we each have a choice to make—will we or will we not love other people? But keep in mind, *God loves us even when we don't deserve it.*

But God demonstrates His own love toward us, in that while we were still sinners, Christ died for us. (Romans 5:8)

Love begins with a choice. Even when we don't feel like loving, by *choosing* to obey God and act like Christ, we set our life on a different path. The power of this decision will cause our emotions to begin to align themselves with the nature of God, then His same nature can live through us!

When we choose to love others, it affects all those around us. A mother wrote to us how her unconditional love for her son and a tape of my testimony led to his decision to throw his drugs away.

Dear Pastor Huch,

I recently ordered your tape series, "Breaking Family Curses." I loved the tapes and sent them with my 21-year-old son to listen to as he made the twelve-hour drive back to college this fall. He was battling with decisions about using marijuana, among other things, and unbeknownst to his father and me, before leaving town he stopped to purchase drugs and paraphernalia.

Dave went to college to play football. Two years in a row he was kicked off the team after two positive drug tests. His dreams for his future were now destroyed. His father and I were devastated, hurt, and hopeless. His life was on a downhill slide. As Dave was driving to college, he listened to the tape of your testimony while he was preparing to do more drugs. Suddenly, the Spirit of God touched his heart as he heard you share how God had changed your life. Dave listened for a while, then pulled his car over, threw his drugs away, and gave his heart back to Jesus. He immediately felt different inside, and he knew things were going to be different on the outside too.

When he got back to college, a miracle had already taken place. He was offered an opportunity to practice with the baseball team and try out for the team. This is a very dramatic turnaround for him, but I realize he will probably have battles to fight very soon, if not already.

I write all this to say that my son has dramatically responded to your anointed teaching and timely message. My husband and I have prayed for years for our son, and it seemed like no matter how much we prayed and how determined Dave was to be a successful Christian, trouble would result. It definitely was a curse! The men in our family had a history of failure. They all had tremendous opportunities for success, but they all met with failure. Thank you for praying for us to break that generational curse of poverty and failure on our family.

PTL!

Karen

Love is the victory! Jesus didn't suffer the pain, agony, and humiliation of the cross because He wanted revenge. He made Himself to be our sacrifice out of love for people—for men, women, and children—and through His act of love, Satan was defeated.

Love was the reason God sent Jesus to this earth. (See John 3:16.) Jesus came to restore man back to a right relationship with God the Father because He loves us!

No matter how terribly someone has hurt you, you can release the blessing of love toward them. When you do this, you get blessed and so do they!

Let's seal this with prayer.

Dear Lord,

I realize how important it is for me to keep a right heart toward You and toward people, so I ask You to forgive me for any bitterness, strife, contention, jealousy, anger, unforgiveness, gossiping, or slandering that has been in my life. Today, with Your help and strength, I am going to walk in love, kindness, peace, joy, and patience. From this day forward, I choose to have Christlike attitudes, no matter what comes my way. I know You forgive and love me in spite of all my flaws, and I choose to forgive and love all those in my life in spite of their flaws. From glory to glory, You're changing each one of us. Thank You, Lord.

In Jesus' name, amen.

Step Four: Release the Power of Love

Discussion Questions

1. Fill in the blanks of the following verse found in Colossians 3:14.

   But _____ all these things put on _____, which is the bond of perfection.

2. What are we commanded to do in Matthew 22:37–40?

3. What do you think *"not discerning the Lord's body"* means in 1 Corinthians 11:28–30?

4. According to Romans 1:29–32, what does walking in sin rather than love bring into our lives?

5. Who else besides God are we to love according to 1 John 4:20–21?

6. Read Revelation 12:10 and fill in the blanks:

   Then I heard a loud voice saying in heaven, "Now salvation, and strength, and the kingdom of our God, and the power of His Christ have come, for the _____ of our brethren, who accused them before God day and night, has been _____ _____."

7. In Proverbs 6:16–19, how does God say He regards gossips and slanderers?

8. What does Galatians say about sowing and reaping?

9. The spiritual world reacts according to the law of sowing and reaping just as the physical world does. What are Jesus' very words in Mark 4:26–28?

10. When you need to forgive others, focus on these promises from the Bible.

Joel 2:25

Proverbs 6:31

Romans 8:28

11. Is there anyone you are finding it difficult to forgive and love? Give them to God and leave the outcome in His hands.

12. When you fulfill your responsibility to love your enemies and to do good to them who despitefully use you, what kind of reward does God give you according to Luke 6:35?

Chapter Twenty

Step Five:
Success Is No Accident

I HAVE BEEN thinking of writing another book to be entitled *Success Is No Accident.* I was inspired in this area recently as I was flying back to Portland after meeting with a group of pastors. It was apparent to me that over the years some of them had experienced very little growth in their churches or in their personal walk with God.

I don't say that to be cruel or judgmental because, truthfully, it made me sad. As I thought about my own life, I realized that my life and ministry have changed drastically over the last few years. By the grace of God, every area of my life has skyrocketed. Please understand, I don't say that to sound boastful, but to make a point. I know, beyond any shadow of a doubt, that it is because of God's grace, and I honestly give Him all the glory.

When I was thinking about that, a very important thought occurred to me, which was, *Success doesn't happen accidentally or automatically.* It has been said, "When you see someone on the mountaintop, know one thing: They didn't accidentally fall there." Winning comes through deliberate plans, purposes, and actions. Through the years of my own life experience and from dealing with thousands of people, I have learned a number of principles and keys that have led me to victory and allowed me to release the blessing of God in my life, but one of the most important has to do with attitude.

Develop a Godly Attitude

The number one thing that has propelled my life forward in the last few years has been my decision to develop a positive attitude. I decided to set my sights on the promises of God and then align my thoughts, my words, and my actions with those promises. A good attitude doesn't make everything go perfectly all the time. Matthew 5:45 tells us God *"sends the rain on the just and on the unjust,"* but our attitude determines whether the rain will water the seeds of our harvest or wash those seeds away.

Set your mind on things above, not on things on the earth. For you died, and your life is hidden with Christ in God.

(Colossians 3:2–3)

> Is your mind set on the things of God, or is your mind so filled with worldly problems that you can't even think about God?

A positive attitude is a result of having our faith in God, putting our trust *completely* in Him. Is your mind set on the things of God, or is your mind so filled with worldly problems that you can't even think about God? Are you complaining or rejoicing?

Rejoice in the Lord always. Again I will say, rejoice!

(Philippians 4:4)

In everything give thanks; for this is the will of God in Christ Jesus for you. (1 Thessalonians 5:18)

Having a positive attitude does not mean we are to praise God for the bad things that happen to us. Don't miss this important point: Scripture does not tell us to praise God *for* all things. Rather, we are to praise God *in the midst* of all things. There's a big difference between *for* and *in*!

When your pocketbook does not have more than a dime in it, you are at a fork in the road. You can look at your situation in the natural and get really depressed, or you can say, "Even though I don't have any money, my faith in God is not going to waver. Praise God that in this situation, He is going to prove Himself mighty. Praise God for the financial miracles that are about to happen. Praise God for the financial plan He is giving me." Find out what God's Word promises you, and then confess that and only that! Learn to *work the Word*. Learn to stand on the promises of God, not the circumstances of life, and then obey Him. When this becomes your attitude and your prayer, the enemy is defeated because praise stills the avenger. (See Psalm 8:2.) Our praise to God binds up the devil so that he cannot operate in our lives.

God Is the Good Guy

The thief does not come except to steal, and to kill, and to destroy. I have come that they may have life, and that they may have it more abundantly. (John 10:10)

God does not bring sickness, disaster, or poverty into His children's lives, so we should not praise Him for those things. It is Satan who comes to steal, kill, and destroy. Satan is the evil mastermind behind all the bad things going on around us or happening to us.

God is a giver, not a taker! Jeremiah said that He has a great future for our lives.

For I know the thoughts that I think toward you, says the LORD, thoughts of peace and not of evil, to give you a future and a hope. (Jeremiah 29:11)

When Scripture says we are to praise God in the midst of all things, you may ask, "How can I praise God in the middle of a battle? How can I rejoice in the Lord in the midst of my situation? The devil has attacked my home, my business, my body, and my ministry—how am I supposed to praise God?" By choosing to have faith in God, no matter what!

> If bad things do come into our lives, we can still have faith in God to make good out of bad.

Because of our faith, we can expect good things, but if bad things do come into our lives, we can still have faith in God to make good out of the bad. Christians have every reason to have a positive attitude in every circumstance. If we keep a right heart and attitude and allow God to have His way, we will see Him accomplish His purposes for our good and His glory in our lives.

God Will Use It for Good

Let's look at the life of Joseph. (See Genesis 37–50.) Joseph had a vision from God about his future. He told his brothers about his vision, and they became jealous. They seized him, threw him into a pit, and left him to die. From there, he was sold into slavery. Finally, he ended up in Egypt in the house of Potiphar, one of Pharaoh's chief officers. Potiphar's wife made immoral advances toward Joseph and then accused him of attacking her when Joseph refused her. To add insult to injury, Joseph was thrown into prison.

At this point, things looked very bleak for Joseph, but through a series of God-ordained events, he was released from prison and rose to become the second most powerful man in Egypt. Years later, the very brothers who started the whole chain of disasters in Joseph's life stood before him asking for help. When Joseph's brothers asked for forgiveness from him for selling Joseph into slavery, he said to them, *"But as for you, you meant evil against me; but God meant it for good"* (Genesis 50:20). Joseph knew that no matter what harm or trouble Satan brought his way, God could use it for his good.

Joseph's brothers had purposed evil against him, but God meant it for good. I believe the word *"meant"* suggests "to weave together as a beautiful tapestry." That is what God was doing through the events of Joseph's life. Like Joseph, we usually don't see the whole picture. Things happen to us, and from our limited perspective, our lives sometimes look pretty messed up. We need to recognize that God is still at work behind the scenes—all for our good.

Whose Perspective?

Have you ever seen a woven tapestry? On the top side you see a beautiful, intricately designed picture or pattern. Look at the back side and it looks like a big mess! God sees our lives from the top and is weaving every detail into an incredible tapestry. We are looking from underneath, wondering, *What is all that about?* We do not see the complete picture as God sees it, but we can trust that God is working all things together. With this perspective, there is never any reason to be angry or upset, and that is why we can *"rejoice in the Lord always"* (Philippians 4:4). And when we rejoice always, our God who brings the answer is at hand.

A successful person is someone who can build a firm foundation with the bricks that are thrown at him!

In my own life, I can see how God has taken the *"all things"* (Romans 8:28) of my life and used them for good. It wasn't God who made me a drug addict, but what Satan meant for evil, God used for good. (See Genesis 50:20.) Because of my testimony of deliverance from drugs and alcohol, I have seen thousands of other addicts set free through the power of God.

It wasn't God who made me an angry, violent young man, but now I can tell you and the world that *"if the Son makes you free, you shall be free indeed"* (John 8:36).

It wasn't God who brought turmoil into my marriage, but now Tiz and I can tell others that there is deliverance and joy for their marriage too!

I really believe that in every situation, Christians can rejoice in the Lord because God is in the process of weaving all things together for good. God even uses our sinful past and turns it into blessing in our new life in Christ. I know this saying is old, but when the devil throws me lemons, I'm not only going to make lemonade—but through Jesus, I'm going to own the lemonade business!

> In every situation, Christians can rejoice in the Lord because God is in the process of weaving all things together for good.

The Choice Is Yours

To maintain a positive, godly attitude, we must realize that sometimes our flesh just enjoys feeling bad. There is a high in being low. Human nature loves to brood over problems. Paul spoke sternly to Timothy when he told him to *"stir up the gift of God which is in you*" (2 Timothy 1:6). He said, "Timothy, *you* have got to get your attitude straight." When the people were talking of stoning David, he *"strengthened himself in the LORD His God"* (1 Samuel 30:6). David encouraged himself! No one can raise your attitude but you. You have to accept responsibility for yourself.

No longer are you the old creature, but you have been made a new creation in Christ. *"Old things have passed away; behold, all things have become new"* (2 Corinthians 5:17). But you must choose to live from the new nature instead of the old.

Applying this principle as a pastor, instead of getting down and depressed if people quit my church, I convince my spirit that God is making room for growth.

A positive faith attitude goes much deeper than simply an upbeat personality, however. People sometimes say to me, "You're just a naturally happy person." That may be true to some degree, but believe me, when I'm facing trials and pressures, I have to *choose* to stay positive.

If you lose your job, don't go dragging into your house depressed, angry, negative, and whining, "How will we ever make it?" or "I'll never get a decent job." Instead, go home with your head held high, a smile on your face, life in your voice, and say, "Glory to God, all things work for the good. God must have something better for me! God is still in control!"

There is a familiar saying that goes, "Accentuate the positive; eliminate the negative." We are not to ignore our problems; we are to deal with them. But we are to do that by focusing on the answers, not the problems. Many times the determining factor between our success and our failure is our attitude.

None of us are immune to problems. We are real people with real needs, and we're fighting a real devil. We also have a real God with real solutions. The more you see God move on your behalf, the more your confidence in Him grows. This gives you the strength and *"the peace of God, which surpasses all understanding"* (Philippians 4:7) and which overrides *all* of life's circumstances!

Step Five: Success Is No Accident

Rejoice or Complain?

Your attitude is an evidence of your faith. We have a saying in our church about being an overcomer that goes like this: "We're not going under—we're going over!" If you walk around defeated, complaining, and murmuring, you are giving evidence that you do not believe you are going over. You believe you are going under. You are to *"rejoice in the Lord always"* (Philippians 4:4). It doesn't matter what is going on around you. You can be a person who rejoices because you know that the good things that your good God has planned for your life *will be accomplished!*

Moses sent twelve spies ahead to spy out the land of Canaan before the people crossed over the Jordan River. Ten of the spies returned with an evil report after seeing the giants in the land, saying, "We are going to die." (See Numbers 13.) They literally talked themselves out of the blessing of God. God did not allow those who complained to enter the Promised Land.

> *And the LORD spoke to Moses and Aaron, saying, "How long shall I bear with this evil congregation who complain against Me?...Say to them, 'As I live,' says the LORD, 'just as you have spoken in My hearing, so I will do to you: the carcasses of you who have complained against Me shall fall in this wilderness, all of you who were numbered, according to your entire number, from twenty years old and above....But your little ones, whom you said would be victims, I will bring in, and they shall know the land which you have despised.'"* (Numbers 14:26–29, 31)

When we praise God, we invite the power of God. When we murmur and complain, we invite the destroyer of the blessing of God.

Opportunity or Impossibility?

First Samuel 17 tells the story of David when he saw Goliath challenge the armies of Israel. When David arrived at the camp, all the Israelite soldiers were afraid and had fled from the giant because they were looking at Goliath's size. When they looked at how big Goliath was, they saw how small they were. When David looked at how big God was, he saw how small Goliath was. David asked, "Who is this uncircumcised Philistine who has no covenant with God? I fought the lion and the bear, and this enemy of God is going down!"

Israel saw Goliath as too big to beat. David saw Goliath as too big to miss.

When Tiz and I came to Portland, we were told it was a hard city, one of the most unchurched, ungodly, unresponsive areas in America. It has been a stronghold for every kind of rebellious and occult group. We could have looked at Portland as an impossibility, but we chose to look at it as an opportunity. Where sin abounds, grace does much more abound!

Every opportunity has a difficulty, and every difficulty has an opportunity.

I'm told that some Chinese dialects have no word in their language for "trouble." The closest word they have means "dangerous opportunity." We chose to view Portland and its problems as dangerous opportunities instead of insurmountable impossibilities, and God has blessed us beyond our wildest dreams!

Where Is Your Focus?

I was holding a meeting for a pastor who was struggling in his church. That week, the Lord brought in all kinds of visitors who were excited about tying into that church. Many were coming back each night and bringing their friends. We were having great meetings, and his church was thrilled to see how God was moving.

After the last night of the meeting, the pastor drove me back to my motel, and I could tell he was upset about something. Suddenly, he burst out with the question, "Did you see that guy making trouble in the back tonight?"

I said, "No, what happened?"

He said, "This guy sat in the back row, his arms folded, shaking his head in unbelief, and giving us all dirty looks!"

I told him, "Brother, with all the fantastic things God did this week, and with so many new people tying into your church, why would you focus on one troublemaker?" This man's life, just like so many others, was not crippled by a lack of abilities or skills but by wrong focus.

One of the enemy's tactics is to try to get us to take our eyes off all the powerful things God is doing and focus on the problems. When God is at work and good things are happening, there will be disruptions and challenges because motion causes friction. Each of us must decide where we will fix our focus. We can look at what God is doing, or we can focus on the distractions. Where we focus our attention will determine our attitude. What we aim at is usually what we hit.

You can sit on the most beautiful ocean beach in the world and enjoy watching an incredible, picture-perfect sunset. Or you can pick up a tiny pebble, hold it up to your eye, pull it so close that you block out all the beautiful scenery, and you will see only that chunk of rock. The pebble will block out your ocean view. Is your focus on the ocean or on the pebble?

Get serious about where you are going with God by getting your attitude lined up with God's Word, having faith and trust in Him.

Discussion Questions

1. What does Colossians 3:2–3 tell you to set you mind on?

2. Is your mind set on the things of God, or is your mind so filled with worldly problems that you can't even think about God? Are you complaining or rejoicing? What do Philippians 4:4 and 1 Thessalonians 5:18 tell you to do?

3. Read Jeremiah 29:11. What kind of thoughts does God have about you? What does God want to give you?

4. When his brothers asked Joseph to forgive them for selling him into slavery, what did he say to them in Genesis 50:20?

5. We need to recognize that God is still at work behind the scenes—all for our good. For this reason, we can do what Philippians 4:4 tells us to do, which is:

6. In 2 Timothy 1:6, Paul spoke sternly to Timothy when he told him to *"stir up the gift of God which is in you."* What did he mean by that statement?

7. Second Corinthians 5:17 says,

    _____ *things have passed away; behold,* _____ *things have become* _____*.*

8. Moses sent twelve spies ahead to spy out the land of Canaan. What blessings did they see in this new land according to Numbers 13:27?

9. In spite of all the blessings, what kind of report did ten of the spies give in Numbers 13:28–33?

10. These ten spies literally talked themselves out of the blessings of God. What action did God take regarding those who complained? Read Numbers 14:26–35.

Chapter Twenty-one

Step Six: Align Your Words with God's Words

I AM SURE you have heard of the Nobel Peace Prize, which was named after Alfred Nobel. However, you may not have heard *why* he established this award.

Alfred Nobel was a Swedish chemist who made his fortune by inventing dynamite and other powerful explosives used for weapons. When his brother died, a newspaper accidentally printed Alfred's obituary instead of his brother's. It described Alfred as one who became rich by enabling people to kill each other in unprecedented numbers. Shaken by this assessment, Nobel resolved to use his fortune from then on to award accomplishments that benefited humanity.

Nobel had the rare opportunity to evaluate his life near its end yet live long enough to change that assessment. Most of us will never see our life's story from that perspective, but we can take an honest look at ourselves, and no matter where we are today, we can move forward. We can't change our past, but we can change our future!

But where do we begin to make the changes we want to see in our lives?

How do we change from being negative and destructive to being positive and productive?

The same way we eat an elephant—one bite at a time!

Step Six: Align Your Words with God's Words

I want to give you three key principles that I believe will help you make the changes you want to see in yourself. If you will catch the revelation and power of what I am showing you, your life will never be the same.

1. EXCHANGE YOUR NEGATIVE WORDS FOR POSITIVE WORDS.

How often have we done or said something negative at a bad moment and later tremendously regretted it? We go to that person we lashed out at and apologize by saying, "I'm sorry. I didn't mean it. I take it back." We are truly sorry, and we really didn't mean the harsh words that were said, but once those words are spoken, they can never be taken back. The damage is done.

Most people don't understand the creative, spiritual force at work in the words they speak. When God created the world, He simply spoke and the world was formed. He tells us that this same supernatural, creative power lies in the words we speak.

Death and life are in the power of the tongue, and those who love it will eat its fruit. (Proverbs 18:21)

You are snared by the words of your mouth; you are taken by the words of your mouth. (Proverbs 6:2)

He who guards his mouth preserves his life, but he who opens wide his lips shall have destruction. (Proverbs 13:3)

I said, "I will guard my ways, lest I sin with my tongue; I will restrain my mouth with a muzzle, while the wicked are before me." (Psalm 39:1)

Let the words of my mouth and the meditation of my heart be acceptable in Your sight, O LORD, my strength and my Redeemer. (Psalm 19:14)

James 3:5 says that our tongue is such a little member, but it directs the paths of our lives. Our words have spiritual power. There is life and death in our tongues. Our words are evidence

233

of our faith, so the Bible admonishes us to put guards on our mouths!

I believe the main reason people don't fulfill God's destiny for their lives is because they dwell on and speak things that are contrary to the promises and plans of God. Do the words you speak agree with the good things God has planned for you? God desires for you to be *"the head and not the tail"* (Deuteronomy 28:13), to *"prosper in all things and be in health, just as your soul prospers"* (3 John 1:2), and to be *"more than conquerors through Him"* (Romans 8:37). In other words, God desires for you to walk in peace, joy, happiness, and victory in every area of your life. Are your words reflecting that?

Our words give evidence of our faith, and they should reflect God's good purposes for us. When we speak negative words that run contrary to God's will for us, we are testifying that we doubt God's goodness. Jesus said, *"According to your faith let it be to you"* (Matthew 9:29). When we read this, we usually think it speaks about applying our positive faith to yield positive results, such as healings, miracles, blessings, and so forth. Although that is true, Jesus wasn't making that distinction. He said, *"**According** to your faith be it unto you."*

> Do the words you speak agree with the good things God has planned for you?

Positive faith produces positive results, and negative faith produces negative results.

When God brought the Hebrew children out of Egypt, His plan was to take them into the Promised Land, a land of their own that flowed with milk and honey, and a land where they could truly be God's people and know His blessings. (See Exodus 3:8.) He never said it would be easy, that there wouldn't be any battles along the way or giants to defeat. He simply told them, "I'm a giant killer and a miracle worker, and I will get you to the Promised Land and give it to you."

Israel praised God and rejoiced when everything was going smoothly, but like most of us, when obstacles and trials came along, they murmured and complained. When the Israelites came out of Egypt, they were singing, dancing, and praising God. When they got to the Red Sea and saw Pharaoh's army chasing them, they panicked and started telling each other, "We're going to die! We're going to die!" They had nowhere to go—the Red Sea was ahead of them and the chariots were closing in behind them. But instead of letting His people die at the hands of Pharaoh's men, God parted the Red Sea and the Israelites crossed safely. Then God closed the waters, which swallowed up the entire Egyptian army. (See Exodus 13:17–15:21.)

After they saw God perform this incredible miracle for them, surely one would think the Israelites would trust God completely and never speak unbelief again. Not so! When they came to the desert and were out of food, they started complaining and speaking out, "We're going to die! We're going to die!" But God miraculously provided by causing manna to fall out of heaven. (See Exodus 16:2–35.) When they ran out of water, they cried again, "We're going to die. We're going to die." Once again, God performed another miracle and brought water out of a rock to quench the thirst of three million people. (See Exodus 17:1–6.)

God's plan was for all the Israelites to enter the Promised Land, not just Joshua and Caleb. But the Israelites literally talked themselves out of the Promised Land. Let's look again at Numbers 14:26–29.

> And the LORD spoke to Moses and Aaron, saying, "How long shall I bear with this evil congregation who complain against Me? I have heard the complaints which the children of Israel make against Me. Say to them, 'As I live,' says the LORD, 'just as you have spoken in My hearing, so I will do to you: the carcasses of you who have complained against Me shall fall in this wilderness, all of you who were numbered, according to your entire number, from twenty years old and above.'"

Notice the power in these verses. In verse 28, God said, "What I'm about to say is as true as the fact that I am alive." God is the Alpha and Omega, the beginning and the end. There is none before Him and none after Him. There is not a truer statement in all the world than this—God lives! He told the Hebrew children that what He was about to say was as absolutely true as the fact that He was alive.

This is what they had been speaking in God's ear.

At the Red Sea—"We're going to die."

When they needed water—"We're going to die."

When they needed food—"We're going to die."

God lamented, "How long must I put up with this evil congregation that speaks against Me?" (See Numbers 14:27.) Every time the children of Israel said, "We're going to die," they were actually saying, "We know You promised to take us into the Promised Land, God, but we don't believe it! You're going to let us die!" Their words were evidence of their lack of faith.

As they approached Canaan, Moses sent twelve spies into the land to search it out. Ten of the spies came back with the negative report, "We're going to die." And they received the evidence, or the results, of their faith. They missed out on the Promised Land.

Joshua and Caleb spied out the same Promised Land and said, "Yeah, there are giants, but our God is able to take them out! We can take the land!" They received the promise. Joshua and Caleb saw the same giants but chose to believe that God was bigger. As a result, they received the evidence, the positive results of their faith. They entered into the Promised Land.

> God wants all of us to be more than conquerors and to enter into the Promised Land He has for us.

God is no respecter of persons. He doesn't choose some people to win and other people to lose. He wants all of us to be *more than conquerors* and to enter into the Promised Land He has for us.

How can you enter that place of God's blessing? Don't speak the doubts, feelings, and fears that try to dominate you. Only speak what God has promised. You must put a guard on your mouth, stop speaking negative words of death, and start speaking positive words of life.

Stop telling God—and everyone else—how big your problem is!

Start telling your problem—and everyone else—how big your GOD is!

Step Six: Align Your Words with God's Words

Try this short exercise to demonstrate to yourself the power of your words. Silently repeat these words to yourself over and over in your mind, "I'm a failure, I'm a failure, I'm a failure." On about the sixth time, say out loud, *"I can do all things through Christ who strengthens me"* (Philippians 4:13). (Stop reading and do this now.)

What happened to your thoughts about being a failure when you spoke out loud? They disappeared, right? God designed us in such a way that our spoken words override our thoughts! As a matter of fact, the Bible says, *"Faith comes by hearing"* (Romans 10:17). This means an *inner ear* hearing. Have you ever seen a singer who has a finger in one of their ears while they are singing? This is so they can hear themselves and harmonize with other singers. When you speak God's promises, you are hearing yourself harmonize with God and faith will come. Remember the Bible says that if two believers *"agree on earth concerning anything that they ask, it will be done for them by My Father in heaven"* (Matthew 18:19). We should agree with God! He has the answers. So speak out loud the promises of God. It's not enough just to think about them. Speak them out loud so you can hear them, the devil can hear them, and God can hear them. Your words seal your faith!

The devil will try to bring in negative thoughts to get us to doubt God and to doubt ourselves. Someone said, "You can't keep birds from flying over your head, but you can sure keep them from nesting in your hair." Negative thoughts will always try to come into your mind, but you have the power in your words to drive them out.

A woman at New Beginnings Christian Center realized she had let the enemy's thoughts control her thinking about herself. When she began to reject those thoughts, it started a process that has set her free from deep childhood pain and has brought new joy into her life.

Dear Pastors Larry and Tiz,

In your sermon, you shared how the enemy talks to you to remind you of what you have done in the past and why you ought not to be in the ministry you are in today. When you said that, something broke free within me; for some time I thought I was the only one who the enemy talked to like that. Actually, the enemy would start the conversation and I would finish it for him with my own negative self-talk! Now I know where these words of condemnation are coming from, and I can rebuke them off my life.

Second, you also shared with us about your own feelings of abandonment. Pastor, thank you so much for sharing that. Because of years of inner pain I too have kept people at bay, in spite of how much I love them.

I was adopted as a nine-month-old baby. Although I've always known I was adopted and felt the love of my adoptive parents, I couldn't get past the feeling that my own birth mother didn't want me. I lived with this spirit of abandonment and inadequacy for years. Before I was 25 years old, I had had an abortion, was in a drug-ridden marriage, suffered from serious depression and total loss of self-worth, had three children, and had developed self-destructive habits.

At twenty-seven years of age, I found my birth family and found out that my mother did want me, but my birth father did not. In fact, they had given up three other siblings for adoption before me. My mother died from injuries she received when my birth father hit her with a car. At twenty-eight, God delivered me from my self-destruction and I got out of my abusive marriage.

Sometime later I met Jim. We became friends, fell in love, married, and found New Beginnings Christian Center. I became pregnant, and when I went to the doctor for an ultra-sound, I found out there was no baby inside, just a yolk sac. I had gone to the radiologist with the expectation of looking at my baby and left the office empty and in shock. There was no baby. Jim reminded me that God is a restorer and that I was not being punished for my past sin of abortion. Later that year, I became pregnant with our new baby, Jeremy. He is a major manifestation of God's great restoration power in our lives.

Thank you for saying yes to God in all that you do for Him. Your yes to God is part of what restores a wreck like me. Be encouraged, know that it is worth it. There is a work being done in all of us.

We love you!

Connie

Connie exchanged the negative words of the enemy for the powerful, positive promises of God and is living proof that God is still in the restoration business!

2. EXCHANGE YOUR NEGATIVE THOUGHTS FOR POSITIVE THOUGHTS.

Our thoughts are the beginning of our destiny. Where we end up in life is determined by how we start.

- Sow a thought—reap an act.
- Sow an act—reap a habit.
- Sow a habit—reap a destiny.

All our actions begin with a thought. Our thoughts actually become the "blueprint" for our lives. Solomon wrote that as a man thinks in his heart, so is he. (See Proverbs 23:7.) In other words, *If you think you can, you can. If you think you can't, you can't.* The outcome of our lives has less to do with outside circumstances than it has to do with our thinking. *If you want to control your future, you must first control your thinking.*

God told Joshua, "Don't let My Word depart out of your mouth. Meditate on it day and night." (See Joshua 1:8.) *Webster's Dictionary* defines the word *meditate* as "reflect upon; study; ponder...plan or intend."[13] When we seriously begin to meditate on God's Word and take His promises into our lives, our thoughts literally will become a blueprint for our actions, and our actions will produce the results that determine our destiny.

Guard your mind. You are who you hang out with, and you are what you read because words are seeds that get planted into the soil of your spirit. Whatever you allow to be planted in your spirit will produce a harvest.

Negative words, fears, doubts, and bad feelings will always try to enter our minds, but the Bible tells us to grab hold of these and cast them down to shatter them violently by submitting them to the truth of Jesus Christ.

> *Casting down arguments and every high thing that exalts itself against the knowledge of God, bringing every thought into captivity to the obedience of Christ.* (2 Corinthians 10:5)

Every day you and I will have plenty of opportunities to let our old, negative nature run wild. It is up to us to decide whether we will let our old nature continue to control us or whether we will take another step toward getting a grip on our thoughts and words. The Bible teaches us that the way to break those old strongholds and habits is to capture negative thoughts and feelings and take control of our minds by replacing the negative thoughts with thoughts that are true, honest, just, pure, lovely, of good report, virtuous, and praiseworthy. (See Philippians 4:8.)

To release God's power and blessings in your life, you must retrain your mind to think the way God thinks. Any thought that doesn't match the Word of God literally needs to be kicked out! Every imagination or thought that tries to rise above God's Word should be "cast down." Our transformation into the people of God takes place by having our minds made new.

> **To release God's power and blessings in your life, you must retrain your mind to think the way God thinks.**

And do not be conformed to this world, but be transformed by the renewing of your mind, that you may prove what is that good and acceptable and perfect will of God. (Romans 12:2)

I can't emphasize enough how critical this issue is. Christians love to blame the devil for everything. I admit that he is definitely out to destroy us, but many of our problems are self-inflicted. We have seen more people miss out on their destinies, lose their families, leave their church, turn their backs on God, lose their jobs and their friends, not because of Satan, but because they refused to renew their minds with God's Word. Anger, anxiety, depression, self-pity, jealousy, lust, greed, unforgiveness, bitterness, or selfishness are strongholds that will control your mind and destroy your future if you do not meditate on the Word of God.

When I was a child, I spoke as a child, I understood as a child, I thought as a child; but when I became a man, I put away childish things. (1 Corinthians 13:11)

It's time to grow up, to mature, to take responsibility for our lives, and to put away—render inoperative—childish things. Our society has allowed us and even encouraged us, as grown adults, to continue to act emotionally immature. As Christians, though, God calls us to rise up and grow up to become the men and women He wants us to be.

We've all heard about the light at the end of the tunnel. Let me show you how Tiz and I see that. If we're going through some battle, a black tunnel, we keep looking until we find the light. It might be small, but we keep looking until we find it. We focus on the light, God's Word, not the darkness, which is the problem. And I'll tell you something I've told very few. If we can't see the light, we make it up. That's right, we create it. Just like God did in Genesis. God said that we're made in His image, so we can call those things which are not as though they were. (See Romans 4:17.) And in dark tunnels, Tiz and I speak light into our situation!

You may say, "I've asked God to remove this anger from my life, but He hasn't done it yet." No. We are instructed to put away these childish behaviors.

> *But now you yourselves are to put off all these: anger, wrath, malice, blasphemy, filthy language out of your mouth. Do not lie to one another, since you have put off the old man with his deeds, and have put on the new man who is renewed in knowledge according to the image of Him who created him.*
>
> (Colossians 3:8–10)

The power of God that was victorious over death is available to us to transform our lives.

God's power is available to us to change and to mature *if* we determine to do so. No matter what anyone does or says to us, if we decide we are going to be different, we can change with God's help.

> **The power of God that was victorious over death is available to us to transform our lives.**

> *Put off, concerning your former conduct, the old man which grows corrupt according to the deceitful lusts, and be renewed in the spirit of your mind, and that you put on the new man which was created according to God, in true righteousness and holiness.*
>
> (Ephesians 4:22–24)

Thankfully, we are not left to the strength of our own will-power to become the person God created us to be. Human will-power will not get us very far. But as believers, we have God's power available to us, and His power is resurrection power! The same power that raised Jesus Christ from the dead is available to us today.

How does this apply to changing your attitude? Through His power, you can exchange your old way of thinking for a renewed way of thinking. You can exchange negative thoughts for a peaceful mind. Our actions are a result of our thoughts, so when negative thoughts begin to rise, you have God's power within to capture them and get a grip on them. You can take control of your thinking.

> *Rejoice in the Lord alway: and again I say, Rejoice. Let your moderation be known unto all men. The Lord is at hand. Be careful for nothing; but in every thing by prayer and supplication with thanksgiving let your requests be made known unto God. And the peace of God, which passeth all understanding, shall keep your hearts and minds through Christ Jesus.*
>
> (Philippians 4:4–7 KJV)

The term *"moderation"* means "forbearance, patience, and gentleness."[14] It means we are not to get irritable or stressed out but to let patience and kindness take over and control us. Paul explained how we can make this happen, and that is by being *"careful for nothing." "Careful"* means anxious or uptight.[15] Instead of carrying your problems and trying to work them out by yourself, take them to God in prayer, thank Him that He's going to work things out, and then leave them in His hands!

"Let the peace of God rule in your hearts" (Colossians 3:15). When we discipline our minds this way, that peace passes all understanding and takes over our hearts and minds (See Philippians 4:7.) His supernatural peace overrides *all* of life's difficulties!

> *Casting all your care upon Him, for He cares for you.*
>
> (1 Peter 5:7)

When the Bible says God cares for us, it means He does more than sympathize with our problems. He gives us the answer: Jesus and His love. When we take our needs to God, He gets involved by equipping and strengthening us from within, then working to change our circumstances. When the reality that God is going to work things out gets down inside our spirits, we will begin to calm down.

Faith is not a gimmick, and it is not a mind game. Faith is a deep conviction that affects our lifestyle. It is believing God and His Word to the point that it changes who we are and how we live.

When I go duck hunting, I obviously have to aim at something in order to hit it. I don't just sit there, point my gun at the sky, start shooting, and hope a duck will fly over. No, I see a duck, aim my gun, and fire. The spiritual realm operates by the same principle—what you aim at is what you will hit. Whatever you aim at or focus on in your mind is what you are going to reap in your life.

I make a decision every day not to focus on problems but to focus on solutions. In fact, no matter what is happening in my life, I always look to find something good to focus on. I look for the possibilities of God in every situation because *"with God nothing will be impossible"* (Luke 1:37).

Walking in faith and working to have a positive attitude does not mean that we ignore or deny problems but that we view them and deal with them from God's perspective. *Before we ever realize that we have a problem, God has already worked out the solution.* We need to align our thoughts, words, and actions with that confidence. Rather than focus on the problem, focus on the One who has the answer!

3. EXCHANGE YOUR NEGATIVE ACTIONS FOR POSITIVE ACTIONS.

Having the desire and the understanding to change and having the faith to change doesn't accomplish anything until we *do* something to change. We are co-laborers with God, which means we work together with Him. He does His part, and we do our part.

> But do you want to know, O foolish man, that faith without works is dead? (James 2:20)

Goliath didn't fall until David picked up the stone and threw it. Gold coins didn't appear until Peter went fishing. Water didn't come until Moses struck the rock. The walls of Jericho didn't fall until the Israelites marched around them. Peter did not walk on the water until he got out of the boat. Do you see the pattern?

Faith requires action. God does His part, but it is up to you to do your part.

I want to encourage you. My life did not change completely overnight! It has been and continues to be a process. It will be the same way with you, so don't allow yourself to feel overwhelmed or discouraged. You will win the entire war, but you must win it one battle at a time.

> Faith requires action. God does His part, but it is up to you to do your part.

Let's look at a couple of areas where you can gain some important victories.

- **First thing in the morning.** Every runner knows that a good start sets the pace for a good finish. George Müller said, "The first thing I do each day is make myself happy in God."

My voice You shall hear in the morning, O LORD; in the morning I will direct it to You, and I will look up. (Psalm 5:3)

Set your emotional course for the day by entering into the blessings of God each morning with praise and thanksgiving. Determine that with God's help you are not going to fall into the old negative patterns that used to govern your life, no matter what comes your way. Determine that absolutely nothing will make you irritable, negative, or disillusioned, causing you to miss out on the blessings God has for your day. Establish your mind, emotions, and spirit in the goodness of God and not in what you feel about your circumstances.

- **Before you leave home.** Do not, under any circumstance, leave your house in a bad mood. Keep the peace of God in your heart. Practice smiling. It's amazing what smiling and laughter will do for you.

Step Six: Align Your Words with God's Words

*A merry heart does good, like medicine, but a broken spirit dries
the bones.*   (Proverbs 17:22)

Laughter actually releases hormones called endorphins into
your system—the same hormones your body releases to heal a
wound and restore your health. So do yourself and your body a
favor and "lighten up."

• **Drive time.** A bumper sticker seen in California reads,
"Keep honking, I'm reloading." Driving seems to be ready-made
for tempers to explode. Driving used to be one of my biggest pit-
falls for losing my temper. I was so bad, in fact, that Tiz wouldn't
let me put Christian bumper stickers on my car. She finally let
me put one on that said, "Christians aren't perfect, they're just
forgiven."

I especially remember one time when I was at my worst. One
day, Tiz and her friend were driving in the friend's car, and they
thought they saw my truck coming toward them. They were certain it was I, however, once they saw me yelling and shaking my
fist in rage at another driver.

Whether to an extreme degree or just to the degree of
"heightened blood pressure," there's no sense in letting your
daily drive take this kind of toll on your health, sanity, and
spirituality for the sake of a few minutes of time. Take time to
listen to Christian tapes. Turn your driving time into growing
time.

We have a saying around our house to help us maintain perspective:

1. Don't sweat the small stuff.

2. It's all small stuff.

Most people spend way too much time and energy on insig-
nificant, petty things. Nothing warrants going off the deep
end or angry outbursts that blow everything out of proportion.
Determine to get off the emotional roller coaster and become
emotionally grounded in God. He has incredibly good things in
store for you. Focus your time and energy on building toward
your future in God.

Motivation to Change

I will be the first to admit that it is not easy to change your life. The changes we need to make for our lives to be transformed are radical—we are changing from a person with a negative outlook to a person with a positive attitude based on our faith in who God is, what we know He is doing, and what He still wants to do. In short, we are making a 180-degree turn, changing the whole orientation of our lives!

Change can be difficult, and it is not always comfortable. It can seem overwhelming when you look at the whole picture. But remember that He is changing us from glory to glory—one step at a time. You'll be amazed at how easily and how quickly the victories come once you start moving in the right direction! Take my word for it, every positive change is worth the effort. God has so many incredible blessings ahead for you. It's time to enter into your Promised Land!

Discussion Questions

1. What do each of the following Scriptures say about our words?

   Proverbs 18:21

   Proverbs 6:2

   Proverbs 13:3

   Psalm 39:1

   Psalm 19:14

   Do the words you speak agree with the good things God has planned for you?

2. What do the following verses say God desires for you?

   Deuteronomy 28:13

   3 John 1:2 KJV

   Romans 8:37

3. Our words give evidence of our faith, and they should reflect God's good purposes for us. What did Jesus say about this in Matthew 9:29?

4. The Israelites left Egypt rejoicing, but when they got to the Red Sea and saw Pharaoh's army chasing them, what did they do according to Exodus 14:10?

5. When the Israelites came to the desert and were out of food, what did they start complaining about in Exodus 16:2–3?

   What did God miraculously provide for them in Exodus 16:4?

6. When they ran out of water in Exodus 17:2–3, did the Israelites believe God would provide or did they start murmuring again?

   How did God provide for them in Exodus 17:6?

7. What does the Bible say about faith in Romans 10:17?

8. All of our actions begin with a thought. Our thoughts become the "blueprint" for our lives. What did Solomon say about this in Proverbs 23:7?

9. What does the Bible tell us to do with negative thoughts in 2 Corinthians 10:5?

10. The Bible teaches us that the way to break old strongholds and habits is to capture negative thoughts and feelings and replace them with what? See Philippians 4:8.

    How does Romans 12:2 say we are transformed?

11. Read what the Bible says in 1 Corinthians 13:11 and fill in the blanks.

    When I was a child, I _____ as a child, I _____ as a child, I _____ as a child; but when I became a man, I put away _____ things.

12. God's power is available to us to change and to mature if we determine to do so. How does Ephesians 4:22–24 prove this is true in our lives?

13. Read Philippians 4:4–7, and explain what it says about having peace of mind.

Chapter Twenty-two

Step Seven: He's God, Our Daddy

A FEW YEARS ago, I attended a Bible conference where the main speaker preached a message entitled, "We Are Mud, Misery, and Maggots in the Eyes of God." He had even dug out Scriptures he thought proved his three points! This saddened me because it is vitally important that we understand that God does not see us this way, and it's equally important that we don't see ourselves this way either!

When our self-esteem is assaulted, we have a hard time loving others and a hard time receiving love from others. Romans 12:3 tells us not to think of ourselves more highly than we ought to think, *"but to think soberly, as God has dealt to each one a measure of faith."*

We are not to be puffed up in pride, but we are also not to be insecure and easily intimidated. God wants us to have confidence in ourselves, a positive self-image, and healthy self-respect. He wants us to know and understand who we are in Christ. We are not just God's little boys and girls; we are power-filled men and women of God. He made us to be joint heirs with Jesus Christ! (See Romans 8:17.)

Most of us bring all our old personal insecurities into our relationship with God. We think He is out to get us or is waiting for us to mess up so He can bring judgment upon us. But He loves us, and He proved it through Jesus:

> *For God so loved the world that He gave His only begotten Son, that whoever believes in Him should not perish but have everlasting life.* (John 3:16)

Step Seven: He's God, Our Daddy

Sometimes we are convinced that God loves the whole world, but we are not as confident that God would love someone like us.

Our problems and failures make us feel condemned. We feel like we can never quite measure up to God's expectations, and that He is most likely disgusted by our weaknesses. That is exactly what Satan wants us to think about God, that He is a hard, impossible-to-please, demanding taskmaster. Satan wants us to think that we will never be good enough to be accepted by God. That is so far from the truth, because in fact, we are the very ones for whom Jesus gave His life!

Your Heart toward God

Jesus described His whole purpose on earth in this statement:

The Spirit of the LORD is upon Me, because He has anointed Me to preach the gospel to the poor; He has sent Me to heal the brokenhearted, to proclaim liberty to the captives and recovery of sight to the blind, to set at liberty those who are oppressed.
(Luke 4:18)

When the Pharisees accused Jesus of hanging out with messed-up people like you and me, Jesus explained that these were the very people He came to help.

Those who are well have no need of a physician, but those who are sick. (Matthew 9:12)

We don't go to the doctor to tell him how good we feel; we tell him where we hurt so he can fix it. In the same way, when we admit our faults and shortcomings to God instead of trying to cover them up, we are healed. He wants us to come to Him for help:

The sacrifices of God are a broken spirit, a broken and a contrite heart; these, O God, You will not despise. (Psalm 51:17)

I believe the greatest asset we can have is a tender, repentant heart before God. We can try to do all the good that is possible, but it is our contrite and tender heart He delights in. As long as we are willing to bring our needs before Him, He is willing to help us meet them. In my own life, I have always tried to be quick to admit when I have blown it and quick to get up and try again.

In spite of all his mistakes, David was a "man after God's own heart." He prayed in Psalm 51:10, *"Create in me a clean heart, O God, and renew a steadfast spirit within me."* No matter what mistakes you have made, God can create a clean heart within you. God is not looking for perfection, He is just looking for a heart after His heart that is willing to keep trying and not willing to give up!

Accept God's Acceptance

Years ago, a young woman came to our church and gave her life to Jesus. We knew she had been in the world and was making some serious lifestyle choices. For months, she attended church faithfully and seemed to be doing great, but Tiz and I sensed that there was a cloud of oppression hanging over her that was dragging her down.

> The greatest asset we can have is a tender, repentant heart before God.

I felt that the Lord showed me the cause of her oppression, but it made no sense to me. Finally, we called her in to talk, and as the conversation progressed, I asked her if she had ever been involved in lesbianism. She burst into tears, confessed that she had, and was ashamed and embarrassed. We comforted her and told her, "That's why we've got a Savior! None of us came in walking on water!"

At that moment, something powerful happened. When she saw that we would accept her and not condemn her because of her past, she realized that God would also accept her and love her. The oppression that had so weighed her down was broken, and she went on to become a powerful woman of God in our church.

I used to wonder why God would use someone like me with my background of drugs and violence. Then I realized that when people come to me with their problems, there isn't anything they could tell me that I haven't heard about, seen in others, or experienced myself. Because of that, I can understand who they are and what temptations and struggles they face. When people see that I don't reject them, they begin to understand that God won't reject them either. I tell them, "Hey, that's why we have a Savior!" Each and every one of us needs a Savior.

> *There is none righteous, no, not one.* (Romans 3:10)

Jesus didn't come to condemn us or punish us. He came to give us hope that our lives really can be different. We don't have to live under the burdens of pain, hurt, shame, or sorrow. All the power in heaven is available to you and me to set us free from every chain that binds us! Corrie

> God won't reject anyone who comes to Him. Each and every one of us needs a Savior.

ten Boom said, "There is no pit so deep that God's love is not deeper still."

> *If God is for us, who can be against us?* (Romans 8:31)

God is on our side! He wants us to win today and every day forward.

> *"In righteousness you shall be established; you shall be far from oppression, for you shall not fear; and from terror, for it shall not come near you. Indeed they shall surely assemble, but not because of Me. Whoever assembles against you shall fall for your sake.... No weapon formed against you shall prosper, and every tongue which rises against you in judgment You shall condemn. This is the heritage of the servants of the LORD, and their righteousness is from Me," says the LORD.* (Isaiah 54:14–15, 17)

Let me say it again, *"If God is for us, who can be against us?"*

Speak Truth to Yourself

> *So then faith comes by hearing, and hearing by the word of God.* (Romans 10:17)

Our faith is not built so much by what others say as it is by what we hear ourselves say. Remember, we need that inner ear to hear what we are telling ourselves about God, about other people, and about ourselves.

Hearing yourself say what God says about you will build you up. This may sound corny, but the first thing you should do every morning as you walk past the mirror is to say out loud, "You are not a loser; you are a winner." You are not trying to convince God of who you are; you are convincing yourself! God already sees you this way! I teach our people to pray out loud. When we pray silently, it is too easy to be flooded by negative thoughts from Satan, but in speaking God's words and promises out loud, it is *impossible* for negative thinking to overpower godly speaking.

The devil tries to assault our minds with negative thoughts. So, when he attacks, we have to counterattack. The devil will always bring up our shortcomings, flaws, and weaknesses. Remember, he is the *accuser* of the brethren. (See Revelations 12:10.) We can wage war against Satan's assaults when we override his thoughts with God's thoughts.

Can you imagine the thoughts that went through Abraham's mind when God spoke to him at age ninety-nine that he would become the father of many nations? (See Genesis 17:4.) Abraham and Sarah had to counterattack the negative thoughts with positive ones. God changed Abram's name to *Abraham,* which means father of many nations. And when Sarah would say to him, "Oh, Abraham, father of many nations," she was calling those things which did not exist as though they did, just as Romans 4:17 tells us to do.

Get Straight

It is critical that our view of God's love for us is in correct alignment with the Word of God. When we realize how much God really loves us, we begin to move from *insecurity* to *security* in our relationship with God and others. When we are secure in that relationship, we are freed from the curse that keeps us from becoming the person God created us to be.

It is also vital that we have a right understanding of who God is. Many Christians think of God as a hard taskmaster or a controlling, angry father. When people have a negative image of their earthly fathers, it is difficult to develop an intimate relationship with their heavenly Father and understand how much He loves them. But we have to allow our thoughts and lives to be shaped by the truth of Scripture, not by a bad experience we may have had growing up.

When we lived in Australia, there was a series of ships that had run aground, causing them to be beached. The ships had followed the channel markers closely, but for some unknown reason, they ended up off course—and in trouble! After investigation, it was found that during a severe storm, the channel markers had shifted slightly. The ships were crashing because their markers were in the wrong place.

One of the greatest revelations we have ever received came when I realized what the Lord's Prayer was really all about.

The disciples had come to Jesus and said, "Teach us how to pray." They weren't asking to be taught the mechanics of prayer. They were Jews who had been trained in the ritual of prayer since they were children, so they already knew the mechanics. But when Jesus prayed, the results were obviously different from when they prayed. When Jesus prayed, storms ceased, lepers were cleansed, and blind eyes were opened. When the disciples prayed, nothing happened. Seeing the difference, they came to Him wanting to learn the keys to this power.

> When Jesus prayed, storms ceased, lepers were cleansed, and blind eyes were opened.

Jesus said, "Okay, when you pray, say 'Father.'" He didn't say, "Pray 'King of Kings,' 'Lord of Lords,' or 'Almighty One.'" When you go before Almighty God, you are going before your Father. Just like those ships that ran aground and wrecked because they didn't have proper alignment, many of us crash in life because we have not had a proper father figure before us. This affects our image of God, our heavenly Father. In my first fifteen years of serving God, I actually believed God was out to get me. I was afraid He would take my health, my kids, and my finances to test my love for Him.

My life began to change the day I began to think, speak, and act like my heavenly Father loved me. This key has done as much to change my life as getting saved itself! Right before we moved back to the United States, I was in a church service watching people struggling to press in and receive from God. God spoke to me and said, "Tell the world I am a good God." The people responded immediately, and miracles began to happen.

To be honest with you, up to that point I believed and preached that God was a hard taskmaster. God is absolutely the opposite. *He is not a hard taskmaster; He is a loving Father.* This is why Jesus said to His disciples, "When you pray, say 'Father.'" Coming before God and seeing Him as a loving heavenly Father instead of as a hard taskmaster is the foundation for entering into all the blessings He has planned for you.

God our Father wants to give us His kingdom. In fact, it gives Him pleasure to do that. (See Luke 12:32.) Repeat this out loud: "It is my Father's good pleasure to give me His kingdom." It is not His reluctant duty or obligation, but His *pleasure* to do so. If God were a hard taskmaster, He would not be willing or eager to share His kingdom with us.

Assuredly, I say to you, whoever does not receive the kingdom of God as a little child will by no means enter it. (Mark 10:15)

Jesus wasn't talking about the kingdom as the "sweet pie in the sky when you die," but "the kingdom down on the ground while we're still around." We enter into all the fullness God has for us when we go to the Father with confidence. We are to come boldly to God with the confidence of a little child going to a loving Father. His love is not conditional upon anything we do, but we can limit how much of His love we receive by not having confidence in the fact that *He loves us no matter what we do.* That is why God's grace is called *amazing.* It is unearned, unmerited, and an unrepayable favor from God whereby we cry out, "Abba, Father—my Dad!"

> God loves us no matter what we do. That is why God's grace is called amazing.

Yes, He is *God*, yes He is *Almighty*, but He is also *Daddy*.

I start every day saying, "Good morning, Father," reminding my spirit that no matter what I face today, it is the Father's good pleasure to give me His kingdom. And *our* Dad can whip *their* dad every time!

Step Seven: He's God, Our Daddy

Discussion Questions

1. How did God prove His love for you according to John 3:16?

2. Read Luke 4:18 and describe Jesus' purpose on earth.

3. Who did Jesus come to help? Read Matthew 9:12.

4. In spite of all his mistakes, David was a *"man after* [God's] *own heart"* (1 Samuel 13:14). What did he pray in Psalm 51:10?

5. All the power in heaven is available to set you free from every chain that binds you. How do you know this is true according to Romans 8:31?

6. Read Isaiah 54:14–15, 17, and explain how God is on your side.

7. What kind of relationship do you have with your earthly father?

8. How has that relationship affected your relationship with your heavenly Father?

9. Read the following prayer based on Luke 12:32 and Mark 10:15 out loud right now.

Father God,

I believe it is Your good pleasure to give me Your kingdom. It is not Your reluctant duty or obligation but Your pleasure to do so. Today, Father God, I come to You as a little child to receive Your kingdom.

In Jesus' name, amen.

Chapter Twenty-three

Step Eight:
Obedience–The Path to
Your Promised Land

*And all these blessings shall come upon you and overtake you,
because you obey the voice of the LORD your God: Blessed shall
you be in the city, and blessed shall you be in the country.
Blessed shall be the fruit of your body, the produce of your
ground and the increase of your herds, the increase of your cattle
and the offspring of your flocks. Blessed shall be your basket
and your kneading bowl. Blessed shall you be when you come
in, and blessed shall you be when you go out. The LORD will
cause your enemies who rise against you to be defeated before
your face; they shall come out against you one way and flee
before you seven ways.*
—Deuteronomy 28:2–7

BEFORE ADAM FELL, the Garden of Eden was full of blessing. It was a place full of health, abundance, and joy. After Adam's sin and mankind's fall from grace came the curse. The blood of Jesus is the key to the power and blessings of the Bible because, through His shed blood, we have the ability to obey the voice of the Lord. The Bible says in Galatians 3:13, *"Christ has redeemed us from the curse of the law."* People often misunderstand that verse to mean they are not under any restriction.

A young man came up to me and was telling me about this problem he was having. And then he said, "Well, my girlfriend...."

I interrupted, "Are you telling me that the woman you are lying in bed with is not your wife?"

He said, "Yes, that's right."

I said, "You need to do one of two things—move out or get married. If you are sleeping with someone who does not have your ring on their finger and with whom you have not made a vow before God, you are in error and are being disobedient to God." As Christians, our being free from the curse of the Law does not mean we are free from living a moral, godly life. There are some things Christians are not supposed to do!

If you fall, or sin, you can come before God and ask Him to forgive you. You can't say, "And by the way, God, forgive me because I'm going back and doing it again." Forgiveness comes when you repent and truly want to live a new life.

> You can't say, "God, forgive me because I'm going back to do it again." Forgiveness comes when you repent and truly want to live a new life.

Jesus said to the woman caught in adultery, "Woman, where are your accusers?"

She said, "None here, Lord."

Then Jesus said, "Neither do I accuse you. Go and sin no more."

He didn't say, "Sin a little bit less," or, "Try to do better." He said, "Go and do not sin anymore." (See John 8:3–11.)

The Called and the Chosen

For many are called, but few chosen.   (Matthew 20:16)

For the eyes of the LORD run to and fro throughout the whole earth, to show Himself strong on behalf of those whose heart is loyal to Him.   (2 Chronicles 16:9)

Many are called because God makes His love, His power, and His anointing available to everyone. God is calling everyone to be born again and to be blessed by the power of His blood. He wants everyone to be saved and to live a life of blessing. Yet only a few respond. Why is that so? Few people become the chosen ones because most Christians do not obey the voice of God when God is calling them or speaking to them about an area in their lives.

Let me give you a foundation that I believe will open your eyes of understanding. In John 15:14, Jesus says, *"You are My friends if...."* Now we know Jesus was not talking about salvation, because salvation doesn't come from works. Salvation is unconditional and comes by grace lest any man should boast. (See Ephesians 2:8–9.) Jesus was talking about us going from being one of the many saved people who are called to becoming one of the few who are chosen. He is talking about going from being His servant to becoming His friend. It is so important that we become a friend to Jesus!

> *You are My friends if you do whatever I command you. No longer do I call you servants, for a servant does not know what his master is doing; but I have called you friends, for all things that I heard from My Father I have made known to you. You did not choose Me, but I chose you and appointed you that you should go and bear fruit, and that your fruit should remain, that whatever you ask the Father in My name He may give you.*
> (John 15:14–16)

Jesus does not exaggerate, but He says that whatever you ask of His Father—healing, finances, anointing, salvation, buildings, property, children being saved—He will give it to you. Yet many Christians say, "Pastor, my prayers aren't getting answered." Maybe God can't answer your prayers because you are not obeying Him. Sometimes it is that simple.

> Jesus says that whatever you ask of His Father–healing, finances, salvation–He will give it to you.

In a kingdom, *everyone* is a servant. From the queen on down, everyone serves the king. That is why Queen Esther, when she was going before her husband on behalf of the Hebrew people, said, "It might cost me my life," because she too was the king's subject to serve the king's purpose. (See Esther 4:16.)

But Jesus says, "If you obey Me, and if you do what I tell you to do, then you are My friend." He speaks to us in many ways—through the Word, through a sermon, and through that still, small voice. He doesn't just tell us not to smoke, cuss, chew, or go out with those who do; He tells us to obey Him in every area of our lives.

Obedience Is More Than Believing

If we obey what Jesus asks us to do, then we are His friends. That means we now have authority equal to that of Jesus Christ. Jesus told us,

> *Whatever you bind on earth will be bound in heaven, and whatever you loose on earth will be loosed in heaven.*
>
> (Matthew 18:18)

When Jesus was walking with the disciples, He asked, "Who do men say that I am?" They replied that some said He was John the Baptist, some thought He was Elijah, and others thought He might be Jeremiah. Then Jesus asked, "Who do you say I am?" Peter's response was, "You are the Christ, You are the anointed one of God." In other words, "You are the one we are to obey. You are the one we are to follow." And Jesus responded to Peter and said, "Now, Peter, I give you the keys of the kingdom, and whatever you bind on earth is bound in heaven and whatever you loose on earth is loosed in heaven." (See Matthew 16:13–19.)

Not every Christian has the keys of the kingdom. Every Christian has a right to the keys, but to be honest, many of us go around binding and loosing, and nothing is bound and nothing is loosed. I believe the reason is that keys are not automatically given to people who are born again. The keys are only given to those whom God trusts. He knows they will obey Him.

Why is it that Christians don't obey God? If I were to ask a believer, "Do you believe the Word of God is true?" They would say, "Yes." What if I were to ask, "Do you not only believe the Word of God is true but also obey the Word of God?" What would their response be? It is one thing to believe in God; it is another thing to obey God.

We know the Bible tells husbands to love their wives and wives to obey their husbands. We know the Bible says gossiping and backbiting are sins. We know the Bible says to remember the Sabbath and keep it holy. We know the Bible says to tithe and give offerings as the Holy Spirit leads. But when the offering plate went past you at church, did you obey God or rob God? God does not need your money—His streets are paved with gold! But He is looking for your obedience. Why? He is looking for someone He can depend upon, someone who will obey His Word. The church is full of people who are saved, but the church is not full of people who are obeying God.

God has a multitude of blessings for every one of us. When He speaks to us in His still small voice, we will choose to obey or disobey. When God says, "Don't gossip," the devil can't come and grab our lips and make our lips talk badly about someone. It's our choice whether to build up or tear down by our words. It's our choice to obey God's commands or not.

Your Obedience and God's Trust

God doesn't need anything, but He wants our obedience. To obey is another key to overcoming anger...to getting your unsaved kids saved...to having blessing on your marriage...to receiving financial blessing...to having a wonderful, vibrant relationship with God. When we obey, we go from being just "called" and average to being the "chosen ones" of God.

One reason we don't obey God is because we think we are smarter than God. He tells us to do something, and we say, "Yeah, but God, You know what I think...?" Do we honestly think God is up in heaven saying, "You know, I never thought of it that way. Why, in your case, it's different." No, it isn't different for anyone! There are no exceptions. It is the same for each one of us. We are to obey Him no matter what we think or feel!

> You have never seen heaven and you have never met Jesus. You have to receive Jesus by faith, not by sight.

In today's society, people are trained to be highly opinionated and independent thinkers. That is why so many people have a hard time living by faith. When you come to God, you have to believe that two thousand years ago a man died on the cross for your sin, and you have to say, "I receive Him as my Savior." You have never seen heaven, and you have never met Jesus. You have to receive Jesus by faith, not by sight. The Bible says that unless you come as a little child, you cannot see the kingdom of God. (See Luke 18:17.)

Another reason we don't obey God is because we think He is a hard taskmaster, but He is a good God. He is not a taker; He is a giver! Our God has promised us life and life more abundantly. (See John 10:10.) We can trust Him!

Do you remember the old movie *The Ten Commandments?* When God gave Moses the list of, "Thou shalt nots," His voice in the movie sounded angry and upset. That's the way I've always viewed what God was saying. "You better obey Me or else!" But then one day I heard He was a good God, that He was my Father, and I saw the Ten Commandments in another light. He was saying, "Son, you don't have to steal because I'm your dad. I own it all. I want you to have whatever you need or desire. Don't commit adultery. I have a better way. You don't need any other god. I'm the way, the truth, and the life."

Now I see that God tells us to obey Him because He always has good things in store for us. The Ten Commandments are not there to limit us but to release us into the full blessing of our heavenly Father. And to receive His blessing, we must obey solely because He tells us to obey.

Sometimes I would get my kids, especially when they were little, and say, "Come on, get in the car. We're going to church." Now they wouldn't say, "Father, is there plenty of gas in the car? Are the tires inflated properly?" No, they just got in the car because their dad said they were going to church. As children trust their parents, so we must trust our heavenly Father. I promise you, He's much smarter than we are!

When I first got saved, I remember reading the Scripture, *"He who finds his life will lose it, and he who loses his life for My sake will find it"* (Matthew 10:39). I was struggling with learning who God was and knowing for sure that I could really trust Him. This Scripture helped me to understand that if I hold on to certain things that

I think are important, I may just lose out on the really incredible things God has for me. But if I let go of them and trust and obey God, He will give me so much more than I could ever dream possible.

In order to break free from the curses and walk in freedom, you must learn to walk in obedience to God's ways. We don't have to be perfect or without mistakes, but our hearts need to be surrendered and pliable toward God. We need to be moving forward in the things of God every day of our lives. *Today's decisions determine our tomorrows.* There is a miracle on the other side of your obedience.

Decide to choose God's way and trust Him completely in every area of your life. What will the results be? You'll be amazed at the results—a supernatural peace the world can't offer, wisdom money can't buy, and freedom no man can give.

Discussion Questions

1. Is God calling you to be obedient in a particular area of your life? If so, what is He asking you to do?

   Why is it important to be obedient to Him? Read 2 Chronicles 16:9.

2. In John 15:14–16, what did Jesus say we are to Him when we are obedient?

3. In Matthew 16:13–19, Jesus was walking with the disciples and asked them, *"Who do you say that I am?"* (verse 15). What was Peter's response?

   Peter was really saying, "You are the one to obey. You are the one we are to follow." What did Jesus say to Peter?

4. Are you currently living in obedience to God? If not, what are your reasons for not obeying God?

Chapter Twenty-four

Healing the Wounded Spirit

S INCE I FIRST published *Free at Last* ten years ago, tens of thousands of people have been identifying personal and generational curses in their lives. Over that time, I have come to realize that many people are facing more than just a curse on their lives—they are also battling a spirit that has been broken. I have been shocked to discover that the vast majority of people I minister to have wounds on the inside that prevent them from receiving the healing God wants to provide. Proverbs 15:13 says, *"A merry heart makes a cheerful countenance, but by sorrow of the heart **the spirit is broken**"* (emphasis added). Right there, Scripture is telling us that a spirit can be broken.

I have horses, and I have seen them trained. The old way to train a horse was to break it. When I first got into horses, a cowboy friend of mine had a ranch in Colorado where they would break horses. It was brutal to watch. First, the trainer would tie up one of the animal's legs, and then he would frighten it to the point that it would have to lie down and submit to everything the trainer wanted. Unfortunately, in breaking a horse that way, it was discovered that the trainer also broke the horse's spirit.

That is exactly what the Lord is talking about in Proverbs 15:13. Somewhere along the line—maybe in training, maybe in life, maybe in childhood, maybe in marriage, maybe in church—someone has broken your spirit.

Why is that important? I have discovered that many people are having problems in their marriages, problems with their children, or problems in other relationships, not necessarily because of something they have done, but because someone at some time has broken their spirits. They are damaged goods. On the surface, they may look fine. They tough it out or cover it up. But, below the surface, there is a rejection and hurt that affects every area of their lives.

There are three ways a curse can come into our lives. First, we can inherit a family curse. (See chapter 4, "Like Father, Like Son.") Second, a curse can come via something we have done; we can bring a curse on ourselves. That's why it is important that we understand that Jesus didn't just die for us, but He died on the cross. Scripture says, *"Cursed is everyone who hangs on a tree"* (Galatians 3:13; see also Deuteronomy 21:23). Jesus not only took all of our sins on the cross, but He also took all of the curses that result from those sins.

But it's the third way a curse can come on our lives that I want us to look at here. We can suffer under a curse because of something that was done to us. Not something that has been passed on to us or something that we did, but something that has been done to us, and until we learn to break these curses, they can affect every area of our lives. I have firsthand knowledge of this. The most important curse that was broken in my life was not the curse of drugs. Don't get me wrong, drugs *were* a curse in my life, a bondage from which God miraculously set me free. But drugs were a curse that I suffered from for only a few years. The greatest miracle of deliverance I received was a curse that went all the way back to my childhood—the curse of anger. Remember what God teaches us in Proverbs 26:2: *"A curse without cause shall not alight."* I won't go into the details, but I can remember the exact day, the exact place, and the exact moment that something changed me, molded me, cursed me, and broke my spirit. That day I opened up to the curse of anger, and it proceeded to affect every area of my life.

For me, the result was a boiling anger that remained with me as an adult. For a long time, Tiz wouldn't let me put a Christian bumper sticker on our car. The only one she let me put on read "Christians aren't perfect, just forgiven." Why? Because I would get into fights in the car on the way to church. How sad is that? Then, I would walk in the church door as if nothing had happened. All that anger was due to an inner hurt and feeling of rejection I had experienced years before.

We all know people who are like this. I have a good friend whom I recently reconnected with after losing touch for a few years. This guy is tremendously talented. He can build anything and operate all kinds of machinery. But he is also one of those guys who has lost job after job after job. People would say that he had a "chip on his shoulder." Do you know what that means? It means he was carrying something around with him, an inner attitude that showed up on the outside. God has now set him free.

Another friend of mine can be the nicest guy in the world, but if somebody looks at him the wrong way or says the wrong words, he will explode in an angry outburst and continue to seethe on the inside. One day, I met his father, and I recognized that the apple hadn't fallen very far from the tree. There was a tremendous relationship problem there.

> Jesus not only took all of our sins on the cross, but He also took all of the curses that result from those sins.

I have another friend who has gone through several divorces. When I began teaching about broken spirits at our church, he said, "You know, I have this problem when it comes to women." When he was thirteen years old, a teacher stood him up before the class, knowing that he couldn't read very well. Nevertheless, she ordered him to read aloud, which resulted in all the kids laughing at him and mocking him. My friend said, "This teacher—a female—stood me up and embarrassed me in front of people, and I am always waiting for that to happen again." Thankfully, God has set my friend free from this curse.

We first started teaching about broken spirits when we were at a church in Portland, Oregon. Tiz went into Nordstrom's, and one of the salesclerks working there was a woman from our church. She introduced one of the other salesclerks, who was so beautiful she could have been a model. In talking to her, Tiz discovered that her husband had left her, but for five years, he had told her, "You aren't worth anything. Nobody will ever want you. Nobody will ever love you. Nobody will ever care about you." He put her down and put her down and put her down until this beautiful person on the outside was a broken person on the inside. She couldn't see herself the way God saw her, and it was resulting in great depression and stress in her life.

Can you relate to this? Many of you may be longtime believers, but you still suffer from a broken spirit. Something has damaged you on the inside, and it is still causing damage all around you on the outside.

Signs of a Broken Spirit

Jesus said, *"The Spirit of the LORD is upon Me, because He has anointed Me...to heal the brokenhearted"* (Luke 4:18). The good news is that healing is not only possible, but a promise. First, however, you need to be able to recognize the signs that you have a broken spirit. These signs are like symptoms. They are not the disease but rather the outward signs of the inner disease. Let's take a look at several of the outward signs, or symptoms, of an inward broken spirit.

Unstable Emotions

Have you ever known somebody with a roller-coaster personality? This is the kind of person who has everyone walking on eggshells around him. Everyone treats him special because they never know what kind of mood he will be in, or what might set him off and change his mood. The atmosphere is always tense around these people. One moment they are happy, and the next moment they are on the warpath. One moment they are optimistic, and the next moment they are depressed. This is important because God does not want us to be subjected to unpredictable, rolling tides of emotion. Scripture tells us that *"the joy of the LORD is your strength"* (Nehemiah 8:10).

No Emotions

On the other side of the scale, someone with a broken spirit may show no emotion at all. People like this never seem to demonstrate any joy in their lives. They never get upset, either. Do you realize that anger is allowed? The Bible says, *"Be angry, and do not sin"* (Psalm 4:4; Ephesians 4:26). In other words, it is normal to feel righteous anger, but it is not godly to react from it the wrong way. If you are someone whose emotions are flat all the time, it could be a sign of a broken spirit.

A Negative Attitude

This refers to the person for whom the glass is always half empty. If it's sunny outside, it's too sunny. If it's rainy, it's too rainy. Nothing is ever good enough. This doesn't mean you can never feel pessimistic about things, but if you are the kind of person who is always critical and complaining about everything, most likely, you are suffering from a broken spirit.

Constant Defensiveness

Some people with broken spirits are always argumentative and perpetually on edge. You may ask them, "Hey, how are you doing?" and they snap back, "What do you mean by that?"

I can remember always wishing that my dad would have to work overtime because I knew what kind of mood he would be in when he came home—mean and ornery. You can't have a marriage like that. You can't have a family like that. You can't be a leader like that when people are always avoiding you and the verbal abuse you spew.

Low Self-Esteem

Someone with low self-esteem walks with his head down and finds it hard to look others in the eye because he doesn't feel good about himself. It is like the woman at Nordstrom's who was beautiful on the outside but thought she was ugly because of what her husband had said to her over and over again. I believe that this is actually a form of witchcraft. It is the parent who constantly tells his kids, "You are a failure; you are never going to get ahead; you will never amount to anything." Low self-esteem comes from a broken spirit that screams, "I'm not worthy. I'll never be good enough."

Let me give you some hope. I don't care how old you are. This may have happened to you ten, twenty, or thirty years ago—or more—but everything the devil has stolen from you can be returned. Jesus says you are so worthy that if you were the only one on earth who would ever receive the Lord Jesus Christ as Savior, He would have died on that cross for you, anyway. Why? Because you are worthy.

The Bible has much to say about our battles with pride, and it should. Proverbs 16:18 says, *"Pride goes before destruction, and a haughty spirit before a fall."* I've found, however, that many Christians don't have a problem with thinking too highly of themselves but with thinking too lowly of themselves.

The Tendency to Be Easily Offended

Someone who is easily offended is the person whose feelings are easily hurt. He is very sensitive. If someone doesn't shake his hand or say hi to him, he goes home from church or work or school and sulks with hurt feelings. If nobody offends him, then he will create some kind of fictitious offense so that he can hold a grudge against the world. This, too, is a sign that, somewhere along the line, someone or something broke his spirit.

Extreme Possessiveness

The extremely possessive person always has to know where his or her spouse is. He lives his life in fear, holding on to people too tightly and not allowing them to breathe. In doing so, however, he finds that he is actually pushing others away. There has to be a release taking place. As I said, this is a fear-based emotion that refuses to trust in God or anybody else. This person assumes the worst and expects it to happen.

An Overly Critical Nature

An overly critical nature always puts others down. The person with this trait deals in gossip and slander and extreme criticism in order to lift himself up. He revels in making others look worse in order to feel better about himself.

Eight Root Causes of a Broken Spirit

Of course, all these things are merely the surface results of an inner broken spirit. When we see these signs pop up, whether in others or in our own lives, our tendency is often to try to treat the outward symptoms. We'll try hard not to be angry or critical or pessimistic or possessive or emotional, but these efforts are doomed to end in frustration if we are not getting at the root cause of these signs in the first place—a broken spirit. I have identified eight root causes of inner brokenness. There may be more, but these are the ones I encounter most often.

Broken Relationships

A broken spirit may come from a broken relationship, whether it was broken recently or as far back as when you were in pre-school. When Tiz and I were pastoring in Australia, a lady came to the front of the church for healing three nights in a row. She was crippled from a hip disease, and we prayed and prayed for her. On the third night, as I was praying for her, God spoke to me, saying, "Who is it she is bitter against?" This woman was a leader in the church and had been a Christian for many years. When I asked her this question, she suddenly burst into tears. She was probably in her mid-fifties at the time, but when she was sixteen, her sister had stolen a boyfriend from her and married him. After she expressed this confession, I asked her to let it go. We prayed with her as she said, "Lord, forgive me for being bitter." God healed both of her hips that night. That is a good example of how a broken relationship can cripple you, not only on the inside, but also on the outside.

Rejection

Rejection comes in all shapes and sizes. You may have been rejected because you were not tall enough, or because you were too tall. You may not have been thin enough, blonde enough, or rich enough. There are few things more damaging than experiencing intense feelings of rejection. Perhaps you were always the last one picked for the team or the one who couldn't get asked on a date. Today, you may try to laugh these things off, but they still hurt. Maybe people called you names in school. You can repeat "Sticks and stones will break my bones, but words will never hurt me" all you want, but you know that's not true. Words hurt.

There are people reading this book who have felt rejection because of the color of their skin. They walk into a place and are treated differently than others. I have prayed with people of mixed race who have found themselves rejected by both sides.

Let me tell you something. The world may have rejected you because of what is on the outside, but God made you absolutely perfect. You are perfect in His eyes. We live in a world obsessed with looks and appearances. The kinds of judgments we face every day are not that much different from those we faced all the way back when we were children. This is why Scripture says: *"By this all will know that you are My disciples, if you have love for one another"* (John 13:35). God knows we need to feel accepted, and He intends for that acceptance to be based on love and not on our appearances.

Adoption

Some of you were adopted as children. I am not talking about someone who was adopted because his or her parents passed away—although that is traumatic enough. I am referring to those whose birth parents gave them up for adoption. You may have had a single mom who gave you up to be raised by a relative. Or, maybe your mother—whom you've never met—simply didn't want to be burdened with the responsibility of being a parent. You may have been raised by a perfectly capable and loving adoptive family, but, over the years, somewhere inside of you, the root of a broken spirit has grown because the woman who gave birth to you didn't love you enough to keep you.

Lack of Love

Maybe you weren't abandoned as a child, but it was obvious that your parents—or one of your parents—simply didn't love you. For whatever reason, they were distant and didn't show you the love you needed. Maybe they were workaholics or alcoholics or simply were emotionally distant because of their own brokenness. Whatever the reasons, day in and day out, their actions demonstrated quite clearly that they didn't love you.

Excessive Criticism

Some of you felt as though you could never please your parents, and you suffered under their relentless criticism. "Why can't you be like your brother?" "Why can't you be like your sister?" "Why aren't you good at sports?" "Why aren't you smarter?" Few things in life hurt as much as the rejection of a parent—especially a father.

Emotional or Physical Abuse

Some of you were beaten as children. Others of you were verbally assaulted. Now, twenty, thirty, or forty years later, the memories are still fresh, and the hurt remains. Unfortunately, the wounds from this root are apt to be carried on from generation to generation—unless you break the generational curse. Experts tell us that those who have been abused have a strong likelihood of passing on that abuse to their children. It's time for God to break that curse.

Sexual Abuse

Experts say that as many as 85 to 90 percent of those who have been emotionally, physically, or sexually abused will pass that abuse on to their children. They may not necessarily sexually abuse a child—although that is a possibility—but emotional damage will be passed on to the next generation.

One night, at a healing service, I called out for anyone who had ever been sexually abused by a pastor. I had never done that in the twelve years I had been teaching on breaking curses. I thought that perhaps one brave soul would raise a hand. To my surprise, around ten people raised their hands to say that they had been abused sexually by a leader in the church.

It's amazing how many of those who have gone through the trauma of sexual abuse suffer not only from the pain of that abuse, but also from the pain that it was somehow their fault. Many have seen their parents divorce because of this and feel that they are to blame—therefore suffering a doubly broken spirit.

Racial Abuse

Today, many people continue to suffer from the scars of racial abuse. Perhaps you've been put down, passed over, or picked on because of your race or the color of your skin, and the hurt and the scars still remain. I remember seeing a show on TV—not a Christian program but a documentary about Dr. Martin Luther King Jr. They were interviewing an old preacher who had marched with Dr. King. He was asked how he felt America was doing today in regard to racism. He said, "We have come a long way, we still have a long way to go, but the church is the last to catch on."

I believe the church of Jesus Christ should look like a rainbow. Years ago, once again in Australia, I saw a television commercial that featured a little Caucasian girl on a swing. Soon, an Aboriginal child walked by, and then an Asian child walked by. Then, the little girl on the swing asked her mother, "What color is Jesus?" Good question, isn't it? In the commercial, the mother said that Jesus is the light of the world, and pure light is made up of every color of the rainbow. Let's begin to reverse this curse right now, in Jesus' name.

> Jesus is the light of the world, and pure light is made up of every color of the rainbow.

The Divine Exchange

Earlier, we read a verse from Luke in which Jesus said that He came to set the captives free. When He said that, Jesus was actually reading from a prophecy from Isaiah concerning His life.

The Spirit of the Lord GOD is upon Me, because the LORD has anointed Me to preach good tidings to the poor; He has sent Me to heal the brokenhearted, to proclaim liberty to the captives, and the opening of the prison to those who are bound; to proclaim the acceptable year of the LORD, and the day of vengeance of our God; to comfort all who mourn, to console those who mourn in Zion, to give them beauty for ashes, the oil of joy for mourning, the garment of praise for the spirit of heaviness.
(Isaiah 61:1–3)

Jesus said this was the reason He came. I call this "the divine exchange." He took our sickness so that we could be healed. He became poor so that we could become rich. He became a servant so that we could rule. He came to heal the brokenhearted and exchange the spirit of heaviness for the oil of joy.

Where Jesus Was Rejected

Another part of the divine exchange is that Jesus was rejected so that you and I could be accepted. You might wonder exactly where Jesus was rejected.

In the Womb

In Jesus' day, if a woman became pregnant out of wedlock, she was guilty of adultery and could be stoned to death. Mary had to go to Joseph, her fiancé, and tell him that she was with child. "Don't worry, Joseph," she said, "God got me pregnant." We read this now as a cute little Christmas tale, but this was a traumatic scandal in their lives. (See Luke 2.)

In my line of work, a lot of people come to me with outrageous claims. I have met people claiming to be the angel Gabriel, Michael the archangel, and even Moses. I can't imagine how I'd react if somebody came to me and said, "Pastor, would you agree with me in prayer? I'm pregnant, and it is God Himself who got me that way." I promise you, my next call would be to security. But that is exactly what happened. Joseph was crushed, and his first inclination was to quietly divorce Mary. (See Matthew 1:19.) Right there in the womb, before Jesus was ever born, His earthly father rejected him.

You've probably heard of those who insist that expectant mothers should talk to their babies while they are in the womb. They say you need to tell your unborn child that you love him or her. Can babies hear the words? I don't know, but I believe they can feel your spirit. And if babies can feel love in the womb, it only figures that they can also feel rejection in the womb.

If you were rejected, even in your mother's womb, God wants to exchange the rejection you experienced for acceptance. Your mother was going to get rid of you. She had already made plans for a grandmother or some other relative to care for you. Maybe she even considered getting an abortion. Jesus knows that feeling and He wants to give you a divine exchange. He was rejected so you could be accepted.

At the Inn

Jesus was rejected a second time before He was even born. When Mary and Joseph arrived in Bethlehem for the census, they went to an inn, but there was no room for them. Imagine, the Son of God is about the enter humanity, and there is not even a bedroom available for Him.

For some of you, there was no room for you in your family or in your parents' lives. Jesus wants to give you a divine exchange: people may have rejected you, but God has accepted you.

As a Child

I am convinced that Jesus was likely rejected as a child. Most of us have probably experienced the cruelty of other children at one time or another. Kids can do the math. "Let me get this straight, Jesus. Your mom and dad were married, and You were born six months later?" If a woman was eligible to be stoned for having an baby out of wedlock, then surely Jesus faced rejection by others in His youth due to the stigma attached to being an "illegitimate child." I believe that Jesus felt that kind of rejection, and that, today, He can break your spirit of rejection.

Because of His Background

Jesus was also rejected because of where He came from. He came from what we would now call "the wrong side of the tracks." When the Lord came into His ministry, one of His future disciples asked, *"Can anything good come out of Nazareth?"* (John 1:46).

> Some of us may never know who our earthly father is, but we do know who our heavenly Father is.

People can be rejected because of where they are from, what color they are, or what their nationality is. Jesus felt that same thing.

I am from the inner city of south St. Louis, which had a reputation of being the 'hood, or the ghetto. I can remember dating a girl in college, and her parents wanted to know where I was from and what my background was. I remember feeling that sense of judgment and rejection. Have you ever felt that? Some of us may never know who our earthly father is, but we do know who our heavenly Father is. No matter where you are from, you have that divine connection.

By a Friend

Jesus sat with His closest followers at Passover and said, *"One of you who eats with Me will betray Me"* (Mark 14:18). Judas was a trusted friend of Jesus for three years, yet he betrayed Him. I believe that one of the things that hurt Jesus the most, however, was the rejection of His close friend, Peter. When Jesus told His disciples that He was going to die, Peter wouldn't hear of it. He promised to follow Jesus no matter where it led. He promised, *"Even if all are made to stumble because of You, I will never be made to stumble"* (Matthew 26:33). Have you ever had anybody promise that they would never leave you? Maybe it was a close friend, or maybe it was a spouse who promised "until death do us part."

But Jesus said, *"I say to you that this night, before the rooster crows, you will deny Me three times"* (verse 34). Before the sun came up, Peter did betray Jesus three times! After Peter's betrayal, Jesus came to him and asked him, "Peter, do you love Me?" Peter replied, "Yes, Lord. You know that I love You." What did Jesus say? "Feed My lambs." Then, Jesus asked again, "Peter, do you love Me?" Once again, Peter said, "Yes, Lord. You know I love You." And Jesus said, "Tend My sheep." Then, for a third time, Jesus asked, "Peter, do you love Me?" Once again, Peter replied, "Lord, You know all things. You know I love You." And again, Jesus said, "Feed My sheep." (See John 21:15–17.)

Why did Jesus have Peter repeat his vow of love three different times? Was He merely being repetitive? No. Peter had denied Jesus three times, and Jesus knew that the spirits of rejection and condemnation were on Peter's life. Each time Jesus asked the question and Peter responded, a curse was broken. Jesus was saying, "Let's break this curse of rejection. Feed My lambs. Tend My sheep. Feed My sheep." Jesus knew that Peter would never be able to accomplish the things God wanted him to accomplish if he allowed this curse to affect the rest his life.

Many of you have also experienced rejection. I can remember when I was first saved. My pastor said, "Larry, someday, you are going to have to let that wall come down and let people love you." He knew that I had this wall up because of my father's earlier rejection. He knew that I would cause damage in my future relationships because of the spirit of anger that I carried as a result. One day, years later, I knocked my son down when he was only three years old. At that moment, I realized that I was just like my dad—like father, like son.

Today, you can break the spirit of rejection in your life. God wants to tear down the walls you've erected around your life. Maybe you have helped people who then betrayed you. You bailed people out, and they turned on you. Think about Jesus. Think of all the multitudes He healed and blessed and ministered to, who, at the hour of His greatest need, cried out, "Crucify Him!" Can you imagine giving your life for people who turn around and cry out for your death? Jesus was rejected by those He loved so that you and I could have a divine covering of acceptance.

On the Cross

He was hung on a cross naked, which amounts to sexual abuse. Can you imagine that kind of humiliation? Not only was He crucified, but He was also stripped of His clothing and physically abused. It amazes me when I see the statistics and realize how many of you, if you felt safe enough to admit it, have been sexually abused by someone in authority, someone you trusted. Jesus knows that kind of rejection. Today, He can give you a divine exchange and turn your story around.

By His Father

Finally, Jesus was rejected by the Father. Jesus was rejected by God. Scripture tells us that when Jesus hung on the cross, every sin that I have ever done, every sin that you have ever done, and every sin that mankind has ever done was put upon this sinless Lamb of God.

> *All we like sheep have gone astray; we have turned, every one, to his own way; and the LORD has laid on Him the iniquity of us all.* (Isaiah 53:6)

The Son of God, who had never known jealousy, became jealousy. The Son of God, who had never hurt a soul, became murder and abuse. Every sin that had ever been committed fell on Jesus at that cross. That is why, at the end, Jesus cried out, *"Eloi, Eloi, lama sabachthani?', which is translated, 'My God, My God, why have You forsaken Me?'"* (Mark 15:34). At that moment, for the first time ever, God the Father turned His face away from Jesus and rejected Him. He did it so that, for the first time since the garden of Eden,

He could find us. It was the divine exchange. Jesus became poor so that, by His stripes, we could become rich. He became sick so that we could be healed. He was rejected so that we could be accepted.

When I came to church for the first time, I had needle marks up and down my arm. I had federal warrants out for my arrest. I was a drug addict and an outcast of society. But, in a moment of time, there was a divine exchange on my behalf. I may have walked into that church a heroin addict, but I walked out a child of God. Jesus took on my rejection so that no matter who I was, what I had done, or what had been done to me, I could be accepted and blessed by my heavenly Father.

> *"Do not fear, for you will not be ashamed; neither be disgraced, for you will not be put to shame; for you will forget the shame of your youth, and will not remember the reproach of your widowhood anymore. For your Maker is your husband, the LORD of hosts is His name; and your Redeemer is the Holy One of Israel; He is called the God of the whole earth. For the LORD has called you like a woman forsaken and grieved in spirit, like a youthful wife when you were refused," says your God. "For a mere moment I have forsaken you, but with great mercies I will gather you."*
> (Isaiah 54:4–7)

This translation says, *"I have forsaken you,"* but a closer translation would be the following:

> For a mere moment, it feels as though I have let you down. It feels like that, but with great mercy, I will gather you. It seems as though I hid My face from you for a time, but with everlasting kindness, I will have mercy on you.

The Final Step

If you are nursing a wounded or broken soul, now is the time to break the curse. This is the final step in throwing the enemy out the door of your life. Perhaps, you are reading these words and realizing that there is a brokenness in your spirit. At some point in your life, something damaged you on the inside. You may put up a good front to the world, but there is damage in your spirit that God wants to heal.

The devil's trick is to tell you that you are the only one who feels like this. From experience, I can assure you that almost everybody reading this book has a brokenness in his or her spirit, to some extent.

God will never reject you. If you are dealing with your parents' rejection because you were adopted, God wants to bring you healing. If you didn't feel loved by one or both of your parents, God wants to bring you healing. If you suffered constant criticism and felt that you were never good enough in their eyes, God wants to heal you. If you suffered from verbal or physical abuse, God wants to heal you. If you were sexually abused at any point in your life, and nobody was there to protect you, God wants to heal you. If you have felt rejection because of your race, God wants to heal you. I want you to understand that once you place that pain and rejection on the cross, they are no longer yours to carry.

Do you know what my greatest joy is as a pastor? I get to see God touch people's lives. Today, what Satan meant for evil, God is going to use for good. (See Genesis 50:20.) I want you to allow the Lord to take out that wounded heart and breathe the breath of life inside of you. If you are ready to get rid of the pain and rejection, I want you to pray this prayer with me:

Father,

Release Your healing in me now. Wash me from the inside to the outside. Father, I break the curse of low self-esteem. I break the curse of rejection. I break the curse of abuse. I break the curse of mental torment. I break the curse of feeling as though I am not good enough. Father, I break the curses of verbal, physical, and sexual abuse. I break them right now in the name of Jesus. From this day forward, I forbid Satan and his lies from taking root in my life. Now, Lord, by Your Spirit, sweep across my life in divine healing. Amen.

I want you to lift up your hands and receive God's healing. That's what you are feeling. I want you to know that you are more than a conqueror. You are made in the image of God. You were divinely designed. You are exactly the look that God needs. You are exactly the color that God needs. Man may have rejected you, man may have abandoned you, but Jesus said, *"All that the Father gives Me will come to Me, and the one who comes to Me I will by no means cast out"* (John 6:37). You are divinely accepted. You are divinely anointed.

Receive your healing. Receive your deliverance. Receive your destiny. Receive back everything that was stolen from you. Every lie the devil ever brought against you is being reversed in your life right now in every area. Men who have been rejected and are full of anger and disappointment can receive their deliverance. Women who have never seen the beauty that God bestowed on them can receive their healing. Today, there is a restoration of joy, a restoration of peace, a restoration of self-esteem, and a restoration of family. Today, there is total victory in the name and by the blood of Jesus!

> Today, there is total victory in the name and by the blood of Jesus!

Let me leave you with one last step to total freedom. There is one more thing that you need to do. When you do this, it will shut the door and lock it forever so the enemy will never come back in again. **Forgive!** We need to learn who to forgive and who to blame. Forgiveness is the key that locks the enemy out. Yes, I know somebody may have hurt you, but look at what God's Word tells us: *"We do not wrestle against flesh and blood, but against principalities, against powers, against the rulers of the darkness of this age, against spiritual hosts of wickedness in the heavenly places"* (Ephesians 6:12). Whenever I teach this, I ask two questions. Now, I will ask them of you. First, if I pray for you and you receive healing, who is it that has healed you? When I ask people this, they always say, "God did." And they would be right. Second, if I hurt or wound you, who is it that has harmed you? When I ask people this, they always say, "*You* did!" You see, we know to give God the glory when the credit is His. Now, however, we need to learn to blame the devil when the damage is his. We need to forgive the people and assign the blame where it truly belongs. When you discover who the thief is, then everything he has stolen from you—joy, peace, happiness, etc.—will come back into your life multiplied by seven! And always remember, *"If the Son makes you free, you shall be free indeed"* (John 8:36).

Conclusion

Today is your day to go from being one of the many who are called to being one of the chosen—those who see the fullness of God's blessing and joy. Today you can go from being one who just hears the Word of God to being one who understands and receives the blessings of God. Today you can go from being one who just hears about miracles to being one who actually experiences miracles. Simply having a Bible in your house will not change you. God's Word will not do one thing for you until it goes from your head to your heart—your spirit.

As a child of God, you have direct access to the throne room of God. You have God's Word and all His power available to you at all times. No longer do you have to live under a generational curse of death and destruction because the Spirit gives life. (See 2 Corinthians 3:6.)

Once the generational curse is broken off your life, fill your mind and spirit with the Word of God. Replace your old thought patterns and habits with godly thought patterns and habits. How do we get God's thoughts to become our thoughts? By the renewing of our minds with the Word of God.

Reading and dwelling on the Word of God causes us to enter into God's destiny and releases His promises into our lives. The mind has major control on a person's life and destiny. When we start thinking differently, we start acting differently. The mind is the foothold for poverty or prosperity. The mind is the foothold for sickness or health. The mind is the foothold to obey our spirit man or ignore our spirit man.

As Christians, we must renew our minds daily. Our actions follow our thinking, and our thinking must follow the Spirit of

Conclusion

God. Our conduct changes when our thinking changes. The only way we can change our destiny is to change our thinking.

> *And be renewed in the spirit of your mind, and that you put on the new man which was created according to God, in true righteousness and holiness.* (Ephesians 4:23–24)

Listen to me carefully. Once you've broken the chain of generational curses, your life will be an ongoing process of change. Don't get discouraged if you stumble—just get up, repent, and keep on going. It's an ongoing transformation.

Our actions will be guided by the transformation of our lives, which comes by the renewing of our minds through reading and meditating on the Word of God. The way we move from being angry to being loving is by the renewing of the mind. The way we move from being sad to being happy is by the renewing of the mind. The way we move from always being poor to always being blessed is by the renewing of the mind. The way we move from being defeated into being victorious is by the renewing of our minds. And renewing the mind is a process!

Our potential is not limited by what we have experienced. Many think they can go only so far in life because they have failed so many times. But there is a transformation that takes place by the renewing of our minds. It is a spiritual metamorphosis. When we think right, our words are right; when our words are right, our actions are right. Our potential is multiplied hundreds of times beyond anything we can think, but it happens through a metamorphosis of God's Spirit changing us by the renewing of our minds.

> *And do not be conformed to this world, but be transformed by the renewing of your mind, that you may prove what is that good and acceptable and perfect will of God.* (Romans 12:2)

We have the ability to exchange our limited ideas and strengths for God's unlimited ideas and strengths. We can exchange our limited natural realm for His unlimited supernatural realm.

The principles I have shared in this book are not simply facts I read somewhere. These are truths that have changed my life and can change your life too. I heard that the number one selling tattoo in America today is, "Born to Lose." Why anyone would permanently tattoo that on their body is beyond me, but what is even more distressing is that there are multitudes of others who have tattooed that message on their hearts.

Without Jesus Christ, my own life was destined for failure, but through the resurrection power of God, I became destined to win. The keys I learned and put into practice have launched my life into joy and blessings that I never dreamed possible. My marriage, family, ministry, and financial prosperity are a testimony of God's amazing grace! I share this only to boast in the Lord and to tell you that God is no respecter of persons. What He has done for me, He will do for you. (See Acts 10:34 KJV.)

God brought me to a point in my life when I knew where I wanted to go, and then He showed me the steps to get there. Are you at that point in your life? Remember, the Lord has an incredible destiny planned for you. Make the decision today to enter into all that He has for you. Let nothing stand in your way. You're not born to lose. You are born to win and born again to conquer!

Trust God today to help you be true to His Word. Trust Him to help you overcome your addictions or shortcomings by the power of the Holy Spirit. Obey Him with every breath you take and in every move you make. In choosing God's way, you are choosing *victory*. It's time to believe in the God who believes in you!

Notes

1. James Strong, *The Exhaustive Concordance of the Bible* (Nashville: Abingdon, 1890), "Greek Dictionary of the New Testament," #3466.

2. Ibid., #458.

3. Adam Clarke, *Adam Clarke Commentary.* 6 vols. PC Study Bible. Version 2.1J CD-ROM. Seattle: Biblesoft, 1993–1998.

4. Strong, "Greek Dictionary of the New Testament," #4129.

5. World: Americas, "U.S. prison population hits record high," Wednesday, May 10, 2000. <http://news2.thls.bbc.co.uk/hi/english/ world/americas/newsid%5F296000/296884.stm>

6. Strong, "Greek Dictionary of the New Testament," #4982.

7. Ibid., #3528.

8. Strong, "Hebrew and Chaldee Dictionary," #3084.

9. T. Rees, "God," *New International Bible Encyclopedia,* vol. II (Grand Rapids, MI: Wm. B. Eerdmans Publishing Co., 1956, reprinted 1980), p. 1254.

10. Strong, "Hebrew and Chaldee Dictionary," #2250 and "Greek Dictionary of the New Testament," #3468.

11. Strong, "Hebrew and Chaldee Dictionary," #693.

12. *Webster's New World College Dictionary,* Third Edition, s.v. "wiles" (New York: Macmillan, Simon & Schuster, Inc., 1986).

13. Ibid., "meditate."

14. Strong, "Greek Dictionary of the New Testament," #1933.

15. Ibid., #3309.

About the Author

L ARRY HUCH IS the founder and senior pastor of DFW New Beginnings in Irving, Texas, a church that ministers to over five thousand people. During the past three decades, he and his wife, Tiz, have pioneered seven churches in America and Australia. The success of these churches is due to their enthusiasm and love for people, their personal commitment to evangelism, and their excellent and effective teaching. They have a heart to assist believers in becoming successful and fulfilled in all areas of their lives. The focus of the Huchs' ministry centers on connecting Christians to their Jewish roots as well as breaking generational curses.

One of the hallmarks of their church is its racial, economic, and cultural diversity. DFW New Beginnings defies the old adage that "11 a.m. Sunday is the most segregated hour of the week." Pastor Larry boldly declares that God is a good God and His love for all people can transform them regardless of their past. This powerful message is carried to the world through their television program, *New Beginnings,* which reaches millions of households.

Pastor Larry's personal testimony of coming out of a life of drug addiction, crime, and violence through the saving power of Jesus Christ is only part of the impact of his ministry. His testimony of how the Lord then delivered him from the generational curse of anger is a powerful illustration of his teaching on how the iniquities of the fathers are passed from one generation to the next. Because of this life-changing message, thousands are being set free and staying free.

Pastor Huch is a nationally recognized ministry leader, conference speaker, and author. His books, *Free at Last, 10 Curses That Block the Blessing,* and *The Torah Blessing* are transforming people's lives around the world.

Pastors Larry and Tiz are the proud parents of three wonderful children, all of whom are active in ministry. Their grandchildren, their "Sugars," are the loves of their lives!

For more information on Pastor Larry Huch's ministry, visit his Web site at www.larryhuchministries.com.
